THAI
PEASANT
PERSONALITY

Thai
Peasant
Personality

The Patterning of Interpersonal Behavior

in the Village of Bang Chan

HERBERT P. PHILLIPS

UNIVERSITY OF CALIFORNIA PRESS
Berkeley, Los Angeles, London

University of California Press
Berkeley and Los Angeles
California

University of California Press, Ltd.
London, England
Fourth Printing, 1974

BB
1/9

For Barbara, Katherine, and Elizabeth

Preface

In a felicitous bit of phrasing, the psychologist Abraham Maslow (1954) characterized the research activities of American social scientists as either "problem centered" or "means centered" in their basic purposes. By the former he means studies that are concerned with describing and analyzing a problem that is important or interesting in its own right, and in which the question of *how* the study is conducted is self-evident, secondary, or unstated; by the latter he means studies concerned with illustrating the merit or validity of a particular research strategy or method, and in which the research findings themselves are subsidiary to the precision, elegance, or thoughtfulness of their formulation. Maslow's characterization applies with particular cogency to the writings of sociologists and psychologists. However, it is also relevant to anthropology, a field in which, on the one hand, authors continue to write splendid ethnographies without devoting more than a paragraph or two to how they collected their data, but in which, on the other hand, the editor of the *American Anthropologist* can introduce an article in his journal by saying (Spindler 1963: 1001): "The paper is intended as a solution of a procedural problem in data ordering, and nothing more, but one of the significant trends in modern anthropology is just this."

In culture and personality studies there has in recent years been an attempt to break through this tendency toward intellectual separatism. Some of the most significant contributions to the field have in fact been dual research efforts. Thus, despite their titles and theoretical concerns, such studies as Wallace's *The Modal Personality Structure of the Tuscarora Indians*, Kaplan's *A Study of Rorschach Responses in Four Cultures*, Gladwin and Sarason's *Truk: Man in Paradise*, and Spindler's *Sociocultural and Psychological Processes in Menomini Acculturation* have given from one-third to one-half of their total volume to problems of research design and method.

The present study is written in terms of this emerging syncretic tradition. It is concerned with two different but closely related problems: the description and analysis of selected aspects of the psychological life of Central Plain Thai peasants, particularly aspects of the villagers' daily encounters with one another; and the presentation of an approach for dealing with some of the problems involved in designing and carrying out cross-cultural personality research. Although all the chapters deal with both issues, certain chapters emphasize one more than the other. Readers interested mainly in the description of Thai peasant personality are urged to go directly to chapters I, II, and the first part of III, V, and VI; those interested primarily in the theoretical and methodological framework of the study are referred to the Introduction and chapters III and IV.

This study is also a product of the recent anthropological trend toward team research. If the author had been a lone field researcher, working in a completely unknown community, he could never have undertaken the kind of specialized project reported here. As will be seen below, it was only because considerable ethnographic material was already in hand, providing the cultural framework so necessary for intelligent psychological analysis, that the research was at all feasible. It is left to the reader to determine whether this kind of study is simply an anthropological luxury or whether it adds a new dimension to traditional anthropological approaches.

Acknowledgments

Sincere appreciation is extended first to the people of the village of Bang Chan for providing the information for this study and for affording me twenty-two of the most stimulating months of my life. Special thanks are due my Thai co-workers, Mr. Khamsing Srinawk, Miss Sumon Sudbhan-thad, Miss Sucharit Iamamnuaj, Mr. Titaya Suwanajata, and Mr. Withun Layraman, without whose dedication and intelligence the field research would not have been possible. I am indebted to Drs. J. Marvin Brown, Margaret Stephan Dalton, Kamol Odd Janlekha, Robert B. Textor, and Mr. Robert Golden for their many different kinds of assistance while I was in Thailand. Mr. Sombhund Ruangvaidya and Miss Phongsri Liangphibun assisted me in translating the Sentence Completion materials from Thai into English, and I wish to thank them; however, the responsi-bility for the accuracy of these and other translations is mine. Others associated with the Cornell Research Center in Bangkok also deserve grateful acknowledgment.

I feel a very special sense of gratitude to my friend and colleague, Professor David A. Wilson, for his encouragement as well as for the many enjoyable hours we have spent together discussing aspects of Thai culture. I owe a similar debt to my other dear friends, Professor Lucien M. Hanks, Jr., Dr. Jane Richardson Hanks, Dr. Marjorie M. Burtt, and to my sister, Mrs. Harriet Lefley. Professors Michael Moerman, Hortense Powder-maker, Bernard Gallin, Charles Hughes, Bert Kaplan, Mrs. Barbara Schott Mainster, and Mr. Joseph Spielberg read and criticized portions of the work, for which I am also grateful. Mrs. Betty Messenger and Professor Eugene Hammel, both of whom know little about Thailand but a great deal about anthropology, suggested major revisions in the earlier version of the study, and my debt to them is considerable. Additional thanks are extended to Phyllis Killen and to Beppie Anne Duker for their editorial contributions.

The Ford Foundation, through its Foreign Area Training Fellowship Program, provided the funds for the field research and some additional time for writing, and for these I am extremely grateful. I also wish to thank the Cornell Research Center in Bangkok and the Fels Foundation for providing funds toward special parts of the research.

The teachers who served on my graduate committee at Cornell University and who supervised the writing of the earlier version of this study were Professors Lauriston Sharp and Morris Edward Opler. My debt to them far exceeds the usual obligations owed to benevolent, if hard-headed, readers of a doctoral dissertation: it is primarily from them that I received much of the knowledge and inspiration that bear on my present professional interests. Others who contributed to my training and to whom I am warmly grateful are Professors Robert M. MacLeod, Robert J. Smith, William W. Lambert, and my undergraduate instructors, Professors Daniel J. Levinson, David M. Schneider, and the late Clyde Kluckhohn.

Acknowledgment is due Harper & Row, Publishers, for permission to quote several passages from essays in *Studying Personality Cross-Culturally*, Bert Kaplan, editor; to the Addison-Wesley Publishing Company for permission to quote from Alex Inkeles' and Daniel J. Levinson's "National Character: The Study of Modal Personality and Socio-Cultural Systems" in *Handbook of Social Psychology*, Volume II, Gardner Lindzey, editor; to The RAND Corporation and Stanford University Press for permission to quote from David A. Wilson's "Thailand and Marxism" in *Marxism in Southeast Asia*, Frank N. Trager, editor; to Routledge and Kegan Paul, Ltd. and to Beacon Press for permission to quote from Johan Huizinga's *Homo Ludens: A Study of the Play Element in Culture*; to the World Publishing Company for permission to quote from Clyde Kluckhohn's "Common Humanity and Diverse Cultures" in *The Human Meaning of the Social Sciences*, Daniel Lerner, editor; and to the editors of the *American Anthropologist* for permission to quote from several articles that have appeared in their journal over the years.

Finally, my appreciation is deepest to my wife, Barbara, for her contributions—practical, intellectual, and emotional—during every phase of this work.

Berkeley, California
August 1964

Contents

Note on the Transliteration of Thai

Thai terms (excepting titles and proper names) have been transcribed according to the Haas phonetic system (Haas, *Thai Vocabulary*, 1955, and *The Thai System of Writing*, 1956. Washington D. C., American Council of Learned Societies). However, the five tonal markers have been omitted.

Briefly the system is as follows: voiced unaspirated stops are written *b, d,* and (only in final position) *g;* voiceless unaspirated stops are *p, t, c, k,* and *?;* voiceless aspirated stops are *ph, th, ch,* and *kh;* voiceless unaspirated spirants are *f, s,* and *h;* voiced semivowel sonorants are *w* and *j;* voiced nasal sonorants are *m, n,* and *ŋ;* the voiced lateral sonorant is *l;* and the voiced trill sonorant is *r.* The vowels are written thus: front unrounded, *i, ii, ia, e, ee, ɛ, ɛɛ;* central unrounded, *y, yy, ya, ə, əə, a, aa;* and back rounded, *u, uu, ua, o, oo, ɔ, ɔɔ.*

Introduction

The purpose of this study is twofold: (1) to provide a *basic* description of the dominant personality traits of the adult members of a Central Plain Thai community; and (2) to demonstrate a procedure for dealing with many of the methodological problems, theoretical and technical, that are encountered in cross-cultural personality research. The primary data are observational materials and the responses of 111 Bang Chan villagers to a Sentence Completion Test, a so-called "projective technique."

Several considerations have prompted this work, its planning, emphases, and aims.

In 1955, when I participated in the preparation of a sociological handbook on Thailand (Sharp *et al.* 1956), I had the task of writing a description of the "social values and personality patterns of the Thai," using as sources all available materials in the English language. These sources consisted largely of the writings of travelers, businessmen, and government servants who had worked in Thailand, the comments of introspective Thai, and some preliminary ethnographic studies (R. F. Benedict 1946, Embree 1950, Sharp *et al.* 1953, deYoung 1955, Kaufman 1955, and unpublished field notes of the Cornell Thailand project). It quickly became apparent that these documents—written originally for purposes quite removed from those of psychological analysis—could provide little more than cursory impressions or intriguing clues to the psychological functioning of the Thai, and that a focused, systematic study of Thai personality was a problem for future research. The account that finally emerged from my review of the literature was hardly more than a vocabulary for describing some of the stereotyped forms of Thai social interaction: politeness, the maintenance of a stoical mien in stressful situations, the love of fun, and the like. Although worthy of note, such a lexicon obviously did not represent a thorough or intensive portrayal of Siamese personality. It was with the aim of redressing this situation, therefore, that in the winter of 1956 I undertook a twenty-two-month field research project, a major portion of which is presented in this monograph. Since the research concerns only the members of the village of Bang Chan, its descriptive universe is limited to this sample of the relatively homogeneous peasant population of Thailand's Central Plain.

A fundamental problem of cross-cultural personality research, however, is the question of precisely what to study and how to study it. Culture-personality studies are now universally acknowledged to be a legitimate part of the anthropological endeavor, but it should be remembered that the first research in this area, Mead's *Coming of Age in Samoa* (1928), is less than four decades old.[1] Forty years is not a long period in the development of a field of study, and much of the research during these years has necessarily been given to experimentation and the pursuit of randomly emerging problems. There is as yet no widely accepted "universal personality pattern," equivalent to the "universal culture pattern" in anthropology proper, to organize and guide psychological studies in non-Western cultures and, by specifying invariant points of reference, to expedite the overriding aim of such research: the determination of the range and variation of human personality. Too, despite the fashionableness of the field, there have in fact been comparatively few research projects that have focused *primarily* on the delineation of personality. With a few notable exceptions (DuBois 1944, Leighton and Kluckhohn 1947, Wallace 1952, Gladwin and Sarason 1953, Kaplan 1954, Hallowell 1955a, Spindler 1955a, Spiro 1958, and isolated life histories) the majority of psychological studies by anthropologists—and most of the personality research in the non-Western world has been done by anthropologists, not psychologists— have been peripheral to the field worker's major concern, ethnographic description, with the result that much of our personality material to date is scanty or ill-collected. Finally, as Inkeles and Levinson have pointed out (1954), the vast majority of personality-in-culture studies have been based not upon descriptions of individual human beings, the loci of personality, but upon descriptions of the institutions by which they were reared or the

---

[1] Questions of origins are of course always debatable. By stretching the concept of personality, one might make a case for Myers' and Rivers' work on the Torres Straits Expedition, 1898, or for Kroeber's three Gros Ventre biographies (1908) being the first culture-personality studies. During the teens and early and mid-twenties, Radin's Winnebago biographies (1913 and 1926), Elsie Clews Parsons' anthology (1922), Malinowski's work (1927), and Sapir's theoretical papers (1924 and 1927), although not in themselves culture-personality studies, certainly helped create a felicitous intellectual climate for Mead's research and for Benedict's *Psychological Types in the Cultures of the Southwest,* published the same year. In his synoptic review, Kluckhohn (1944) credits the Mead–Benedict–Sapir triumvirate with providing the groundwork for culture-personality studies in 1928. On the other hand, LaBarre (1958: 279) says: "Culture-personality studies essentially began in the 1930's at Yale University, when Edward Sapir and John Dollard began the first seminar on 'Culture and Personality.'" Milton Singer in his more recent historical review (1961) points to both events as marking the beginnings of the field.

collective cultural products they have created: myths, folktales, religious conceptions and practices. In these instances, personality has been conceived of as either a hypothetical construct linking two sets of cultural institutions (child training methods and adult collective products) or the seat of unconscious processes for the handling of anxiety (created primarily by the child training methods and unconsciously expressed in the adult collective products). Although there is considerable cogency in this last approach (Kardiner 1939 and 1945, Erikson 1950: 98–160, Whiting and Child 1953, Whiting 1961), I would suggest that limiting the meaning of personality to a mechanism for handling anxiety represents a somewhat narrow conception of its functions and attributes. Several scholars (Opler 1936 and 1938, Hallowell 1941, Kluckhohn 1943a, Spiro 1952, among others) have ignored the issue of child rearing and have focused on the psycho-cultural functions of the collective products—both as sources and outlets for the anxieties as well as the realistic problems of adult life. These studies have been concerned not so much with portraying personality as with bringing psychological perspective and insight to the interpretation of ethnographic materials.

These comments are made not in criticism of past research, but rather to note that there are still few firmly established conventions for precisely how a cross-cultural personality study should or can be conducted. Much personality data in the past has *had* to be scanty, simply because the careful collection of ethnographic facts—a fundamental prerequisite to the interpretation of psychological data—is in itself so time-consuming.

Given this lack of a clear methodological mandate, I formulated the following general strategy for the study of the personality characteristics of Siamese villagers.

First, it was decided to concentrate on the description and analysis of the typical dispositions, feelings, conflicts, character traits, and psychological defenses of individual adult informants viewed within the setting of Thai peasant culture. This meant that the point of departure would be a series of psychological states and processes characteristic of individuals rather than a series of cultural institutions which might or might not reflect such states. It was clear, however, that this approach would be practicable only if substantial ethnographic data on the villagers were in hand to provide both general background information and the local cultural meanings necessary for interpreting the personality data. The issue of local cultural meanings will be amplified in a later section; for the present it is sufficient to note that I proceeded from the premise that a study concerned *primarily* with the portrayal of personality would be effective to the extent to which, on the one hand, it rested on solid ethnographic data and, on the other, freed the researcher from devoting his time and energy to collecting such data. Fortunately, the conditions for putting this plan into effect were present in the Thai situation, where extensive ethnographic studies had already been conducted in Bang Chan by Sharp and his colleagues (Sharp *et al.* 1953, Janlekha 1955, L. M. Hanks 1959*a–c*, J. R. Hanks 1959, Textor 1960). To a large degree, the design and phrasing of my project was predicated on the prior existence of these materials.

Second, it was assumed that the states and processes referred to by the concept of personality are among the most complex of phenomena, with as many dimensions and attributes as there are to the concept of culture. This "primitive assumption" was made of course not to acknowledge an obvious truth, but to affirm the necessity that research designs for the study of personality in non-Western societies explicitly exhibit a recognition of the complexity of the task. I would suggest, for example, that collecting a set of Rorschach or TAT protocols during the last hurried weeks of one's field work—not an atypical practice (see Nadel 1955, Spindler 1955*b*, and Hallowell 1955*c*)—and then assuming that the personality portion of one's field work has been "done" is like collecting a list of kinship terms and assuming that all the complex emotional, economic, and juridical elements of actual kinship relationships have been covered. Although most anthropologists recognize the limited intellectual reference of kinship terms (Kroeber 1909 and 1952: 172, Opler 1937 and 1955: 190, Murdock 1949: 113–183, Edmonson 1957, Wallace and Atkins 1960), relatively few have taken an equally circumspect attitude toward the meaning of projective test materials, at least insofar as they have represented themselves to readers. The point is not that TAT protocols or kinship terms are unimportant, but rather that they should be seen as forming only a portion of a complex, cumulative research process, each stage of which should be carefully executed and aimed at dealing with a specific descriptive task. If personality is as involved and multi-dimensional as we all tacitly assume it to be, we should be willing to work with research designs that are equally involved and multi-dimensional.

It was with the above in mind that I worked out a five-stage cumulative research program, the first two stages of which are represented by the data and interpretations in the present volume. The main body of this book has been limited to the two initial stages principally to permit a more complete exploration of the issues involved while at the same time keeping the report to a manageable size. The complete design is outlined below solely to provide the broader theoretical and methodological setting of the present study and to indicate its precise limits.

The first stage (chaps. II and VI) is perhaps descriptively the most interesting, but methodologically the most vulnerable. It involves sketching a naturalistic portrayal of the villagers' dominant personality traits on the basis of their overt behavior, and the patterning of these traits in their interpersonal contacts. Basically this entails trying to arrive at several generalizations about the villagers' characteristic types of response, drawing from several areas of cultural life—kinship, religion, gossip-group behavior, and so forth—and ignoring for the most part detailed situational considerations, deviations, and differences of age, sex, and status. The purpose of such a description is not to provide a precise picture of psychological modes and variations, which is a task in and of itself (stage two), but to sketch in broad strokes for the Western reader some of the manifestations of Thai character which are strikingly different from our own and are important elements in their pattern of expectancies. The emphasis here is on the psychological dimensions of interaction and on those traits which are possible, expectable, and—most important—inimitably Thai, not on those traits which are most frequent in a statistical sense. "Interaction" and "interpersonal contacts" are discussed mainly as attributes of the personalities of individual villagers rather than as attributes of the sociocultural system in which these individuals exist.

It must be emphasized that since the first approach is based on a spectator's observations of overt behavior, it cannot be expected to provide information about how, from a subjective viewpoint, villagers perceive their own behavior and feelings (particularly in psychologically loaded situations), what sentiments they feel but do not express, how they deal with such sentiments psychodynamically, what their unconscious defense mechanisms and private fantasies are (as contrasted to codified beliefs, which in some cases may be institutionalized fantasies); this type of information, commonly assigned to "deeper levels" of personality, is best dealt with in subsequent sections of the research. The major aim of the first section is to provide a general psychological map upon which finer points can later be traced.

The second stage (chaps. IV—VI), involving the use of the Sentence Completion Technique, is concerned with delineating in a statistical sense the subjectively held dispositions of the villagers in various areas of psychological concern: aggression, dependency, achievement, and the like. These dispositions refer not to a series of characteristics consistently shared by any distinguishable segments of the Bang Chan population but rather to the modal and variant characteristics held by villagers in different psychological situations. Since villagers who have similar dispositions in an aggression situation, for example, may have different ones in an achievement situation, it is expected that the frequencies of modes and variants, and their representative memberships, can change from area to area. Our modal and variant types therefore represent not a composite but a profile of the villagers' psychological tendencies.

This second stage of the research differs in intent from the first on several counts.

First, in contrast to the earlier emphasis on what the observer sees as the villagers' most typical behavior, the second section focuses on how villagers themselves perceive situations, or pychologically relevant states, and how best to deal with them. The statements of the Sentence Completion Technique describe a series of relatively unstructured but highly realistic situations and states—"When I realize other people do not like me, I feel . . ."; "When he was asked if he wanted to become boss, he . . ." —to which informants are asked to respond, and in so doing reveal their own needs, wishes, and experiences. It must be emphasized that the completions thus provided do not necessarily represent a description of how informants would in fact behave "when they realize other people do not like them," but do portray their predispositions to react in the manner indicated. The analytic meaning of the response is explored fully in chapter V, but for the present it suffices to note that a basic aim of this section of the research is to present in a systematic way the villagers' internal views and definitions of psychologically significant experiences.

Another aim of this section, of a different order from that above, is to shed some light on a problem that has been the subject of considerable interest, and also considerable obfuscation, from the very beginning of culture-personality studies: the question of a culturally modal personality. (Some representative studies or theoretical statements on this problem are: R. F. Benedict 1934, Belo 1935, LaBarre 1945, Gorer 1948, Mead 1951 and 1953; some representative criticisms, Lindesmith and Strauss 1950, Farber 1950 and 1951, Hart 1954, Piddington 1957; some representative analyses, Wallace 1952, Kaplan 1954 and 1957, Inkeles and Levinson 1954, and Farber 1955.) I am convinced that one of the major sources of difficulty surrounding the use of the concept of modal personality—or its over-inflated version, "national character"—has been the tendency on the part of some field workers to confound inadvertently the culturally interesting or different with the culturally typical. Researchers have been so intent on communicating to readers the unusual nature of the characteristics of the people they have been studying—those characteristics they encountered most personally and directly in the field—that they have often reported unusual characteristics that occurred with *sufficient* frequency to be impressive as actually occurring *most* frequently. I would suggest that it is precisely this kind of confusion that prompted the criticisms (Malinowski 1936 and Thurnwald 1940) of Mead's descriptions (1935) of the psychological transmutability of the sexes among the Arapesh, Mundugu-inur, and Tschambuli, and to a lesser extent those directed against R. F. Benedict's (1934) and Thompson's (1945) views of Pueblo Indian character by Goldfrank (1945), Eggan (1943), and Titiev (1944 and 1946). The issue here is not that traits occurring most frequently are ultimately any more reliable than interesting ones occurring sufficiently frequently or even rarely—these latter are perhaps the best evidence for the variegated and innovative richness of human personality—but simply that the two should not be confused when presenting descriptions of modal personality.

Setting aside for the moment the substantive differences between an "external" (stage one) and "internal" (stage two) approach to personality, it seems clear that the most sensible way for a researcher to proceed to make statements about modal personality—the most frequently occurring personality characteristics in a group—is not by naturalistic portrayal, but by presenting to several members of the group a series of standardized stimuli, the responses to which are then examined for modes and variants and the degree of modality and variation actually expressive of the group. At first glance, naturalistic portrayal may seem the more desirable approach to modal personality, but empirically it entails serious methodological difficulties. A researcher who employed such an approach with reasonable precision would have to (1) record literally everything that occurred around him in order to insure a complete set of observations upon which to base his determinations of modality; (2) identify in these data equivalent social situations for all individuals observed, which, given all the relevant factors present that must be permuted, would vastly reduce his total number of cases; and (3) attempt to tease out modal and variant psychological responses to these situations while working with a very small sample indeed. Moreover, there would always be certain areas of psychological functioning—in Bang Chan, for example, direct aggression between adults, undisguised adult sexual behavior—which would be either closed to him or radically altered *because* of his presence. Unhappily, it is often these very areas in which he may be most interested.[2] With a method such as the

---

[2] I know of no case in the anthropological literature in which a study of adult modal personality in the terms just outlined has ever been seriously attempted—undoubtedly for the reasons specified. Roberts' study (1951) of three Navaho households may seem stylistically similar but actually deals with a totally different problem. It may be noted that the anthropologist who has argued most vigorously for a naturalistic observation approach to personality—Jules Henry (1955, 1958, and Mensh and Henry 1953)—has at all times confined his illustrations to observations of children or children with adults, never adults with adults. The major and unexplicated reason for this limitation is the fact that the behavior of relatively unsocialized children is of an entirely different order from that of adults: it is more spontaneous, motoric, uninhibited, and less verbal than adults' behavior, so much of which is guided by social role requirements. Stated in another way: a Bang Chan child would

Sentence Completion Technique, however, the researcher obtains data that are the product of all individuals responding to the same stimuli, describing the same situations (although in the nature of the technique, hypothetical ones—and this is precisely what permits the handling of topics that may be taboo), and interviewed under generally the same conditions.

Another major aim of this section is to illustrate the usefulness of the Sentence Completion Method for the cross-cultural study of personality. The specific advantages of the technique are elaborated upon later, but the point to be emphasized here is the necessity for phrasing *any* study of personality (or a principal part of it) in a non-Western culture in terms of a technique that will yield comparable data from *any other* culture. I am firmly convinced that only by using a method that can be easily adapted and freely translated from culture to culture can we begin to deal in earnest with the underlying theoretical justification of all culture-personality studies: the determination of the range and variation of human personality. As Spiro (1955: 257) has so persuasively argued:

> one of our main interests is to discover the extent to which culture influences personality; and for this purpose I believe that the Rorschach (*or any other culture-free unstructured stimulus*) is of crucial significance, for it provides us with a yardstick against which genuine personality variables, in contrast to patterned-response variables can be measured. This proposition requires some explanation. A culture, psychologically viewed, consists of a configuration of stimulus situations and the customary responses to these situations which have been learned by the members of a given society. Hence, in demonstrating, as we have successfully done, that emotional and behavioral differences are to be found within different sociocultural contexts we have not demonstrated the existence of personality differences at all. We have merely shown that different stimuli evoke different responses. What we must demonstrate, if we are to show personality differences, is that peoples reared in different sociocultural contexts respond differently to the *same* stimulus. We must, in short, be able to observe the responses of different peoples to a stimulus that is identical for all of them. . . . If under

---

have few qualms about kicking another youngster in the presence of an observer, but a Bang Chan husband would think twice before beating his wife in this setting. Similarly, a mother might make love to her child in the presence of an observer, but never to her husband.

Henry himself recognizes the difficulties of using a naturalistic approach with adults (personal communication 1958), a conclusion shared by other researchers who have attempted naturalistic observation in psychological field work (personal communication from William Lambert with regard to the Whiting–Child–Lambert cross-cultural studies in socialization). Boggs (1956) provides an excellent illustration of the use of naturalistic observation with children. The work of Barker and his colleagues (Barker and Wright 1951, Barker 1963) represents the most sophisticated application of naturalistic observation to the *description* of behavior (although not necessarily personality), but again the focus is on children.

these circumstances we find differences in response, we can be fairly confident that we have a true measure of personality differences and not a measure of how well these people have learned their respective cultures [first italics added].

In my view, the Rorschach, not being a language-mediated instrument, is descriptively and analytically limited to too narrow a sector of psychological functioning (primarily to perceptual processes). It was therefore not used in my own research. However, the major condition of Spiro's argument is admirably fulfilled by our Sentence Completion Technique, the statements of which—covering a broad spectrum of psychological experiences—were expressly designed for, and are capable of, use not only in Thai peasant culture but in several other cultures of the world.

The next two basic stages of the research are intended eventually to provide analytic depth and descriptive detail to the earlier formulations. The third stage, involving the use of the Thematic Apperception Test— eleven of the original Murray–Morgan "American" cards which were redrawn to suit Thai conditions—is concerned with portraying the fantasies and unconscious sentiments of the villagers to the extent to which they are willing or capable of articulating material which reveals such sentiments. This last point is important. I used the TAT in Bang Chan on the premise that this technique would elicit the type of data it is theoretically designed to elicit; that is, when informants are presented with highly ambiguous pictures and asked to make up stories describing what is occurring in the pictures, they will project through these stories their own unconscious sentiments and preoccupations. The rationale here is that since the stories and the pictures which stimulate them are so highly fanciful, with no realistic consequences or constraints, informants will give free rein to their imaginations and reveal those concerns that are not usually expressed in the more inhibiting and realistic circumstances of ordinary life; and being fantasies, the stories represent projections of unconscious materials. It is this fanciful element that differentiates the TAT data analytically from the considerably more realistic SCT materials.

To a large extent, these theoretical expectations were fulfilled in the informants' responses to the TAT. The villagers' inordinate preoccupation with aggression and social conflict in the stories, for example, was almost the antithesis of what one would predict from observations of overt behavior, but made considerable sense to an investigator who always found it hard to believe that their marked non-aggressiveness at the behavioral level did not betray something quite different at more latent levels.

Despite successes of this sort with the TAT, there were several instances when informants did not seem to articulate analytically useful material. This was either because some pictures held little psychological significance for them (and this happened, I might add, with cards that were expected to be among the most stimulating) or, more important, because the informants' stories were getting psychologically too close to home: the "unconscious sentiments" they were supposedly projecting onto the figures in the cards were becoming uncomfortably conscious and knowingly self-descriptive.

Thus informants would often get their story "heroes" into emotionally difficult or painful situations, and as if recognizing what they had done—"I will reveal this much, but not more"—would resist elaborating, working through, or even resolving the fanciful but personally distressing situations they had created.

I mention these difficulties primarily to emphasize that despite the usefulness of an instrument like the TAT for evoking the unconscious feelings of informants—and doing so more efficiently than other techniques heretofore devised—the extent to which such feelings will in fact be articulated depends largely on the informants' emerging awareness of their feelings, or lack of same, a characteristic which may well vary from culture to culture. In assessing TAT responses or any other fantasy materials, therefore, it is well to remember that the obtained data may eventually tell us just as much about the process of accepting and rejecting unconscious feelings as it will about the content of "unconscious" feelings as such.

The fourth section of the research consists of several detailed life histories. The major aim here is to provide in the most naturalistic terms possible what it means to feel and think like a Thai peasant. Except for highly general, open-ended questions ("Thinking back on your life, what are the most important things that ever happened to you?"; "What kind of childhood did you lead?") and occasional probes, the data are completely the product of the villagers' own assumptions, trains of thought, and emphases.

Having collected and worked with all the foregoing data, I would suggest that the life histories are clearly the most descriptively rich and psychologically revealing, especially when coupled with individual analyses of the projective test materials. However, being life histories, they are also highly idiosyncratic—perhaps an inevitable concomitant of their richness. It is precisely for this reason that the analyses of life histories were (and should be) undertaken toward the latter part of a research program, after a basic picture of psychological modality and variation, as well as a general description of villagers' unconscious processes and preoccupations, has first been provided. It is only in such a context that their representative character,[3] as well as their substantive significance, can be intelligently

---

[3] I am referring here to *psychological* representativeness, not to the more familiar problem of *social* representativeness—age, sex, occupational roles—that has been bruited about in the literature (Lindesmith and Strauss 1950, Mead 1953 and 1955,

determined. So frequently the provocative, interesting, or delightfully human life histories found in the anthropological literature (Dyk 1938 and Tirabutana 1958 come immediately to mind) are so simply because they are the products of the more imaginative, articulate, and introspective members of the culture in question. The issue of course is not that a biography elicited from an articulate individual is to be considered ultimately any more or less valuable than one obtained from a more "typical" member of the culture—Kluckhohn's "Mr. Moustache" (1945) is ample evidence of what an articulate interpreter can do with the life history of a relatively inarticulate informant—but rather that it be accurately seen against a background of the psychological responses of the members of the community as a whole.[4]

The final stage of the research program is perhaps the most complex. Following the outlines of a recommendation originally made by Inkeles and Levinson (1954) and Inkeles (1959), it aims at presenting a systematic analysis of the *relationship* between the personality tendencies of the villagers, as determined through the foregoing materials on the one hand, and the functional requirements of Thai peasant society, as determined through ethnographic data, on the other.

An analysis of this type rests on at least three premises: (1) that there is just as likely to be a lack of congruence between the psychological capacities and proclivities of a group of people and the psychological demands that are made upon them by their own social institutions (demands that must be met if the institutions are to be maintained effectively) as there is likely to be a close fit, and that a crucial, empirical task of any culture-personality study is to detail the specific areas of congruence and non-congruence; (2) that human beings can bear considerable psychological strain—precisely how much we really do not know—and still function effectively, maintaining both their prevailing personality patterns and

---

Mandelbaum 1953, among others). The issue is the extent to which the psychological tendencies of life history informants—their readiness to respond and modes of response in various situations, their assumptions and unconscious premises—are typical of other villagers.

[4] I am reminded here of my own ambivalent reaction to a comment once made by a villager who, intrigued by the fact that I was collecting life histories, said: "I have heard about those people who are telling you their life stories. You're smart—getting interesting ones like them. Some of those people can really *phuud keŋ.*" To *phuud keŋ* means to "speak well," but more particularly to speak cleverly, fluently, deceptively, convincingly, or beautifully (in an aesthetic sense). Actually, there were numerous individuals in Bang Chan who, in local terms, could speak considerably more *keŋ* than the life history informants. However, as the villager's remark suggests, the ability to be "keŋ-ful" in one's speech is something to which Bang Chaners give considerable attention, often to the extent of seriously modifying the intellectual content of their speech, and is one more factor that must be dealt with in assessing the content of a biographical document.

established social structure, albeit in a state of stressful equilibrium; (3) that too much strain will eventually lead to major changes either in their personality patterns or social structure or both, in either a social-psychologically integrative or malintegrative way.[5] Some preliminary illustrations of this approach can be found in Phillips (1963).

I have gone into considerable detail in the above discussion in order to indicate the broader context of the present volume and also to illustrate the necessity for thinking in terms of a multiple-stage research program, each part of which concentrates on a circumscribed descriptive issue. The point is that each stage of the design has *of necessity* its intrinsic strengths and limitations. At the very outset of this book it was noted that the purpose of this study is "to provide a *basic* description of the dominant personality traits" of the villagers. It is hoped that it will indeed provide that—by which is meant a portrayal of the villagers' most distinctive personality traits as expressed in overt behavior and an account of their subjectively held dispositions as revealed in responses made to a series of hypothetical but realistic situations. In the latter instance, special attention is given to the issue of psychological modality and variation as well as to the larger problem of cross-cultural comparability. However, the presentation will neither deal in any detail with fantasies, unconscious sentiments, or psychodynamic processes, nor will it have the descriptive—and idiosyncratic—richness that can be found in life history documents. The emphasis throughout is on the personality characteristics of the members of the community as a whole.

A final word should be said about the theoretical model which underlies the entire effort. The basic organizing principle of a study of this kind is that human beings can be most effectively described in terms of their *typical, characteristic,* or *stable* psychological responses. These terms refer not to the superficiality or depth of such responses (which may be con-

---

[5] This last premise is mentioned for purposes of formal completeness, not as a practical predictive principle. We have as yet little idea of the amount of psychological strain individuals can endure before making changes in their personalities or social environments, although in a loose *post hoc* way we have often been able to specify in individual cases the conditions which lead to such changes. Also, we obviously have no way of foretelling whether changes resulting from personality-institutional strains will lead to integrative social psychological responses (Manus culture during the past twenty-five years; the abolition of the taboo system in Hawaii in 1819); or simply to more intense strains, the most extreme examples being revolution (Burma during the early and mid-1950's, the Congo) or cultural malaise (many Melanesian and American Indian tribes). The crucial issue here may well be the time factor: how short- or long-lived these responses prove to be, or whether they are instrumental or conclusive. The Hawaiian abolition of taboo, for example, was inconsequential relative to what occurred five months later after the first missionaries arrived; but the recent chaos in the Congo may in time prove to be only a minor episode in the establishment of the nation.

scious or unconscious), but to their *constancy*. Thus when we speak of a "polite," "fun-loving" people—or a "narcissistic," "self-accepting" people— we mean that there is great likelihood that these persons will respond or will be predisposed to respond in the manner indicated, especially in novel or ambiguous situations. Indeed, ambiguous situations provide the best evidence for how typical the responses actually are, a point that should be kept in mind later with regard to the Sentence Completion data.

It is recognized of course that this model cannot possibly account for all human behavior and feelings. Even the most polite people will have their moments of boorishness, and the most narcissistic their moments of selflessness. Also, responses that occur relatively infrequently, or under very special circumstances, may often prove to be among the most psychologically revealing. Yet the psychological tendencies of human beings are remarkably constant. People do act repeatedly in similar and often almost identical ways, and it is primarily this attribute of psychological predictability that brings order both to their lives and to our analyses.

I

The Village of Bang Chan

Geographical and Cultural Setting

The heartland of Siam is the Mɛɛnaam or Caw Phrajaa Valley, a vast alluvial plain stretching out for some 250 miles north of the Gulf of Thailand and the capital city of Bangkok, where approximately 40 percent of the nation's 26.3 million persons (1960) live.[1] This Central region is distinguished geographically, and to a lesser extent culturally, from the three other major areas of Thailand: the North, a forested mountain area dominated by Chiengmai, Thailand's second largest city, and in whose outer reaches live many of the tribal peoples of Siam; the Northeast, a broad plateau region which is the largest and economically poorest area of the country; and the South, or Peninsular Thailand, a jungle and mountain area where the heaviest concentration of Thai Malay–Moslems live.

The community of Bang Chan is located some 31 kilometers northeast of Bangkok on what is essentially a flat, seemingly endless rice field, broken occasionally by tall Asiatic pines, strings of houses along canals, or clumps of trees shielding some isolated homesteads. A person seeing Bang Chan for the first time is struck particularly by the intense green of the landscape and, once off the macadam road that connects the village to Bangkok and to the market town of Minburi four kilometers to the east, the stillness of the setting, even along the thickly populated main canal where voices are muffled by the heavy foliage surrounding each house. Often in the early hours of the afternoon the only sound that one can hear in Bang Chan is the dip of the paddles of boats moving up the canal or the barking of dogs.

---

[1] There is no general agreement on the precise boundaries of the Mɛɛnaam Valley. Zimmerman (1931), Andrews (1935), Blanchard *et al.* (1958), and most Thai government documents use the term synonymously with "Central region," which would include the provinces east and southeast of Bangkok to the Cambodia frontier, west to the Burma border, and north of the Gulf of Thailand. Credner (1935) and deYoung (1955) on the other hand limit the term to only that portion of the Central region which falls north of Bangkok, equivalent to what Pendleton (1962) calls the "Bangkok Plain." Our population figure refers to the former usage.

Houses in the village vary considerably in appearance: from the bamboo and thatch dwellings of the poorest families to the sturdy, great gabled houses of teak built by Bang Chan's original settlers to the tiled and corrugated iron-roofed homes of the newly rich. Most, however, follow the traditional Siamese pattern of being built on posts two to ten feet off the ground, mainly as a protection against flood waters. Many homes in Bang Chan give the impression of being permanently unfinished, the bamboo houses because they require constant refurbishment, the wooden dwellings because they are made of teak which seasons best when left untreated and exposed directly to the elements. The merging upper-class urban pattern of painting teakwood has not yet reached Bang Chan.

The major thoroughfare of the community, bisecting it in a north-south direction and perpendicular to the Bangkok-Minburi highway, is Khlɔɔŋ (or Canal) Bang Chan, which links with Khlɔɔŋ Sɛɛn Sɛɛb three kilometers south of the village. The latter, dug in the 1840's and originally intended as a military route to the Cambodian frontier, is one of several major canals dug during the mid-nineteenth century as part of the vast canal system that was constructed in the Central Plain when the region was opened for commercial rice production. Together with the highway built since World War II, a one-hour bus ride to the capital, Khlɔɔŋ Sɛɛn Sɛɛb, provides the villagers with their major access to Bangkok and the rest of the Central Plain. By motorboat a trip to Bangkok via this large, bustling canal takes approximately three hours.

Despite these relatively good communications facilities and the long-standing Thai peasant tradition to paj thiaw ("to go around"—for fun, on visits, pilgrimages, often for long distances) few people outside the immediate vicinity of the village have ever heard of Bang Chan. The community is neither a landmark nor is it located near one; it is not famed for any activities (other than having become the research site for the "American professors"); and because it is not a spatially integrated village, Bang Chan cannot even be found on any map of Thailand. Like most Thai settlements, Bang Chan has a Buddhist monastery and a government elementary school. It is these two structures that give the village its identity and the local people a sense of belonging to a community. People say that they live "at home in Bang Chan" because they make their merit at the monastery of Bang Chan and send their children to the Bang Chan school. Approximately five square miles in size and inhabited by 1,771 people living in 296 households (1956 village census), Bang Chan seems in physical appearance and social significance like the thousands of other communities that dot the rice fields of the great Central Plain.

To what extent Bang Chan may be considered "typical" in an analytic sense of other villages of the Mɛɛnaam Valley, or even of the country as a whole, depends in large part on one's frame of reference.[2] In the most general terms, the people of Bang Chan are like almost all ethnic Thai peasants (excepting on some counts Thai Moslems and some of the economically disenfranchised people of the Northeast) in that they have a keen sense of membership in the nation-state with a deep loyalty to the Crown, speak the Thai language, are Therevada Buddhists, are outwardly highly deferential to the authority of the Central government, and have a conception of the good life that stresses fun, physical comfort and security, intellectual simplicity and practicality, and a moral (as contrasted with a natural) ordering of the universe. Too, like the vast majority of their rural compatriots,[3] they are engaged in the production of rice, an activity which to them is not only an economic operation (Ingram 1955, Janlekha 1955) but almost a way of life, being bound up with their social structure, dietary habits, religious practices, and even their philosophical (J. R. Hanks 1961) and aesthetic conceptions.

-----

[2] For readers unfamiliar with Thailand, the nation-state, it should be noted that the country is predominantly rural; 84 percent of the total national labor force is in agriculture and there are only ten towns with populations of 20,000 people or more, in which 6 percent of the national population (1947 census) live. Although Bangkok has a population of approximately 1,200,000, the second largest city, Chiengmai, has only 60,000 (1957 estimate).

The nation also has a high degree of ethnic homogeneity, 82 percent of the population considering themselves native Thai (1957 estimate). The largest ethnic minority group is the overseas Chinese, comprising 11.3 percent of the population (1953 estimate, from Skinner 1957), the balance being Malays, Cambodians, and Indians; the so-called tribal groups number in toto only about 150,000 people.

The religious composition of the country is 94.1 percent Buddhist, 3.9 percent Moslem, 0.5 percent Christian, and 1.5 percent "others," many of whom are tribal animists. Thai Buddhism is of the Southern (Therevada, Hinayana, or "Lesser Vehicle") variety and as practiced by most Thai, has syncretized within it many Brahmanic and traditional Southeast Asian animistic elements (see the chapter on "Religion" in Sharp et al. 1956, and Textor 1960). The largest minority religion, Islam, is practiced by ethnic Malay living in the four southernmost provinces of Thailand, as well as by some ethnic Thai—many of them descendants of former Malay slaves or war prisoners—scattered through the areas north and east of Bangkok, including Bang Chan, where they comprise 9.8 percent of the local population. Relationships between Buddhists and Moslems, at least in Bang Chan, are quite amicable and except for ideal prohibitions against intermarriage and occasional off-hand remarks such as "Moslem women are loose" or "Moslems kill animals," there is little overt hostility between the two groups. Certainly few Bang Chaners ever distinguish between their Buddhist and Moslem neighbors when arranging a work group, selecting a drinking partner, or even compiling a guest list for a son's ordination. .

[3] Janlekha (in Sharp et al. 1953: 110) indicates that 55 percent of the total national labor force is involved solely in the cultivation of rice—which occupies approximately 90 percent of the total cultivated land area—and as many as 92 percent of all agricultural households are rice households. The 55 percent figure excludes all those people who are involved in the transportation, milling, storing, and distribution of rice. Eighty-five percent of the population of Bang Chan (1953) are rice farmers.

In addition to these widespread national patterns, Bang Chan has certain characteristics that seem relatively distinctive of villages of the Central Plain. Not of least importance is the demographic arrangement of the community: either isolated homesteads surrounded by rice fields and connected to larger canals by small tributaries or groups of households strung out along both sides of the canals. The former pattern is more commonplace and historically more recent, and is the result of an expanding population trying to live on a land that has been so committed to the commercialized cultivation of rice that the only available house sites are on the fields themselves. This "typical Central Plain" pattern contrasts with the "cluster" type villages found in the North and Northeast (deYoung 1955) where houses are integrated into compact communities around which are located the rice fields. Although it is difficult to draw precise relationships between demographic arrangements and psychological characteristics, it is noteworthy that the isolated locale of so many Bang Chan households is not out of keeping with the independent and individualistic propensities of the villagers. As one villager expressed it, "If people live far away from each other, there will not be any trouble."

Related to the above pattern and characteristic of other communities of the Central region (cf. Kaufman 1960) is the absence among village residents of any strong sense of identification with the needs of their community as a whole. Except for religious activities and the reciprocal work groups organized for rice transplanting and harvesting—the rewards for which are directly personal—the villagers simply are not predisposed to participate in communal projects. Thus, activities which require large-scale coöperation or organization to be effective—clearing or deepening canals, repairing the unusable road that leads from the main highway to the school, building a playground for the school—are either not carried out or are effected only with extreme difficulty. Although a few villagers recognize these as defects of social organization, it is clear that the majority find it easier to live with them than to try to change the basic institutional framework that sustains them; maintaining their own freedom of action is simply more important, and more culturally "natural," to the villagers than getting involved in public service projects. Again, this pattern seems to contrast with that found in the villages of the North (deYoung 1955) where individuals regularly contribute labor to their communities by repairing village streets and maintaining irrigation systems, even when such efforts require coöperation between adjacent villages.

The inability of Bang Chaners to organize coöperative projects is undoubtedly abetted by the formal governmental structure of the village which, although perhaps more of an administrative nightmare than is normally found elsewhere in the Central Plain, is in its organizational essentials not atypical of the region. Instead of villages being organized administratively on the basis of natural social groupings and demarcations—that is, social centers and groups with which people feel a primary identification, in Bang Chan's case the local Buddhist monastery and government primary school—so that governmental and social units are isomorphic, they are gerrymandered into highly arbitrary administrative units. Thus the village of Bang Chan is comprised of seven *muubaan* or hamlets, at the head of which are seven hamlet headmen; these hamlets are located in two different *tambon,* or communes (four in one commune, three in the other) headed by two commune headmen, neither of whom lives in Bang Chan; the two communes are located in two different districts headed by two different district officers and their staffs; the two districts fortunately are in a single province, Phranakhɔɔn, the same administrative unit in which the metropolis of Bangkok is located. Yet the people who reside in these varying hamlets located in different communes and districts all perceive themselves as living in the single village of Bang Chan. The fundamental organizational problem here is that since the sources and lines of governmental authority do not follow the lines of the natural Bang Chan community, jurisdictional conflicts and confusions arise to threaten the effectiveness of those community-wide programs that occasionally may be initiated. For example, during a diphtheria immunization campaign in the village (Hanks and Hanks 1955), the public health officer from one of the district offices was reluctant to immunize all the children of Bang Chan on the grounds that some of them came from hamlets outside his district's jurisdiction; he yielded, as the Hankses note, only when a perceptive villager pointed out that if germs knew no boundaries why should he?

Not all villages of the Central region have such real or potential administrative difficulties. (And Bang Chan does not have them too frequently either, principally because the government does not initiate too many community service programs.) However, the basic organizational principle which admits them—that houses are grouped together as administrative "villages" on the basis of conceptual neatness rather than socially functional criteria—is a common feature of the administrative structure of the Central Plain.

The foregoing account describes some basic culture patterns which Bang Chan shares with other villages of either the region or the nation. In addition to these broader patterns, Bang Chan has certain traits which inevitably refer to local village conditions and contingencies. For example, the most active and viable social unit in Bang Chan beyond the familial level is the order of Buddhist monks associated with the monastery. It is the only organization within the village that has been successful in mobilizing community activity (Sharp *et al.* 1953), although much of this activity has been religious in nature—getting the assistance of villagers to construct monks' cubicles or repairing the small rest pavilions near the monastery, the "pay" for which is Buddhist merit—or, if secular, infused with sacred attributes, such as when the head monk helped raise funds for the construction of the Bang Chan school by supporting the notion that villagers who gave money to the school would make merit. It is clear, however, that the organizational vigor of the Bang Chan monkhood is mainly a function of the aggressive personality and leadership of Bang Chan's particular abbot, and that with a more retiring, contemplative head monk—a not uncommon or undesirable role for an abbot—the situation would be strikingly different.

In a similar vein, it is difficult to link the incidence of land ownership and tenancy in Bang Chan with any consistent national or regional pattern. At the national level, Thailand is fortunate among predominantly peasant nations in having a comparatively low level of land tenancy, an estimated 80 percent of the cultivated land of the country being owned by the small, independent farmers who work it (National FAO Committee of Thailand 1949). However, within these broad, national parameters there is considerable inter- and intra-regional variation. Zimmerman's study in the early 1930's indicated that the number of peasants without land ranged from 14 percent in Southern Thailand, through 27 percent in the North, to 36 percent in the Central Plain. These regional figures seemed to have remained relatively constant through the years in that deYoung (1955) reports a tenancy figure of 27.7 percent for a village in the North which he studied in 1949, and Janlekha (1955) indicates a figure of 37 percent for Bang Chan, in the Central Plain, in 1953.[4] As close as the Bang Chan figure may seem to its regional average, however, it is of little significance when seen against the background of variability that exists within the region as a whole: for example, in villages near the city of Lopburi, only 12 percent of the villagers are landless, but in the Khlɔɔŋ Rangsit area, not far

---

[4] It should be noted, however, that other indices of economic well-being in Bang Chan have not remained constant. To the extent that his historical materials permit, Janlekha (1955) points out that land holdings have become increasingly smaller, the amount of time newly-married couples must live with one set of parents (in order to accumulate the capital necessary for setting up their own neolocal households) longer, and the price of land higher. Janlekha's data indicate that in the five-year period between 1948 and 1953 alone, the price of agricultural land, as contrasted with considerably more expensive residential land, in and around Bang Chan increased 560 percent!

It is also well to keep in mind Janlekha's observation that, depending upon familial circumstances such as number of children and availability and proximity of labor, a Bang Chan farmer who rents a large plot of land from a benevolent absentee landlord, who is often unfamiliar with Bang Chan crop values, may be considerably better off economically than a farmer who works a small plot of land that is all his own.

from Bang Chan, the figure is as high as 85 percent (Dobby 1950). In these terms, therefore, it is best to view the incidence of land tenancy in Bang Chan as largely a function of local, historical circumstances.

A final word should be said about Bang Chan's proximity and accessibility to Bangkok—the cornucopia of so much that is new, interesting, and desirable (if somewhat equivocally) to most Siamese peasants. It is clear that Bang Chan's closeness to the capital creates certain conditions that would not be present in a community situated, for example, 200 kilometers, instead of 31 kilometers, from the nation's largest city. Simply on practical grounds, this nearness to the city permits the villagers to take advantage of opportunities—economic, recreational, and religious—which those living in distant provinces can obtain only after serious consideration of the financial and psychological expenses involved: "Do I have shoes to wear in the city? Do they treat people from the provinces well? With whom will I stay? Do I have the train fare?" A Bang Chaner who visits the capital does not have to make such financial or emotional commitments, since it is only a one hour, three and one-half baht (seventeen and one-half cents) bus ride back home, although many do share with their up-country cousins the peasant's apprehensions about city manners.

The attractions of Bangkok take several forms: off-season jobs, medical care, kinship ties, special schools, great market places, famed monasteries or fairs, and the many other places where one can go to have fun. A survey conducted in Bang Chan during 1955 (Goldsen and Ralis 1957) indicates that 62 percent of all household heads in the village visited Bangkok more than twice during the year for just such purposes. (Twenty-one percent had not gone to Bangkok at all, and 23 percent had gone more than ten times.) Many villagers, particularly younger men, attracted by the promise of regular wages, lighter work, and the bright lights of the city, leave Bang Chan with the hope that they will never have to return, although of course many do. The Goldsen-Ralis survey reveals that 26 percent of their respondents had lived in Bangkok for a year or more, although for most this was in fulfillment of military service.

Living in Bangkok is not something that is desired in and of itself. Bang Chaners are keenly aware of the disadvantages of city living—particularly its great expense and insecurity—and are impressed only by those individuals who have made a success out of their urban sojourn. Most would agree that a Bangkok coolie, for all his exposure to the wonders of the modern world, lives a considerably less attractive life than they do.

The frequent transit between Bang Chan and Bangkok,[5] however,

---

[5] Of less practical consequence than their direct personal experiences and word-of-mouth contacts, but not to be ignored, are the villagers' contacts with Bangkok by way of radio, newspapers, books, and of course by way of what their children bring

continually brings to the attention of the villagers urban standards and aspirations which, whenever possible, they attempt to apply to themselves. L. M. Hanks (1959b: 19) sees the operation of this characteristic acculturative mechanism in Bang Chan in terms of the villagers' "search for respectability": "A respectable cremation requires an orchestra; a respectable dwelling a tile roof; a respectable sickness an injection; and a respectable family must chaperone carefully its growing daughters. So run a host of points which help to bolster but not necessarily to advance social position."

Yet, after the relationship between village and town has been considered, Bang Chan remains very much a peasant community, whose residents are concerned first and foremost with the cultivation of rice, the maintenance of their monastery, and their own immediate social environment. Despite aspirations, many Bang Chan cremations must go without the orchestra; most dwellings lack the tile roof; injections are taken only by those who can afford them; and the necessity for boys and girls to work together during harvest time, a period of unavoidably infectious joy, precludes any rigidly imposed chaperonage. Perhaps the best assessment of the cultural position of Bang Chan was provided by the writer's field assistant—an individual born and reared in a village in the Northeast who, although in many respects worldly and urbane, maintained an almost passionate identification with his peasant background—who said: "When I first came here to Bang Chan, I never thought that people living so close to Bangkok could be *real* Thai villagers. But they are. They are not as friendly and hospitable as Northeastern peasants, and they are more interested in money, but they have a much greater love of the land. No city person could ever think and feel as they do."

Family Life and Social Organization

In terms of the traditional categories of social structural analysis, the social organization of Bang Chan is strikingly simple. There are essentially only five social units which demand, and toward which villagers express, relatively enduring psychological commitments. These are the nuclear family;

---

home from school, the curriculum for which is written and directed by Ministry of Education officials in the city. Approximately 14 percent of Bang Chan households have battery driven radios (there is no electricity in the village) and approximately 60 percent of the villagers can read, although considerably fewer actually have the proficiency to go comfortably through a newspaper; theoretically the same number of people can write, but few Bang Chan adults have the courage to take pencil to paper without feeling discomfort over their handwriting, spelling, and knowledge of stylistic forms. Newspapers that people bring home from town are passed around and read more for their entertainment than information; the few books that are seen in the village are pulp magazines, religious or moralistic writings, and occasionally do-it-yourself pamphlets ("How to Raise Chickens the Modern Way").

a loosely defined, laterally oriented kindred; the nation-state (mentioned not for formal reasons, but because it actually is psychologically important); and to a lesser extent, the village monastery and school. Of these five institutions, the nuclear family is the principal focus of psychological concern, beyond the individual himself. Otherwise, there are in Bang Chan no castes, age-grade societies, occupational groups (other than the family), neighborhood groups, or groups expressive of village solidarity (such as councils or governing boards) which might impose a sense of obligation on the villagers, or to whose norms or functions the villagers might have to conform.[6] Bang Chaners do not have to contribute their labor to their community, serve as village guards, contend with the dictates of village elders, or even actively coöperate with fellow villagers.

All villagers have additional relationships of varying degrees of intimacy both within and without the community, but these are dyadic, not group, relationships based on implicit expectations of mutual benefit. Such contacts are in nature primarily idiosyncratic (friends), transient (reciprocal work groups, gambling and drinking partners), or contractual (as opposed to affective or kin determined: vendors, landlords, debtors, rice millers, employers, and doctors). It is important to recognize that if some of these latter relationships take on positive affective qualities, they may also assume some of the forms and feelings of kinship. Thus, a young man who is taken on as a hired hand by a family frequently ceases to be considered an "employee" and becomes instead an "adopted son." (This type of gemeinschaft relationship, contrary perhaps to theoretical expectations, is also characteristic of many occupational situations in Bangkok.) In a similar vein, the terms for older sibling (phii), elder uncle (lung), and elder aunt (paa) are used as terms of address and reference between individuals who are obviously not related to each other, but who wish to mark overtly their fondness and respect for one another. The use of these

---

[6] There are two minor exceptions to this generalization: (1) a monastery lay committee whose functions are limited to the secular tasks of monastery administration, and membership in which brings prestige and Buddhist merit to a few selected members of the community; and (2) reciprocal work groups organized for and limited to rice transplanting and harvesting, membership in which is completely voluntary and a matter of mutual convenience (Janlekha 1955). Careful accounts are kept as to how much labor is contributed by each participating family, and responsibility for remitting labor received lies with the individual participant, not the group.

It must be noted that the monastery and its cadre of relatively permanent monks, although the very institution that defines the existence of "the village of Bang Chan," is not from the point of view of its clientele primarily a unit representative of village cohesiveness. It is first and foremost a Buddhist monastery where one may make merit and only secondarily the Bang Chan Monastery. Several members of the community patronize other monasteries, and several Bang Chan monks come from other locales. The keen sense of individual obligation that villagers feel toward their monastery could be directed toward any monastery.

fictive terms is of course sometimes prompted by nothing more than the desire to be polite, but equally often it symbolizes genuine feelings of affection and obligation not too different from what the terms imply when they are used in their original kinship context. Bang Chaners have a wonderfully convenient term, *phyan-yaad,* a compound meaning literally "family friends," which is used to refer both to friends to whom ego feels so close that he considers them members of his family and to individuals whom he considers his friends *because* they are members of his family. The particular persons to whom this term, as well as those noted above, is applied vary widely from informant to informant (expectedly so because they are non-institutionalized terms). However, the point to be emphasized is that for all villagers kinship provides a basic referential mechanism for expressing the degree of psychological affiliation that they feel toward other human beings.

An *awareness* of degrees of psychological affiliation and obligation and of the modes for expressing such sentiments are very much a part of village life. For with the exception of the five institutions mentioned above, most Bang Chaners, as I have noted elsewhere (Sharp *et al.* 1956: 241), are really not obliged—and do not feel obliged—to be beholden to anyone but themselves. In a very real sense, the village is comprised of 1,771 individualists whose major goals in life are to obtain sufficient land to support themselves, their growing children, and their religion, free from physical insecurities and unencumbered by entangling social obligations. When they enter into relationships with other people they do so with an awareness that they are always acting of their own free will.

Despite the conventions of ethnographic reporting, it is difficult to delimit the precise nature of the nuclear family in Bang Chan. The nuclear family clearly is the ideal for all villagers, but because Bang Chaners are just as responsive to convenience as they are to custom, there is considerable variation regarding this ideal. In his study of the economy of the village, Janlekha (1955) found it necessary to distinguish five different kinds of functioning, mutually exclusive household units in Bang Chan: the typical nuclear family (59.4 percent of all households); a limited extended family, consisting of a man, wife, either or both their sets of parents, and unmarried children (8.1 percent); an extended family, consisting of the limited extended family plus married children, the latters' children, and any collateral relatives of any generation (26.8 percent); a one-person family (5.4 percent); and the ecclesiastical "family," consisting of the order of Buddhist monks, the only truly corporate group in the village (0.3 percent). (These variations of the nuclear family, all localized groups, should of course not be confused with what I, following Sharp [1957], have been calling the kindred, with what Kaufman [1960] refers to as spatially and remotely extended families, or with what L. M. Hanks [1959c] calls the multi-local extended family, about which there is more below.)

The variations of the nuclear family, obviously excepting the monkhood, arise primarily out of the large proportion of recently married couples who find it more expedient to continue living with one set of parents while accumulating funds for setting up their own independent households. In the case of one-person families, the variation arises when individuals are unable to live with their kin, are deserted by them, or have none. All the one-person families tend to be poor and are comprised largely of elderly people. In arrangements of the former type, there is a slight (five to three) tendency to matrilocality over patrilocality, and despite the intention of all concerned that the arrangements remain impermanent, there is considerable variability as to how long they are maintained. Analyzing a sample of 96 Bang Chan families, Janlekha found that although 30 percent came into being as nuclear families immediately after marriage, the balance underwent a period of residence with parents ranging from one to twenty years, the average being four years, with 16 percent never moving from the parents' home at all. Most cases of what Janlekha calls "limited extended families" result from a stem family inheritance pattern, although some entail elderly parents breaking up their households and moving in with the family of one of their mature children.

In addition to these basic variations, more accurately labeled "alternatives," there are several other variations of the nuclear family that occur with sufficient frequency to be noticed and at the same time are considered not at all unusual by the villagers themselves. Their significance for us is that they reveal what appears to be an almost nonchalant willingness or acquiescence on the part of the villagers to make modifications and adjustments in their living arrangements whenever necessary. Underlying this seems to be a fundamental assumption that the question of who lives with whom simply is not one of overriding importance: as long as individuals can live together without discord, act in terms of the household's established patterns of superordination and subordination, contribute labor or money to the family larder commensurate with their ages, and not inconvenience each other, they will be welcomed into the household; if unable or unwilling to fulfill such elementary obligations, they may take their leave, even if they are in fact full-fledged members of the nuclear family.

This rather flexible, or what the late John Embree would have called (1950) "loosely structured," approach to family organization is expressed in both centripetal and centrifugal ways.

Consonant with the fact that in all but the poorest Bang Chan families there is almost always enough rice to feed another mouth, it is common in

the village to find dependent relatives—siblings, cousins, nephews, nieces—
who, unable to make a go of it elsewhere, are accepted into a relative's
family, sometimes to the extent of eventually taking over the headship of
the family. Sometimes, on the initiative and invitation of an elderly or
lonely relative, an entire nuclear family will be asked to take over or share a
household. Children of poor or "inconvenienced" families (where a new
child is born before the first is weaned, where there are too many children
for the mother to handle comfortably, where a youngster is simply being
"troublesome") are adopted or "borrowed" by other villagers for varying
periods of time. This is done preferably by relatives, sometimes by neighbors, and often, in the case of boys, by the monastery, where the children
become hand-servants to the monks and are supposed to absorb, by a kind
of osmotic process, righteous ways of behaving. (Of my three male life
history informants, two were given over to relatives at the ages of two, the
third at the age of eight; one spent his childhood with four different
families, another with five families; one describes his adolescence as "wan-
dering from place to place." The psychological implications of such dis-
placement should not be underestimated.) On occasion, two independent
nuclear families—almost always connected by some kinship tie—will join
together for convenience to share cooking facilities, in which case they
effectively become a single extended family. And in some cases, although
rare, one will encounter adult children living in independent households
but handing over their income to a parent, living in still another home, who
disburses the proceeds when necessary.

On the other side, it is common practice in Bang Chan now for a
husband to be away for four or five months at a time earning money in
Bangkok, or during the dry season on a vegetable farm, returning home to
visit his wife and children whenever opportunity permits, with or without
funds. The wife may still maintain their household, but often returns to
live with her own parents.[7] In a similar vein, although obviously more
extreme, it is not unusual to find families in Bang Chan which have simply
"disintegrated," as the villagers say. Much depends here on the circumstances of family members. Bang Chaners usually reserve the term "disintegrated" for families that no longer have the economic wherewithal or
justification for staying together as functioning units. In these instances,
family members simply go their separate ways, if possible back to their
families of orientation or to other relatives, husbands perhaps into the
monkhood, and the children to whomever will take them. Most frequently,
"disintegration" is characteristic of very poor families, and in the minds of

---

[7] This pattern may be related to the old *corvée* labor pattern when able-bodied
village men were away from their families for extended periods of time.

the villagers is contrasted with those cases of separation or divorce which are viewed as resulting more from social psychological reasons: arguments, contrariness, general incompatability, and wasting or not sharing money. The squandering of money is a most frequent cause of family discord contributing to family dissolution, especially when it involves the three aphoristic evils of Thai life: women, whiskey, and opium (although, in fact, I know of only two cases where Bang Chaners have been reputed to smoke opium).

Precise figures on the divorce or separation rate in Bang Chan are un-known, primarily because many marriages as well as divorces are never registered on the government rolls; also, many separations seem to follow an on-again-off-again pattern; the sanctioned occurrence of polygyny (only eight known cases out of the 296 families) and even polyandry (two known cases) complicates the problem even further. However, the fact that *four months* after I had designated a sample of thirty families from which to select informants, six of those families, or 20 percent of the sample popula-tion, had dissolved would strongly suggest that Bang Chan families are not particularly stable.

The causes of family fission in these specific cases are unknown, but what is impressive is the apparent ease with which it takes place and the equanimity with which people seem to accept it. Other informants, re-porting their own experiences or observations, discuss family breakups as if they were among the more normal events of the workaday world and completely understandable. They seem to be of no greater emotional import—in the sense of eliciting recognizable feelings of distress—than losing a good price on the sale of a piece of land or on the sale of some rice. In fact, the latter kinds of situations are considerably more likely to evoke expressions of hurt or exasperation. One repeatedly encounters in Bang Chan instances on the following order: a family breaks up simply because the husband has an inclination to work for a particular person whom he likes; a wife ("she is a touchy woman") runs away every time she has a minor disagreement with her husband (minor even by village standards, for example, "Should I buy my lottery tickets from Mr. X or Mr. Y?"; "Should we invite seven monks or ten monks to officiate at this cere-mony?"). The point here is that these explanations—and the low tolerance for discord, the importance to a person of a boss or job over a spouse, the desire to be footloose, which they imply—are to the villagers completely reasonable justifications for the dissolution of family units.

Many of the family relationships referred to above as "centripetal" in nature are clearly related to or derived from patterns of social organization characteristic of an earlier Bang Chan. Although most evidence indicates that even in the years immediately following the settlement of the village in the 1880's, the nuclear family was the primary social unit,[8] it is equally clear that extended family relations played a highly significant role—considerably more so than they do today—in the total life of the community. The precise nature of that role resists easy terminological formulation. In his reconstruction of the history of Bang Chan, L. M. Hanks (1959c) speaks of two types of "extended families" typical of early Bang Chan, one organized along lineal lines toward a single parent, and the other based on an alliance of siblings. In both cases, members of these groups assisted each other "by working in the fields, sharing food and equipment, helping with chores and celebrating special occasions together," and effectively formed what Hanks calls "extended family hamlets." These larger family units, however, were based on personal compatability, or in the case of the lineally oriented family, on the wealth and leadership of a particularly dynamic individual. They were never based on compelling structural characteristics such as corporate ownership of land or homes. Since many of the individual nuclear families were poor and trying to live off a land that was essentially a frontier, it made sense that they should join together or attach themselves to a wealthier, more powerful individual, and that the primary criterion for association should be the kinship tie with its built-in sentiments of affiliation, familiarity, and trust. However, since the basis of association here was at all times an economic-functional one—it was *reciprocal* and *mutual* benefits that brought people together, not an overriding ethic of familial solidarity—it might perhaps be better to think of such families as associations of "kindred" in the technical sense rather than

---

[8] Since almost all Thai history, by Thai or foreigners, is primarily a court history and concerned with activities of the kingdom at large or activities at the seat of power (where, of course, most of the literati, writers and readers, lived) there is little documentation on the history of the peasant family or any changes it might have gone through. Phya Anuman Rajadhon's profoundly knowledgeable, but highly idealized, essays on "ancient customs" of Thailand (Radjadhon ["Sathien Koset"] 1957 and Rajadhon 1954, 1958) contain references vaguely suggestive of an extended family system among peasants: "the house a groom built always had to be in the home compound of his father-in-law," for example, the time and effort demanded by house-building suggesting a high degree of permanency, the compound implying extended family unity. But the data are too meager and uneven to form the basis of anything more than speculation. On the other hand, comparative distributional data on other Thai-speaking peasants (P. K. Benedict 1943, Seidenfaden 1958); the great emphasis in traditional law, going back to the decrees of Rama Tibodi I in the mid-fourteenth century, on the absence of family responsibility in the commission of individual crime (Lingat 1936 and 1952); and the background commentary in Thailand's great multi-authored love epic of the late eighteenth–early nineteenth century, *Khun Chang and Khun Phaen,* all suggest that the peasant family has remained remarkably stable through the centuries as a nucleated, independently functioning unit linked to other families in the community by loose ties of kinship. The fact that family names did not come into use in Thailand until 1916, and then only by royal decree, further suggests that the extended family was never the major kinship unit.

"extended families." The aim of all Bang Chan families even then was to attain a position in which they would be free from such obligations or would have other families dependent upon them.

In the intervening years the influx of new families into Bang Chan, the increased self-sufficiency of the individual nuclear families and, most important, the increased acceptance of commercial values, have served to break down kindred groups so that today few kinsmen work their fields together and even fewer share their food or equipment with one another, beyond what has been noted above. Perhaps the only remaining *universally* practiced function of the old kindred groups is the celebration of ceremonials involving members of the family, particularly cremations and ordinations, the cost and merit of which are shared among the participants, depending upon their wealth. Very often people do not want to borrow from or lend money or equipment to kinsmen precisely because the intrusion of the kinship tie makes the collection of such debts doubly awkward ("relatives take twice as long in repaying money; I do not want to lend anything to them"). However, the old forms have not been completely obliterated and when necessity requires or personal convenience moves an individual to look to others, the traditions of extended kinship, as indicated earlier, may be invoked.

For purposes of conceptual convenience, two types of kindred may be specified: the kind referred to above which involves kinsmen living in the village and to which Kaufman (1960) gives the name "spatially extended family"; and the type descriptive of relatives living outside Bang Chan, dispersed throughout other villages and provinces or in Bangkok, and called by Kaufman "the remotely extended family" and by L. M. Hanks (1959c) "the multi-local extended family." These terms are of course generic labels descriptive of actual or potential relationships between individuals, not of specifically delimited groups. Sometimes Bang Chaners attempt to extend the definition of the latter type of relationship to individuals who have never heard of them, but who may be in a position to help their son obtain a job in the city or get him admitted into a vocational school. Hanks has shown how the multi-local extended family has to a limited extent in recent years rejuvenated extended kinship ties by becoming the major institutional mechanism through which villagers leave Bang Chan to seek their fortunes elsewhere. (This last phrase is not merely a figure of speech; many young Bang Chan men have what could be called almost a Dick Whittington view about leaving Bang Chan for Bangkok.) A cousin who undertakes to serve as a villager's liaison to a city job or who offers him a place to stay usually does so willingly, for it creates obligations which may be called upon later if need be.

The above description of variations and extensions has been presented in some detail not only to indicate the complex reality of Bang Chan family organization, but to convey—it is hoped with some measure of success by my prolonged, but obviously incomplete, qualifications—some sense of the amorphous nature of village kinship structure. Actually, I feel that any attempt to bring descriptive order to Bang Chan kinship does violence, in the very process of ordering, to the reality of what is being described. This is said neither out of a sense of inadequacy nor apology, but simply to underscore the fact that kinship relationships in Bang Chan are considerably more unpredictable, inconsistent, and chaotic than our descriptive modes typically admit, and that any coherent discussion of them must unavoidably involve an element of reification.[9] Our categories above are by no means inaccurate in indicating functioning kinship units, but they communicate little of the fluidity and tenuousness characteristic of such units. Individuals of all ages recurringly move in and out of families; families splinter, in full or in part, sometimes permanently, but more frequently to be formed again with the same or new members. What is perhaps most distinctive of this flux is the sense of uncertainty that surrounds it—a state that is easily tolerated by the villagers. Often during the course of field work we would enter a home looking for a particular informant only to be told that he had left for Bangkok or for another

---

[9] L. M. Hanks (1959b: 1) has made a similar observation with regard to Thai social structure in general: "The Thai social scene at its most orderly moment seems to flaunt conventional Western requirements for organization and to travel always on the brink of social chaos. Every inclination of the student would give it more regularity. . . ." However, in seeking to account for such instability, Hanks points to such historical circumstances as the freeing of the slaves in 1905, reorganization of the government, the expansion of the population on the new land frontier, the new market economy, and the new ideas and gadgets introduced from the West. One might add the presence of Buddhism and its emphasis on change and impermanence as another contributing factor. I would agree that these social upheavals and the presence of the philosophy represented by the "Wheel of Law" have contributed to the instability of Thai social life, but there is more to it than that, at least with regard to the family. Such explanations simply do not account for cases of a family breaking up because its members accuse each other of stealing lost equipment (why the alternative, "let us look for the lost equipment," is so rarely raised is unknown); or of a father sending his eight- and six-year-old sons to live at the monastery and with relatives because his new wife is annoyed by them; or of the case cited by Hanks of the person who was abandoned by his mother at the age of three months when she ran away out of anger at her husband for taking a second wife, and who later went to live with his grandfather "because he had no one to take care of the buffalo." The point of course is that the primary and immediate factors at work here are psychological ones: an intense narcissism; an assumption that all human beings, even children, are responsible for themselves; a tendency to respond to social discord by rupture rather than an attempt to work it through; in the first example cited, an expectation that others cannot be trusted. The factors that in turn determine these characteristics are of course considerably more difficult to identify, although biographical data (Phillips 1959) suggest that the seeds of such traits are implanted early in the life-cycle.

village; for how long his wife or child did not know: "maybe he will be back next week or next month; it is not certain." In a similar vein, we would encounter a youngster serving at the monastery, a week later working as a chore boy in someone's home, and a few months later living in still another home. And most fascinating of all are those seemingly amicable and placid families—and it should be remembered that Bang Chan is small enough, and in the daily round of life open and quiet enough, so that the slightest manifestation of family tension may easily become public knowledge—which suddenly split apart after a disagreement about something as inconsequential as a missing shirt. Here, the cause of fission is of course not the intrinsic importance of the missing item (although a white "city" shirt is expensive and does have symbolic significance), but rather the villagers' extraordinarily low tolerance for interpersonal conflict and the challenge to their pride: rather than permit the disagreement to mushroom into an emotionally expressive conflict, it is much easier to leave the field. Because the volatility of a dispute is what is often most feared, one rarely hears of any actual argument accompanying the disagreement; instead villagers say, "We had a few words and he left. That's all." [10]

None of the above is meant to imply that family fissions are typical, in a statistical sense, of Bang Chan or even less that discord is what causes them. (Our concern with discord was simply to illustrate that villagers feel so strongly about it that when it occurs, they will take the most extreme measure to avoid it.) However, together with the separations that result from economic opportunities, "arrangements of convenience," and the desire to be footloose, they do occur frequently enough to exist as potentialities in the life of every family; when they happen they are not completely unexpected.

These points have been raised primarily because Bang Chan is in fact a rather placid community, and in discussing kinship it is easy to mistake placidity for inertia, especially when our typical categories of description almost assume the latter state to be the case. However, accompanying this placidity is a kind of quiet dynamic resulting from 1,771 individualists—polite, gentle, non-aggressive, but nevertheless individualists—pursuing their own purposes. These pursuits do not preclude family obligations, loyalties, and love—Bang Chaners repeatedly speak and act in terms of repaying the love that their parents have given them; of repaying them for

---

[10] The desire to avoid emotional climax here seems very similar to what Bateson (1949: 40) found among the Balinese where, when individuals quarrel, there is an attempt at a "formal recognition of the state of their mutual relationship, and possibly, in some sort, a pegging of their relationship at that state . . . this method of dealing with quarrels would correspond to the substitution of a plateau for a climax." In Bang Chan, the "plateau" is achieved by having nothing to do with one's antagonist.

bringing them into the world; of helping siblings because of the kind
things they have done; of loving children so that they will care for them
when they are old [11]—but they do condition how and when such sentiments
will be expressed. It is difficult to recall any instance of a Bang Chaner
being caught in a situation of which *he was aware of* a conflict between
satisfying his own desires and fulfilling his obligations to kin, so it is
difficult to say which sentiment would ordinarily take precedence in his
own mind; but to an observer, it would seem that the former would most
likely have priority. (See Hanks and Phillips 1961 for evidence in support
of this point.) [12] Actually, most villagers seem eminently successful in
keeping the sentiments apart, which helps to account in part for the
"centripetal" forms of kinship arrangement referred to earlier. Self-interest
is of course not the same as selfishness, and when circumstances and
inclinations permit, Bang Chaners can become among the most generous
and hospitable of people (and in no sense paradoxically). Rarely have I
seen, for example, people derive so much genuine pleasure from doing
favors for others. In fact, these are among the first things that one notices
about them: free agents helping others—but also ignoring them—when
they see fit.

---

[11] This phrasing here in terms of *reciprocal benefits* is in the villagers' idiom, not
mine.

[12] It is not insignificant that nowhere in Thai folklore does one find a recognition
of possible conflict between the motives of self-interest and family obligation or of any
moral lesson to be drawn from it; that is, there are no stories of a parent sacrificing
himself for his children, or of children for their parents or, for that matter, of any
moral value at all in self-sacrifice. On the other hand, one does find stories of individuals in conflict over which of two self-satisfying alternatives to select. In *Khun
Chang and Khun Phaen*, for example, Wan Thong, the inconstant lover, could not
make up her mind between love and wealth, and eventually was slain because of her
indecision, the moral being that the person who cannot make up his mind deserves
nothing.

On a more realistic level, one rarely finds anyone in Bang Chan being condemned
for self-interest—the mother who abandons her children or the gallivanting husband
—although one very frequently does encounter sympathy for those who suffer, the
sympathy being elicited by the person or the fact of suffering, not the cause. The
majority of Bang Chaners generally consider the motives of the self-interested party
as the person's own business. This concern with sympathy (*soŋsaan*) for those in
difficulty, and simultaneous indifference to the source of their problem has deep
roots in Buddhist doctrine and should not be glossed over.

To have compassion (*mettaa* and *karunaa*) is among the noblest of Buddhist vir-
tues. It is at one time a kindly expression of concern with others and a recognition of
—or coming to terms with—what is considered intrinsic to the human situation. "Life
is suffering" is the first of Buddhism's Four Noble Truths. However, since such suffering is intrinsic, there is little to be gained by assigning blame for it. Equally important,
villagers assume that a person who suffers may well have brought it upon himself.
The other person, acting in his own natural self-interest, may have simply been an
agent or catalyst. His motives are his own business because they will eventually
contribute, for better or worse, to his own denouement. The dynamics of these attitudes are discussed in detail in the next chapter.

As the reader might by now suspect, it is not easy to determine the basis of the unity of the family. However, of all the factors that keep people living together in amity and affection, two come to the fore: a sense of love, obligation, and respect that is derived from the simple fact of kinship, but which must be continuously confirmed by mutual benefits; and economic considerations.

The economic foundation of the family is significant not only because the family is in fact the sole economic and occupational unit in the community (with the exception of the monkhood and school) but because the villagers themselves think of the family in terms of its economic functions. People say that they marry for wealth or because of the productive capacities of their spouses; [13] spouses stay together because the economic costs of a split are too great; most important of all, people are keenly *aware* of their economic interdependence. Fathers say that they need children to work in the fields and care for the buffalos, that a family needs a mother so that its members will be fed, that siblings are useful because it is easy to borrow from them (although, as noted earlier, some are unhappy about the intrusion of the kinship tie into what they regard to be a commercial transaction). Many villagers extend this economic, transactional type of thinking to other aspects of the kinship relationship. Thus they say that "the purpose of marriage is to have a companion who will take care of you when you get sick," or very frequently that "my parents went to the trouble of bringing me up so they would have a person to make merit for them when they die." The emphasis here is on independent agents serving each other because it is mutually beneficial.

The love and affection that people feel for each other is of course grounded in the close associations that one finds in most nuclear families. However, the attitudes of respect that one sees are perhaps more distinctively Thai. Almost all the literature on Thailand refers, at one point or another, to the patterns of respect (*khwaamnabthyy*) existing between people, both within and without the family. These patterns are based, in the first instance, on the status inequalities that exist in almost all social

---

[13] In responding to the unstructured Sentence Completion Test item, "*He (she) wants to get a wife (husband) who. . . ,*" for example, thirty-one of sixty informants indicated that they wanted a mate who "was a good worker," "earned a living," "was rich," or otherwise had high socio-economic status. Only two persons said that they wanted a spouse for reasons that could be reasonably defined as sentimental: one woman wanted a husband who "would be a good friend with whom she could discuss things," and a man said he wanted a wife whom "he loved." Other informants gave completions distributed among a variety of categories: "polite, well-mannered, handsome, kind, strong, and good" spouses; and six women wanted husbands who would be faithful.

relationships: within the family, usually in terms of the relative ages of people; elsewhere, in terms of age, wealth, power, knowledge, religious or governmental role. Secondly, they are based on the assumption that every individual, regardless of his position in the hierarchy, deserves respect. The first is a respect associated with the proper performance of one's role; the second, a recognition of the essential dignity of every human being.

The role of these respect patterns cannot be emphasized enough. Benedict, in her study (1946) of Thai culture at a distance, referred to the learning of the *waj*, or gesture of obeisance, as "the first teaching the child receives." Although the *waj* is perhaps not the very first social act the child learns, I have seen infants no more than two weeks old being guided by the mother in raising the palms of their little hands to the forehead in expression of deference to superiors. The older infant who can do this on his own almost always receives acknowledgments of approval and delight from the adults in attendance. An older sibling really means it when he says of his relationship with his younger brothers, "when I ask them to do some kind of work, they go and do it. They never disobey, and when there is no disobedience, there is no hatred. . . . Formerly, whenever there was entertainment somewhere I took them with me. My younger siblings love me a lot. . . ." His position in the authority structure assumes the respect of those younger than he, and they willingly grant it for, among other things, he plays his role well as the kindly superior who takes them with him whenever there is entertainment. All the polite little linguistic forms (honorifics, expletives suggesting status and, most important, ordinary kinship terminology with its specification of relative age) as well as kinesthetic forms (lowering the body while passing a seated older person, holding the younger between one's legs and with arms around him in a position of protection) also serve to emphasize the respect that people grant one another because of their differential status. Perhaps the most revealing illustration of the strength of these patterns, at least the authority pattern, was provided by a two-year-old toddler who pointed to the stomach of his pregnant mother and said with pride, "My younger sibling is in there. When he is born he will be *my* responsibility." Little doubt that when the child is born he will give his older brother his due.

With regard to the other respect form, recognizing the dignity of every human being, more than once I have heard parents say that they disliked giving their child a certain medicine "because it offends the baby; he does not like it. It is better not to give it to him than to hurt his feelings." Although I do not doubt that in some instances the parents were annoyed more by the screams of the child than anything else, I am also convinced that for the most part they were respecting his basic individuality and right to choose, even if in this case it was seemingly to his own detriment—he knows what is best for himself. Even the incompetent, helpless infant is an independent soul with his own will and right of determination, and his dignity must be respected.

It must be recognized of course that in the cosmology of Bang Chan the infant is anything but a conative *tabula rasa*. When he enters the world of human beings he brings with him not only a stock of individually accumulated merit (*bun*) and demerit (*baap*) from countless previous lives which will affect his being in this one, but also a host of other forces which predetermine his character: his *khwaan* (soul-stuff), *winjaan* (psychobiological motive power), *caj* (heart), and *nidsaj* or *ʔupanidsaj* (ingrained character), among others. (J. R. Hanks 1959 has a brilliant exposition of the role of these elements.) In a very real sense the infant enters the world of humans as a developed, or partially developed, psychological being. Human influences, particularly virtue and "good habits," can be inculcated into him, but they are ultimately limited by these pre-natally determined characteristics. Much of Bang Chan child rearing is actually a series of perpetual compromises between (a) parents surrendering to what they think are the child's predetermined traits (and while this represents an extraordinary respect for his infantile individuality, it also leads in a developmental sense to much of the solipsism to which we have been referring throughout); (b) parents trying to come to terms with, or overcome, his preordained characteristics by inculcating good habits through example, coaxing, and whipping (the three modes of socialization, in order of priority, although villagers are more prone to talk about whippings than actually give them; most are too tenderhearted, and the rare whipping is almost always the result of sudden rage); and (c) leaving the child to his own devices. The third differs from the first in that it focuses on the parent's concerns rather than the child's and indicates indifference rather than respect. Thus, in contrast to the illustration above, one constantly sees children, generally under eight years of age, "annoying" conversing adults (primarily by making noises, although not necessarily to get the latter's attention) to which the parent responds with continuous but intermittent "tsk, tsks." The adult never raises the volume of his admonition, never gets increasingly disturbed, and eventually gives up while the children continue on their merry, noise-making way. The parent's lack of genuine concern and compulsion is not lost upon the child. Although events of this type are not overly noticeable in Bang Chan—precisely because they occur in such an easygoing and unremarkable way—they do take place repeatedly, and represent one of the principal interactional themes of the parent-child relationship. Children learn quickly that although parents will go through little ritualistic forms of controlling them, the parents often do not really care and children can pretty much get away with doing what they want.[14]

With regard to other expressions of the recognition of individual dignity, one rarely sees in Bang Chan any physical or even verbal coercion. (The rare use of whipping, noted above, is to punish transgression, not to implement action.) Other than in horseplay, children do not push each other around; in my twenty-two months in Thailand, I saw not one case of young children in a serious fight, despite the fact that I looked for it. Very rare indeed is the parent who uses force or the threat of force on his child; there is no Siamese equivalent to the American intimidation, "You had better do that or else. . . ." In general, Bang Chaners proceed on the simple assumption that if people, including children, do not do what you ask them, they have good—and more important, private—reasons for responding that way; there is no need for, or interest in, self-justification. The major means of inducing recalcitrants to conform to your wishes is to cajole, wheedle, and flatter them (see particularly the responses to the Sentence Completion items, *"The best way to treat a subordinate is . . ."*; *"The worst way to treat a subordinate is . . ."* in chapter V). A less conscious but more frequently practiced alternative is simply to withdraw support: the parent who turns his back on the child and walks out (particularly evident in our TAT stories),[15] the older sibling who refuses to take his younger ones with him when there is entertainment to be seen, and the like. It must be noted, however, that social disengagement, although frequently utilized, does not always work; often the individual who is left suspended merely accepts the fact and continues about his business. The major point to be recognized is that villagers do not use forms of direct, blatant coercion on others. If soft words or the withdrawal of love will not move them, then their decision, freely determined, must be respected.

Love and affection within the family appear primarily in two forms. Their most typical expression is shown through the gifts, favors, and services people do for each other. The degree of affection that individuals feel toward one another is in fact explicitly measured in these terms. Thus, a father says that of all his daughters, the one who has given him the greatest pleasure is "the one who sells things . . . When she gets money,

---

[14] In qualification, however, it must be noted that all Bang Chaners are extremely sensitive to social cues—partially as a consequence of having to balance off their individualistic propensities against the demands of the authority system—and here the children ignore their parents only because the latter have indicated by their very halfheartedness that they do not care. The children can, and do, quickly hop to it on the slightest indication of parental seriousness: a stern look, for example. My point, however, is that such looks are comparatively rare.

[15] In another paper, Hanks and Hanks (1963) make the same observation on the basis of behavioral materials.

she gives it to me." In describing his relationship with his maternal grand-parents, with whom he spent all but two of the first twelve years of his life, this same person says:

> My younger sister and I were born one year after the other. So mother gave me to grandmother to be weaned. I lived with her until I became a novice at the monastery at the age of twelve. I lived with grandmother, so I loved grandmother and grandfather more. I loved grandmother even more than my own mother and father. Wherever grandfather and grand-mother went, I went too. Grandmother loved me: she always gave me sweets and toys. I had everything I wanted because I was the only young thing in the house. She loved me. She was going to give her property to me, land and gold, as much as she was going to give to her own children. But it was only a promise. I got the gold, but not the land, because when grandmother died, grandfather got a new wife. She was young. . . . I didn't quite like her. The young woman was too eco-nomical. . . . Sometimes she prevented grandfather from buying good things for me. When grandfather was going to buy gold or anything for me, she stopped him. She wanted him to buy for her more than for his grandchild.

This excerpt, taken from the biography of one of the life history informants and comprising almost the complete portrayal of the relationship between the informant and the individuals with whom he spent the crucial years of his childhood, is by no means atypical. The point is that of all the myriad elements in the relationship, or of all the loving characteristics that in his eyes the grandparents had, he chose to emphasize only the material gifts they had given him as the measure of their love. Other informants are no different: one man said he knew his father did not love him because when he died he left the family home to the Buddhist monastery; and a woman said she admired her father because "when he died there was property left. He was a good man: he did not abandon his children. He was worried about them." (Her other reason for *admiring* him was that "he was the person who brought me into the world.")

The other major form of familial love is evidenced in the camaraderie, warmth, and generosity that surrounds the family in planning and ac-complishing the various tasks associated with rice farming. As indicated earlier, the cultivation and harvesting of rice is not only an economic operation in Bang Chan, but almost a way of life. When villagers must deal with the very real and complex problems of planting and bringing in the harvest, all the individualistic propensities, and even to an extent the authority patterns, with which they normally indulge themselves recede before the coöperative requirements of the task at hand. In a very real sense the functional requirements of the economic activity, particularly during harvest time, serve to create a rite of intensification as family members decide together what work will be done by whom, arise early in the morning to work together happily in the fields—sometimes for as long as fourteen hours at a stretch—and actually see the fruits of their coöperative labor mount up on the threshing floors. The sense of familial solidarity and intradependence, and its associated feelings of love, is experienced by all.[16] Also, since harvesting more often than not involves working reciprocally with other families, the host of a reciprocal labor group giving a feast whenever possible at the end of the day, it serves, although to a lesser extent, to intensify feelings of membership in the larger community.

Summary

In my discussion of the "cultural background," I have dwelt primarily on kinship because the family is functionally the most significant social unit in the village and because it is within the context of kinship that personality is developed and, in Bang Chan, most frequently expressed. None of this is meant to imply a lack of importance for other social units—the monastery, the school, the state—or for the non-institutionalized relationships—friends, drinking partners, and business contacts. However, kinship does provide the basic psychological model for all human relationships in Bang Chan,

---

[16] Although the annual cycle of Thai peasants is described in detail in the available ethnographies on Thai rural life (deYoung 1955, Fraser 1960, Kaufman 1960, Kingshill 1960, Sharp et al. 1953) a few words should be added about the psychological dimensions of this cycle. Thus familial solidarity, intradependence, and love are not the only sentiments that are heightened during the harvest period. Perhaps the most striking quality of this season (December to January) is the increase in the optimism, joy, and general psychic well-being of the villagers: people laugh more loudly than usual; they relish telling about the things they are going to buy; parents take more kindly to the gallivanting of the children. These months contrast with transplanting time (late July to early August) and the period prior to harvest (October to November), when an overabundance of rain can destroy the villagers' rice seedlings or their entire crop. These latter periods are marked not so much by anxiety as by a sense of watchful waiting. All these contrast with the Dry season when things are especially quiet in Bang Chan and when villagers spend their time repairing farming equipment and houses, gossiping, or are working on jobs outside the community. Villagers say that of the three major seasons of the year (Dry, February to June; Rainy, June to January; Cold, January to February) they like the Rainy season best. The season coincides with the rice-growing cycle, is marked by Buddhist Lent and, excepting a final week of Monsoon downpour, is in fact the most comfortable period of the year.

These seasonal activities and attitudes also have direct implications for field work. Thus, while villagers gave freely of their time during the dry season and after the harvest, and during the latter were especially outgoing and benign, many simply would not see me during the weeks of planting and harvesting. The benign attitudes of villagers interviewed after the harvest were reflected directly in the data, as were the noncommittal responses of some villagers who were interviewed during transplanting time.

and not only in the abstract, symbolic sense. Non-kin are approached in the hope that they eventually may be treated as kin; good government officials are unabashedly described as being like "good fathers"; the basic patterns of respect that are learned and practiced in the family are extended to relationships outside of it, although inevitably in more formal ways. There is no *rigid* psychological cleavage between the sentiments of kinship and the sentiments about individuals outside of the family. Conversely the mere fact of kinship does not assure that individuals will be given special emotional treatment: often the love between friends is greater than the love between kin (see the case of "Dang," his father, and father's friends in Hanks and Phillips 1961, or the case cited earlier of the man who left his wife because of his fondness for an employer). Kinship represents to the villager relationships of warmth, familiarity, and conviviality, but also unpredictability and undependability. Such is the nature of most human contact in Bang Chan.

In this type of cultural situation, one does *not* find arising the type of community power struggles or schisms apparently characteristic of many peasant communities (see Foster 1960–61). Bang Chan is indeed a placid community because no family has the organizational means or the quality of familial cohesiveness necessary to assume a dominant social, political, or economic position. Individuals assume important positions and individuals disagree and squabble, but rarely families. In surveying the cultural landscape of Bang Chan, I often wondered whether the basic unit of anthropological and sociological, as well as psychological, analyses was perhaps not the individual rather than the family, monastery, school, or village itself.

II

Naturalistic Observation of
Thai Personality

This chapter is concerned primarily with presenting a picture of the villagers' distinctive and expectable psychological characteristics as expressed in overt behavior. By *distinctive* is meant those traits which are characteristically Thai (although the extent to which they are, strictly speaking, uniquely Thai is unknown) and by *expectable* is meant those traits which fall well within the range of what is culturally probable. Essentially my purpose is to describe those aspects of the villagers' personalities which play a visible role in their ordinary patterns of interpersonal behavior but which are generally unfamiliar to the Western reader.

As indicated earlier, the discussion should not be interpreted to mean that the patterns portrayed necessarily represent those that occur most frequently: it may well be that modal personality characteristics are not the same as those which, because they are unfamiliar or unusual, impress the foreign observer; nor does it mean of course that Bang Chaners may not display several other traits which are characteristic of other peoples as well. The characteristics to be discussed, however, do occur with sufficient frequency to be recognized as normal elements in the psychological functioning and pattern of expectancies of all villagers. And in some cases, to be confirmed later at a different analytic level by the Sentence Completion data, they obviously are also modal characteristics (for example, the gentleness, affability, and politeness evident in most face-to-face relationships).

To provide a critical context for the main body of the discussion, I will first analyze what has been written in both Siamese and English on Thai personality; excepting three recent papers on the people of Bang Chan, there is no literature that focuses exclusively on *peasant* personality.

An Analysis of the Literature

Despite the extraordinary sensitivity on the part of almost all Thai to the subtleties of human relationships and to human foibles and feelings, there is almost no literature in the Thai language that could reasonably be considered psychologically analytic or dispassionately self-examining. This applies not only to the few accounts of peasants but to descriptions of any other identifiable groups in the society. Precisely why this is the case is difficult to determine, although there seem to be at least two factors involved.

First, there exists for all Thai a relatively explicit and unquestioned set of standards of what is proper, desirable, or appropriate behavior. We will encounter some of these below, but the point to be noted here is that almost all native language commentaries on matters relating to personality are inevitably phrased in terms of these standards: the extent to which behavior conforms to them, the remedial steps which individuals should take to conform, or satirical slaps at those who fail to live up to standard. Essentially, Thai psychology, even that represented in the Great Tradition (and perhaps even more so than in the Little Tradition of the peasantry [Redfield 1955] which contains several areas of amoral indeterminacy in its non-Buddhistic aspects) takes the form of moral philosophy rather than disinterested, descriptive analysis.

The second reason, related to the above, is the absence among the Thai literati [1] (those most likely to write about personality) of any strong need to

---

[1] Although this is not the place to go into a detailed discussion of Thai intellectual life and its effects on native psychological theory and the lack of an analytic literature, it might help to realize that Thai intellectual commentators are still principally a *literati* rather than an *intelligentsia*, in the sense that Redfield (1953: 42–44, and Redfield and Singer 1954), following Childe and Toynbee, explicitly used these terms; that is, they are (Redfield and Singer 1954) specialists who "reflect, synthesize and create out of the traditional material new arrangements and developments that are felt by the people to be outgrowths of the old. What is changed is a further statement of what was before. . . . The 'literati' who fashion a Great Tradition do not repudiate the values and outlook of their rural hinterland but systematize and elaborate them under technical specialization." An intelligentsia, on the other hand, is comprised of heretics, dissenters, and marginal men who challenge, interrupt, or destroy the ancient traditions to bring forth totally new intellectual orientations. They are the "cosmopolitan" individuals who historically tend to arise only after the native civilization has come into prolonged contact with or is stimulated by foreign cultures and ideas.

This distinction is not only taxonomically useful, but in Thailand's case seems to fit with actual historical circumstances; that is, by applying related parts of Redfield's formulations, it is clear that Thailand went through the first great "orthogenetic" or "primary" transformation from a precivilized folk society to an urban civilization at least seven hundred years ago with the founding of Sukothai in 1238, although the origins of this civilization (its writing system, art forms, codified legal

challenge or go beyond ethical standards in trying to understand human psychological functioning. It is as if the moral life were the only facet (or comprehended all facets) of the total psychological makeup of individuals worth thinking about. This is coupled with an emphasis on the practical effects of overt behavior rather than a concern with probing those factors that lie behind behavior or which may have prompted it. Although he was writing in an entirely different context, Wilson's comments (1959a: 59–60 and 67) on Thai intellectual life are most apropos here:

> It is evident that in Buddhism the Thai intellectual has a *Weltanschauung* which is both satisfactory and comfortable. This faith in traditional religion has saved him from heart-rending introspection and self-criti-cism and has preserved for him a matter-of-fact approach to life. The Thai intellectual is above all pragmatic rather than speculative . . .
>   . . . Most educated Thai are officials faced daily with the stubborn facts of life. They are not therefore given to flights of imagination. They fit comfortably into an established structure of social organization. They are not stimulated by idleness and failure to an examination of the

---

system) go back even further to Khmer and ultimately Indian civilizations. Throughout these years, the intellectuals, as literati associated with the court (and often the court itself: some of Thailand's greatest poets and dramatists were kings) helped maintain, develop, and glorify this civilization, but not change it radically. Approximately one hundred years ago, with the accession of King Mongkut to the throne, Thailand began to undergo the "heterogenetic" or "secondary" urban transformation involving participation in an international civilization. This self-determined participation, however, has proceeded most selectively and slowly, being confined principally to the technical and formal sides of the governmental (Vella 1955, Wilson 1959b), administrative (Mosel 1957), and technological sectors of the culture. From a long-term historical point of view, this heterogenetic transformation is still probably only in its formative stage, for up to now the emphasis has been on reinterpreting Occidental ideas and practices so they could be integrated into the traditional style of life. All this of course has been abetted by the fact that, unlike all other countries of South and Southeast Asia, Thailand never lost its political autonomy, and thus never experienced either the stimulation or pain resulting from colonial status. In the more purely intellectual and ideological sectors, the heterogenetic transformation, with its concomitant disruption of indigenous cultural values, has hardly even begun to be felt. When Western intellectual formulations are known or used, they are consistently phrased in terms of their relevance to traditional values and modes of thought. Thailand is probably one of the few countries in the world where a leading Marxist intellectual can declare that one of the most influential persons in his life has been Dr. Frank Buchman of the Moral Re-Armament Movement because his writings have helped him to understand better his own Buddhist religion (personal communication from David A. Wilson, based on field interviews). In this type of intellectual environment, still oriented toward the synthesis and integration of the new into the old, it is not surprising to find a Western-trained Thai psychiatrist describe Sigmund Freud as a person "who did not have too much to say because he wrote only about sex." Perhaps the most fitting characterization of the values underlying the purposes of the Thai intellectual is provided by the motto of The Siam Society, the one major association in Thailand approximating a society of scholars, which is "Knowledge Produces Friendship."

fundamentals of that structure or of the ultimate values upon which it is based. In a very real sense, the educated group is a class with a vested interest. Consequently it is conservative and pragmatic rather than radical and speculative . . .

The closest approximation to a psychological literature resulting from these fundamental intellectual orientations are religious and secular didactic essays, public school texts on morality, self-help or "peace of mind" tracts, and satirical or didactic fiction and poetry. (Mosel 1961 provides an excellent discussion of contemporary Thai poetry.)

Addressed to the reading public at large, these writings do not purport to be concerned with any particular group or class of Thai society: peasants, Bangkokians, Northeasterners, or others. Since they are for the most part written by the educated elite, however, they tend to reflect their authors' interests and standards. To what extent their standards differ from those held by peasants is difficult to determine with precision, although impressionistically it would seem that in psychological questions the educated elite give considerably more attention to the importance of social forms, the desirability of pleasing others, and also reveal a greater sense of compulsiveness, achievement, and social uneasiness than do peasants. Villagers simply seem more relaxed and self-accepting. However, these differences are very much a matter of degree. A Bang Chan child who learns about proper modes of behavior from *Sombad Khɔɔŋ Phuu Dii*, discussed below, may not have the same compulsion nor experience the same pressures to implement his studies as does the child of the Ministry of Education official who wrote the text. However, he thoroughly understands the teachings, their relevance and importance; knowing them is part of being Thai. A few illustrations will provide some of the flavor of these writings.

One of Thailand's most famous men of letters is M. R. Khukrit Pramoj, a publisher, editor, author, lecturer, and recently, movie actor. Educated in England and a member of the royalty, he is known to most Westerners as a kind of Siamese equivalent of Henry R. Luce, but to most Thai (although to no more than a handful of Bang Chaners, the majority having never even heard his name) he is known for his all-around knowledge of human affairs. His most popular work is *Panhaa Pracamwan*, or *Problems of Everyday Life*, a multi-volumed set of dialogues based on a column he wrote for his own newspaper in which he answers questions from hypothetical individuals who have "written" for advice on problems of ordinary living. These problems concern such matters as how to handle one's jealousy, how to treat those below and above one in the hierarchy, and how to control one's feelings of spleen and anger.

The following excerpt from volume iv of these essays (1952: 337–339) is not only representative of Khukrit's thinking, but bespeaks a fairly typical Thai problem; it could just as easily be found in the rice fields of Bang Chan as in a Bangkok office building. What is perhaps most revealing is the phrasing of the problem and the very fact that it is considered one, *i.e.*, this is precisely the type of issue that would exercise many Thai.

An individual writes Khukrit describing his relationship with "Mr. Kaw" ("Mr. A"), a friend of eight years with whom he began working in an office a year ago. The person reports that Mr. Kaw is always fawning over their mutual boss, entertaining him, taking his meals with him, and getting up early in the morning and running to the office so that the boss will be aware of him. As a result of his activities, Kaw received both a promotion in status and a raise in pay:

> But I remain in my same position, although we have always worked together and have always been side by side: And when my friend received the better position, he said: "Do not worry. Be patient. I will help you for sure. You should have acted like me and entertained the boss. He will see you and take an interest in you." I answered him: "I entertained him formerly. That's enough. It is not seemly to have meals with the boss all the time. It would seem as if I were currying his favor to get a better job." My friend said: "Things are now good with me. He gave me a better position."
>
> . . . There is something wrong with my friend. He does not esteem his friends. He always makes himself seem more prominent and conspicuous than his friends. And if someone says something, he always says in front of everybody that it is wrong. I myself am not a child. I know what I am doing. But he has treated me like this many times. But I would not say anything because we are friends . . .

The letter writer then poses two questions for Khukrit: (1) "Should I continue to work with Mr. Kaw?" and (2) "If I continue to work with Mr. Kaw, I am afraid he will dominate me or insult me in public again. What shall I do?" Khukrit's reply to all of this is:

> The reason that Mr. Kaw has received a better position than you is because he knows how to please your superior. In this respect, you should not complain about him or blame him for everything, because it is natural to try to advance oneself. At the same time, you cannot blame your superior, for according to your story, Mr. Kaw is the person who always has his face in front of the boss. And it is natural for the boss to think of him first. Mr. Kaw's behavior perhaps shows his good-will. What you have said indicates that Mr. Kaw has the willingness to entertain the boss. He does not stay in bed but gets up and shows himself to the boss . . . So I think you should not break off with Mr. Kaw, because as far as I can see he still respects you as a friend, and has strongly promised to help you get a raise later. Mr. Kaw still has some

goodness: when he advanced in his job, he did not forget his friends. You still go out together and eat together as you used to.

Do not do anything that will give Mr. Kaw a chance to look down upon you. Anyway, you should show respect to him because of his position. You will also be considered a good friend. A person should honor his friend. I myself am always glad when my friends have gone further than I have. I always respect them according to their position. This will induce other people to respect our friends.

Although the above is almost self-explanatory, a few points might be underscored: the attention that is given to the practical consequences of Kaw's actions rather than to his motives; the fact that overt behavior alone is the measure of the man; the necessity to honor a position rather than the person who holds it; and the pleasure that is derived from doing right by a social superior. The fear of being criticized in public is also prominent here, a fairly widespread anxiety related to the great desire to avoid any kind of face-to-face conflict. In fact, the entire letter is suggestive of this desire in that it makes so much sense to a Thai reader to find a person's feelings of displeasure with a friend expressed in a communication to a third party rather than openly and directly to the person himself. Khukrit, the author, simply turns this ready-made cultural expectation to his own literary advantage. Finally, the letter writer's willingness to take the most extreme position possible in dealing with Kaw—to break off the relationship entirely, if not to quit his job—is indicative both of the priority given to interpersonal relationships over all other considerations in the occupational situation and of the characteristic Thai response to leave the field when faced with a problem rather than attempt to work it out. (See Phillips 1960 and Hanks and Phillips 1961 for references to precisely the same kind of response with two individuals in totally different situations.)

Of a somewhat different order from the above is *Sombad Khɔɔŋ Phuu Dii*, or *Characteristics of a Good Person* (Ministry of Education 1959). This is one of a series of pamphlets used in Thai public schools for instruction in morality. Since the school system is operated by the central government, almost every Siamese child is familiar with it. The text is simply a listing of behavioral commandments, and like most listings of this kind is phrased almost completely in terms of prohibitions. Following are some of these dicta, selected at random from the first few pages of the text:

1. Do not touch any person in a disrespectful way.
2. Do not try to act in the same way as your superior [meaning simply, "Know your place"].
3. Do not be concerned with your own comfort before the comfort of your superiors or women.

4. The good person is one who tries to behave in an honest way.
5. Do not shove anything at anybody or throw anything at anybody.
6. Do not make loud noises when people are working.
7. Do not spit or clear your phlegm or yawn in public.
8. Do not gobble your food or scatter things on your plate or chew loudly.
9. Do not sit or walk carelessly or abruptly against other people.
10. Do not touch or horse-play with people who are your close friends.
11. If you are a superior, wherever you go, you should look after the comfort of your inferior.

Again, although the list is almost self-explanatory, note should be taken of some cultural emphases that run through several of the items: the stress on behaving properly toward superordinates and subordinates; the emphasis upon motoric and emotional self-discipline, and conversely, the implicit fear of losing control over one's impulses (as indicated in the dictum against horseplay, even with one's friends); the general stress of respecting the inviolability of every person; and finally, the great emphasis on the importance of the body in human behavior and social relationships. Although this last point may not seem unusual, in that the dicta are addressed to children—with whom one would expect much concern over the body—it in fact represents an area about which all Thai regardless of age are sensitive. In general Siamese, considerably more than Occidentals, tend to be aware of physical bearing, beauty, and ugliness, as well as the use of the body as a communicative device. A person's physical appearance is an indication of his character, particularly his moral nature, and kinesthetic modes are explicitly used for conveying love, regard, and as suggested above, disrespect.[2]

It is worth reëmphasizing that the above items are standards for, not descriptions of, behavior. The attention given to controlling body movements is simply to emphasize for the child that people will decide whether he is good or bad on the basis of the way he handles his body, and he must therefore exercise extreme care in its use. Items one, nine, and ten are not meant to imply anything fundamentally wrong with touching another. Most Thai, particularly members of the same sex, thoroughly enjoy expressing their mutual affection through bodily contact: by holding hands, grasping the leg or arm of the other, and in Bang Chan, sometimes by sleeping with one another. In the last instance, there is absolutely no sexual contact; often during the cold season the practice serves not only friendship

[2] Although it belongs to a different area of behavior, it is not insignificant that in classical Thai dance every body movement—the configuration of the hands, the position of the legs, eye movements—has a specific, conventionalized meaning. In the oldest, or Kɔɔn, version of the dance, the only means of communication other than that provided by masks are body movements.

but the additional purpose of keeping the participants warm. However, the items underscore the fact that touching carries important social connotations and the toucher should be cognizant of these, and beware of what he does; should he touch the wrong person in the wrong way, for example, a social superior to whom he should be expressing respect rather than camaraderie, he will be identified as ill-mannered or uncouth. The point throughout is that manners do count. They define, in a social if not in an ontological sense, the "good" or "bad" person. Also they typify, from an analytic point of view, something of the sensitivity, psychological care, and interpersonal jockeying that is expressed repeatedly in face-to-face relationships, the avowed purpose of which is to keep such relationships smooth and uncomplicated, but which characteristically results in a lack of spontaneity. (The major exception to such a lack of spontaneity occurs when humor is injected into the relationship.) This entire complex will be discussed in greater detail later in the chapter.

The English language psychological literature is not as rich a source of data as the above, but it is more analytically oriented and comprehensive in scope. However, with the exception of the papers on the people of Bang Chan and life history materials, it is similar to the literature in the native language in that for the most part it takes all Thailand as its province and fails to distinguish descriptively between members of any of the various sub-groups in the country. Given the original aims of the descriptions and the nature of their data, this is perhaps not an unpardonable flaw. Also, most of these reports are phrased in terms which suggest that, although the enumerated characteristics may not be attributed to *all* Siamese, they are part of the Thai system of interactive expectations: the personality traits of an upper-class urbanite and a landless Northeastern peasant obviously differ in many respects, as do those of a Bang Chan man and a Bang Chan woman as well as those of every individual Thai. All these people, however, share certain broadly defined expectations about how each is most likely to behave, at least toward one another; were it otherwise, they could not interact.

Despite its brevity, one of the more intriguing English language descriptions of Thai personality is the list of characteristics prepared by a Western-trained Thai psychologist for the Cornell Thailand Handbook (Sharp *et al.* 1956: 231). The account is intriguing simply because it is one of the few, if not the only, publicly offered descriptions by a native Siamese that goes beyond the usual practice of enumerating moral and ethical prescriptions:

The psychologist commented that the Thai in general were hospitable people; that the tempo of their lives was slow; that they possessed con-

siderable equanimity; that many Thai actions had a basis in the Buddhist religion; that the Thai respected age; that the Thai, although
capable of making rapid cultural adaptations at least on a superficial
level, were basically conservative; that ritual and ceremony were important parts of Thai life; that the Thai were not steadfast; that they
were extravagant; that they were bashful, introverted; that they were
not socially minded, that is, they were not joiners; that the Thai approach to life's concerns was empirical rather than theoretical; that the
Thai were indolent; that they were egoistic, self-centered; that they
lacked persistence, "stick-to-it-iveness"; and that the Thai were a mild
people, a non-violent people.

Although this inventory may appear to be simply a list of cultural
stereotypes, it is basically in accord with what most sensitive observers have
said or written about the Siamese in general. The only items requiring
qualification perhaps, from the point of view of an outside observer, are the
references to equanimity and bashfulness. Equanimity *is* very much of a
cultural ideal, with a heritage deep in Buddhist doctrine, but it would seem
more accurate, at least on the basis of the people of Bang Chan, to think of
the typical Thai as possessing not a sense of quiet imperturbability but, on
one hand, a posture of inner control and, on the other, a good deal of
passivity and fatalism. Most Thai are much less prone to a tranquil acceptance of the world as it is than they are aware of their inability to do
anything about it; the problem is to know how to face unusual circumstances (happy as well as unhappy) with composure, *despite* one's feelings.
The reference to bashfulness would seem to merit qualification in that the
social statuses of the persons involved as well as the purpose of their
relationship are always decisive in determining how bashful or assertive a
person will actually be. There is little doubt that a typical Thai will often
choose not to act rather than seem pushy or place another person in an
embarrassing position, but he is less likely to be concerned about these
matters if he is the social superior or if the other individual has something
he really wants. Although it often does take a summoning of courage to
affirm themselves, Siamese can be unashamedly frank in their dealings.
They are aided in this to an extent by an awareness that all human
relationships involve something of a "contract" or an "exchange," and that
it is not untoward to be frank with a person when both parties realize that
each can expect something in return. Again, this whole complex will be
amplified below.

Prajuab Tirabutana's autobiography, *The Simple One: The Story of a
Siamese Girlhood* (1958), is of a totally different order from the above but
deserves mention here because its spontaneously expressive data provides
what is probably the most revealing Thai psychological document in the

English language. Since it is a life history, the essay is completely descriptive and nonanalytic; also, in her readiness to articulate her feelings and in
her ethnic background, the author is not a typical Thai. However, as I
noted in an earlier review of the biography, Miss Prajuab phrases her
experiences in an idiom that clearly reveals their basically Thai source
(Phillips 1960: 537). "She vividly discribes her delight in being pampered
and coddled as a child, her warm relationships with older women but
almost a total indifference to men, her running away from trouble rather
than attempting to deal with it, and her pride in having a good memory—
culturally, the most important measure of intellectual prowess." These and
other events and responses described in the text are immediately recognizable as characteristic experiences in the life of a young, unmarried Thai
woman. The principal value of the essay is its ingenuous presentation of
what it is like to feel and think like a Thai.

The most famous culture-personality study on Thailand is Ruth Benedict's wartime "study at a distance," *Thai Culture and Behavior* (1946).
The essay's fame is due partially to the stature of the author and to the relatively high degree of accuracy she achieved in her portrayal despite the fact
that she had never worked in the country, had to depend on documents
that were essentially unrelated to her purposes, and had to rely on upper-
class Thai informants who, because of the war, were living in the United
States. Written in the style of a "national character" study, the essay is
essentially a psychological analysis of semi-ethnographic materials; that is,
Benedict attempted to identify and analyze whatever aspects of the psychological functioning of the Thai she could discover *reflected* in their social
institutions and cultural products. Thus she discussed the role of male
dominance in Thailand in terms of its expression in Buddhist doctrine and
practice, its appearance in folk tales and proverbs, and the like. Because of
the nature of her data and technique, she could give scant attention to the
functioning of individuals, and her report is in many parts somewhat
idealized and overstated. Thus, in her discussions of "male dominance,"
Benedict failed to note—through no fault of her own—the controlling voice
that women have in financial matters; the essential equality of the sexes in
occupational activities (both may pull the plow, sew, work on road gangs,
serve as midwives); [3] the fear on the part of many husbands that their wives
will turn to other men if they are not sexually satisfied; and despite this, the
widely held stereotype that whatever stability exists in the family is due to
the steady, sensible, tightfisted female, not the wasteful, self-indulgent

---

[3] Perhaps the most impressive example of the equality of the sexes is found in the
boat races which take place during fiestas, in which sturdy peasant maidens can be
seen paddling furiously along with the men as members of the same crew. This is
not a sop to their feminine status, but a simple recognition of their competence.

male. The point of course is that Benedict's references to male dominance in Buddhist belief and in many fables are not incorrect; neither are they complete, however, and to base one's interpretations on them alone is inevitably to invite an imbalanced presentation. Despite these unavoidable limitations, Benedict's essay is clearly a landmark in Thai studies: it is the first serious attempt to penetrate aspects of Siamese character.

A frequently overlooked source of psychological materials is Reginald leMay's *Siamese Tales, Old and New* (1930). The tales themselves are often utilized (as, for example, by Benedict), but leMay's accompanying commentary tends to get slighted, perhaps because he gives the impression of being more concerned with admiring the stories than analyzing them. The fifteen stories are too complex and subtle to try to summarize here, but a few of leMay's reflections *are* worth noting. Most important, he em-phasizes the essentially realistic and pragmatic nature of Siamese thinking as it emerges through the tales (pp. 10 and 163):

> As I hope is clear by now, the Siamese are realists. This is a very wicked world, and everyone is trying to get the better of you in some way or other. Your only means of protection is to be cleverer than your neighbor, and if you gain a reputation for being alert and keen in your business dealings, you will be looked up to and admired. There is little sympathy wasted on the dupe . . .
> . . . I myself have often asked my Siamese friends why in their stories the rascal so frequently comes out on top to the discomfiture of the hero . . . , and I am invariably met with the answer, "But isn't it very often true?"

Related to this is the Siamese sensitivity to the intentions of others, particularly to the possibility that others may want to do them in: "We look at others with our front eyes, but we see ourselves with those behind" (p. 129). I might add that the theme of the end justifying the means, whether the latter involves guile or more attractive procedures, is one that appears repeatedly in these stories; "good results" at all times validate the methods that are used to achieve them.

The summary of materials on Thai personality that I prepared for the Cornell Thailand Handbook (Sharp *et al.* 1956) is, as was noted earlier, essentially a lexicon descriptive of some of the conventionalized forms of Thai social interaction. The discussion focused simply on the description of these forms, with little attention given to the psychodynamics involved or to explanatory or causative factors which lay behind them. The presentation differed from earlier efforts in that it was woven around an exposition of the meaning of various Thai vocabulary items descriptive of attitudes and states for which there are no easy equivalents in English. Included here were concepts such as *kreeŋcaj* (the feeling and attitude of self-effacement and humbleness, involving the desire to avoid intruding upon or embarrassing others, or causing others to extend or trouble themselves); *chɔɔj-chɔɔj* (a state and attitude with multiple forms: simply being quiet or silent, feeling strongly about a situation but expressing nothing, assuming an attitude of indifference or noninvolvement); *maj pen raj* (literally, "it does not matter" or "it is nothing," but a verbal device repeatedly used to shrug off and ignore all the little frustrations and difficulties that occur in daily life; the Thai government once tried, unsuccessfully, to forbid all government employees to use the phrase). These and several other items discussed in the presentation are immediately familiar to anyone who has worked in Thailand as terms which Thai use to describe their own behavior. In the sense that they are so familiar—having been selected from the most ordinary kind of daily discourse—their presentation could hardly be considered a novel contribution.

Robert B. Textor's *From Peasant to Pedicab Driver,*[4] as its title suggests, is not principally a psychological study. However, because the work is interlaced with numerous psychological observations and is the product of a seasoned observer of the Thai rural and urban scene, it merits a few words of comment. The bulk of the monograph is a discussion of the various health and social problems faced by the drivers of the manually-operated pedicabs that, until 1960, abounded in the streets of Bangkok. The majority of the 12,000 drivers were peasant migrants from Thailand's Northeastern provinces, economically the most depressed area of the country. The study, reflecting either Rousseauesque innocence or a misconception of Thai culture, portrays these men as humble rustics whose psychological life is being corrupted by the ways of the city. Textor argues, for example (p. 46), that the longer a pedicab driver stays in Bangkok, "the more calculating a personality he becomes," and the shrewder he becomes in manipulating other people in order to avoid his own work. In another place, he presents a chart which tells us, among other things, that there is less emphasis on "warm interpersonal relationships" in the city than in the peasant sub-culture from which the drivers came. One would hope that our anthropological knowledge of the differences and similarities between rural and urban life had gone beyond the replication of such traditional and simplistic Western idealism. Some of Textor's other observa-

---

[4] The study originally appeared as a chapter in a volume entitled *The Social Implications of Industrialisation and Urbanisation: Five Studies of Urban Populations of Recent Rural Origin in Cities of Southern Asia*, published by the UNESCO Research Centre on The Social Implications of Industrialisation in Southern Asia, Calcutta, 1955. The study cited here is a revised and expanded version of the earlier work, and appears under the title, *From Peasant to Pedicab Driver: A Social Study of Northeastern Thai Farmers Who Periodically Migrated to Bangkok and Became Pedicab Drivers*, Cultural Report Series No. 9, Yale University, Southeast Asia Studies, New Haven, Conn., 1961.

tions are more penetrating, but in these instances he works himself into the more serious problem of interpreting overt behavior without examining the meaning that it has for those who are experiencing it. Thus, in discussing pedicab drivers' relationships with the police, he asserts that the drivers need closer police supervision because they lack strong inner controls. He argues that when they get out of control, they "go all the way," and try to get away with as much as they possibly can, particularly with regard to traffic and license regulations. Textor's *description* of the overt behavior of pedicab drivers and police is accurate, but what is not shown in his *interpretation* is that for a Thai there are, in the relations between authority figures and subordinates, several *other* considerations that take precedence over the need to observe regulations: that authority figures should be benevolent and helpful, rather than demanding; that one tries to avoid placing others, especially subordinates, in embarrassing situations; that in most interpersonal situations, Thai have an extraordinarily high tolerance for deviation from the rules, regardless of the confusion that may ensue (as the most superficial observation of Bangkok traffic would demonstrate). Textor's recommendation in fact flies in the face of these more deeply-rooted norms and expectations. Despite these various shortcomings, Textor's study is an interesting and readable commentary on some of the social psychological dimensions of culture change in Thailand.

Together with Benedict's study, the papers by Hanks and Phillips (1961) and Phillips (1959) represent the few excursions made into the analysis, as contrasted simply with the description, of Thai personality. The article by Hanks and Phillips is a discussion of a portion of the life-history and projective test responses of a young Bang Chan man, focusing on the events leading up to his marriage, his motives for getting married, and the psychological complications that this event entailed. Emerging from the informant's account was evidence pointing to two related areas of psychic tension: (1) a conflict between the informant's desire for independence, based on the expectation of becoming master of his own household and establishment, and the necessity for him to make himself dependent on others, his social superiors, as the very means by which to achieve this end; and (2) a conflict between the desire for the security provided by these individuals and the fear of expressing his hostility toward them when they, involved with their own concerns and never completely independent themselves, are unable to fulfill his untoward demands. The informant resolved these predicaments simply by continuing his demands on others but ignoring any psychological obligations he had toward them. The behavioral implications of this resolution are summarized in the article's final paragraph (655-656):

> From this vantage point, the Thai personality stands more encapsulated, alone, and isolated than the Chinese. Thai resist strong affiliation

as do rejected lovers who fear suffering again. Without strong bonds, they develop no sense of guilt for those they injure and stand ultimately responsible only to themselves, individuals among individuals who differ mainly in the amount of influence they wield. Thus Dang [the informant] can make demands of others but feels little obligation toward them. As he left his father and uncle with scarcely a second thought, so others can leave him. Of course, as was indicated by Dang's projective test data, this form of individualism is not entirely without its psychic toll. But on the level of action and conscious decision, the moral for a Thai runs: invest not thy love in a shadow.

The piece by this writer (Phillips, 1959) is essentially an amplification of some of the findings of the above paper and a confirmation, in the life histories of two other informants, of their typicality. The paper was confined to an examination of the development and expression of the needs for dependence and independence in the lives of these villagers. Three major points emerged from the analysis. First, the most common expression of dependence was in the area of subsistence and economics, in the individual's desire to attach himself to others who would give him sustenance in return for services rendered. Over and over again, the informants viewed their relationships with other people, particularly kin, in terms of the others' economic value to themselves. However, this mode of dependence was not so much an overriding compulsion as it was a basic postulate about human relationships: the measure of another person's love was explicitly the degree to which in material terms he served the self. The second point, in contrast to the above, was that marriage was seen as the means by which a person could free himself from the obligations of economic dependence. This freedom has two aspects: freedom from the frustrations caused by others; and freedom to set oneself up as master of one's own household, thus reaping the psychological satisfactions—status, power, and prestige—of having others dependent on oneself. The third and perhaps most striking point concerned the fact that all these informants spent their childhoods being shuttled from one family to another. Although this experience may not have been culturally modal, it occurred with sufficient frequency to be a possibility for every Bang Chan child. It was further suggested that in part such experiences taught villagers at a very early age that they had to fend for themselves, and that the experiences served as psychological prototypes for the sense of fragility of social relationships that is so characteristic of village life.

In contrast to most of the literature cited above, the last two articles are based on data which are products of interviews heavily weighted toward the psychologically expressive. Two of the informants admitted that they told us things that they had never shared with anyone, and the agitation (a non-histrionic agitation)[5] with which they reported some of their experiences suggested that this was indeed the case. I mention these considerations because the kind of material to come out of the interviews was perhaps not what one would expect from typically affable, easygoing Thai peasants. However, it must be recognized that the material focused only on the private sector of their lives, and indeed a very narrow area of this sector. Thus, although the articles may have been more analytic than previous efforts, they were also considerably more limited in scope.

I have attempted above to describe and evaluate almost all the available literature on Thai personality. There are a few additional sources which might be cited (Ratanakorn 1955, Boesch 1956, Mosel 1957), but their major concerns seem so tangential to our present purposes that it would add little to discuss them. By way of summary, the following points should be noted. The Thai language psychological literature is for the most part an unself-conscious, non-analytic folk literature, and as such is a rich source of data rather than a source of ideas on Thai personality. Illustrations of the value of the literature as data were provided in the text. However, since these data are primarily the product of an urban literati it is difficult to determine precisely to what extent they are also descriptive of peasants, although many of the traits reported seem apposite. There are no psychologically oriented Thai language essays dealing exclusively with villagers. The English language literature tends to be more analytic and broad-ranging in its concerns. Excluding Tirabutana's autobiography, these efforts seem to fall into one of three categories: (1) itemizations of manifest traits with little attention given to the psychodynamics involved (Thai psychologist, Phillips in Cornell Thailand Handbook, Textor); (2) sensitive psychological reflections on incomplete or specialized ethnographic data (R. F. Benedict, leMay); and (3) analyses of a limited set of private psychological issues from a few informants. (Hanks and Phillips, Phillips).

Psychological Dimensions of Village Interaction

Most personality portrayals proceed either by discussing how people behave in terms of a specific set of analytic issues, such as aggression,

---

[5] This is important simply because when opportunity permits—and the life-history situation is clearly such an opportunity—villagers love to tell a good story: full of histrionics, feigned exaggerations, and emotional flourishes. However, our informants were not given to theatrics during the interviews; on the contrary, they tended to tell their stories with an almost poignant seriousness. The fact that we were the first people ever to take such a direct, personal interest in them as individuals played a crucial role here. Being asked to reveal for the first time how they felt about their early lives, their families, and themselves was cause not only for pride but trust, and they often used the interviews as a way of unburdening themselves.

achievement, and dependency, or by discussing those traits which are significant in the daily round of life, irrespective of the analytic categories to which they refer. In this section we will emphasize the latter, more naturalistic approach. Its advantage is that it permits us to identify and develop certain issues which play a crucial role in the interactive world of the villagers, but which might otherwise go unnoticed should they not be represented by, or not quite fit, any of the predetermined categories. The Thai attitudes toward the body referred to earlier, for example, is an issue of extreme importance in their interpersonal relationships, but one that is actually given little explicit attention in most personality studies. This section is designed in part to deal with such problems, although inevitably there may be some overlap between the materials covered here and those discussed in later sections.

The Pleasures of Social Contact

Of all the personality traits that come to the attention of the foreign observer there is perhaps none more compelling than the affability, gentleness, and good humor of the villagers. It is difficult to think of a people more consistently ready, *once contact has been made,* to treat others amicably and convivially than the peasants of Bang Chan. (The italics are necessary simply because the villagers are equally primed to ignore others.) However, this jovial cordiality is not an easy thing to conceptualize. In the earlier paper by Hanks and Phillips (1961) we spoke of these happy characteristics as "not so much the expressions of any basic light-heartedness as they are techniques for implementing the main precept of social interaction: 'Avoid face-to-face conflict!'" Although the villagers' good humor does serve this purpose, I would now suggest that it involves several additional dimensions and motives.

First, there is a whole complex of responses represented here. The tendency to keep situations and conversations jocular, amusing, and at times gently ribald, is perhaps the most relaxed expression of this attitude. It is most obvious in the behavior of village gossip groups and in the relationships between individuals who consider themselves acquaintances but not quite close friends. The essential ingredient of this mode of affability is that interaction should be a great deal of fun but of little social consequence. Of a different order, and more common, is the villagers' ubiquitous politeness. This takes a host of forms: the genial hospitality that is expressed toward a newcomer, usually in the form of "personal" questions serving both to identify the person and to make him feel that others are interested in him ("How old are you? Any children? How much did you pay for your shirt or your land? Why don't you have any children?"); the numerous linguistic

and postural forms expressive of respect cited earlier; the repeated hesitation to place others in embarrassing situations; the hesitation to tell others
bad news so that "they will not feel sad" or will not have to dissemble
(although more often the less delicate reason is the person's fear of embarrassing himself). Of a still different order is the uneasy affability that is
expressed in the nervous giggling accompanying many face-to-face relationships and in the compulsive preoccupation with inconsequential or inoffensive topics while conversing with others. These responses appear to be
either attempts to maintain minimal contact with others while jockeying to
find out what they are really up to, or, in the negative sense, efforts to fulfill
the minimum requirements of interaction while waiting (and hoping) for
the contact to come to an end. And still different from all these is the
affability associated with trying to make a good impression on others
expressed in the constant concern with displaying good manners, with
using pleasing or flattering words, with being a good host, and the like.
Although this category is in many respects behaviorally similar to the
"politeness" referred to above, it seems to differ from the latter motiva-
tionally in that it is concerned not with the state and comfort of others *per
se*, but with ego's effect on others.

As described above in simple summary terms, these responses might
appear quite ordinary and at certain times applicable to any group of
human beings. However, what impresses the observer in Bang Chan is the
insistence and constancy of their use. These are precisely the forms that the
villagers choose in the vast majority of situations for expressing the degree
and quality of contact that they feel toward others. That they are in fact
social forms—stylized, often ritualized, modes of behaving—should not be
overlooked. It is just this characteristic that engenders the theme underlying all the responses and which indeed sets the tone of most Thai
interaction: that the relations between people should be friendly, genial,
and correct, but need have little personal commitment or involvement. As
will be seen below, it is this readiness to phrase most face-to-face contact in
terms of social rituals while at the same time feeling little commitment to
others that actually lies at the root of what has so often been called
Thailand's "loosely structured social system."

Social Play

The first response mentioned above, the tendency to turn social situations
into occasions for play, is probably one of the most common of all human
tendencies (it is certainly one of the earliest), but one that strangely has
received little attention in the psychological literature. The few writers
who have expressed any interest in social play have tended to view it simply

as a release mechanism from boredom or tension (Riesman and Bloomberg 1957, Roy 1959–1960), as a "healthy" escape from reality (Flugel 1954, Bateson 1954), or as a normal and desirable regression to childhood pleasures (Freud 1905 and 1928). Running through all these observations is the obvious Western bias that play somehow is divorced from, or a reaction to, the harsh facts of social reality.[6] On reflection, however, it is clear there is no theoretical necessity, either maturational or social psychological, for play to be limited to cathartic functions, or for regarding it as a less realistic or less mature psychological state than that which causes boredom, tension, escape, or regression. In fact, one might logically argue that the conditions which create the latter states are less realistic and immature because they represent retreats to forms of infantile masochism. Such questions of course belong to the realm of interpretive debate. The essential point is that in the process of learning to adapt to the social psychological realities of one's culture there is no inherent, ontogenetic requirement (other than that imposed by the peculiarities of one's culture) for human beings to renounce their motivations for play. Simply stated, having fun need not be so much a retreat from or defense against adult reality and responsibility as it is something to be sought after for its own sake.

The fundamental analytic issue here may well be whether play is a psychobiological "given" of the human animal, on the same order as hunger, sex, and other precultural needs, or a learned, secondary cultural

---

[6] Of these various interpretations, the most broadly conceived and carefully argued is Freud's, where play activities are linked theoretically to the interrelationships of the id, ego, and superego and the aims of the "pleasure principle." However, even here Freud was caught up in the Western cultural bias that only children, those who have not yet had to come fully to terms with social reality, could easily "afford" the luxury of play. This same cultural bias often appears at a totally different interpretive level in the rather crass pronouncements of journalists and travelers who, in writing about the Thai, refer to the "child-like" behavior of these people who spend so much time, energy, and money in having fun.

Radcliffe-Brown's famous essay on the "joking relationship" (1952) is of course a special sociological case of the "tension release" function of play. In a brief paper, Keesing (1960) lists some seven overlapping functions of play, but here too play is seen largely as divorced from "everyday 'reality' activities." Callois (1958) brings together valuable cross-cultural data in what is otherwise a classification of organized games.

Probably the most comprehensive study of play ever written is *Homo Ludens: A Study of the Play Element in Culture* (1938; English translation 1950) by the late cultural historian, Johan Huizinga. Although Huizinga is concerned mainly with structured play activities (games of skill, chance, guessing games) and with the relationships between play and ceremonials, one of his observations is worth noting: "Nature, so our reasoning mind tells us, could just as easily given her children all those useful functions of discharging superabundant energy, of relaxing after exertion, of training for the demands of life, of compensating for unfulfilled longings, etc., in the form of purely mechanical exercises and reactions. But no, she gave us play, with its tension, its mirth, and its fun. Now this last element, the *fun* of playing, resists all analysis, all logical interpretation. As a concept, it cannot be reduced to any other mental category. . . ."

need. The problem is that we really do not know, although comparative data from primatology (Yerkes 1943, Kroeber 1948: 27–29 and 60–61) clearly suggest that play belongs to the former category. If this is indeed the case it would imply that play is subject to the same degree of cultural influence, channeling, and socialization as are hunger, sex, and aggression, but can no more be fully obliterated than can these needs. Assuming, for the sake of argument, that this reasoning is correct, then the compensatory "escape" and "regressive" functions attributed to play by the authors noted above would not be at all unreasonable: play might well come to serve as an escape from adult reality in the same way that food sometimes serves as an escape from sexual anxiety or sex from food anxiety (Holmberg 1950). However, the point is that these are not the primary or typical functions of these needs, but secondary and defensive ones; although significant, they hardly comprise the necessary conditions for their being. If this approach is valid, we would be considerably wiser in our present state of knowledge (the Protestant Ethic and its intellectual extensions notwithstanding) to direct our attention to identifying the varying forms of play from culture to culture rather than to dwell on its secondary, compensatory functions.

Whatever its ultimate motivational basis, there is no doubting either the spontaneity or ingenuousness with which Bang Chaners turn social situations into occasions for play. For the most part they seem prompted in these situations by the simple desire to have a good time rather than to affect others in a socially pointed way, that is, their humor is not typically aimed at being sarcastic, didactic, or even exhibitionistic, although the person who excels at being funny is quickly recognized as such and is to an extent admired.[7] There is, in the negative sense noted earlier, an element of interpersonal effect operating here: comedy is a technique which almost by definition reduces the potentiality for face-to-face conflict. However, the villagers' play seems aimed primarily at satisfying personalistic function: their *individual* needs for pleasure and amusement.

The forms that these play activities take are numerous.[8] Perhaps their

---

[7] In the more explicitly institutionalized forms of comedy—*likee* (folk dramatic shows) or newspaper and magazine cartoons—these aims do come into play and often assume extreme, sometimes even biting, proportions. However, this is the comparatively safe world of theatre and "literature." Among themselves, in the world of face-to-face contact, villagers are considerably more gentle (or less sophisticated) and do not focus explicitly on such purposes.

[8] We will be concerned primarily with the forms of play, not its content. For whatever reason, humor and comedy seem to be the last refuge of what is genuinely private in a culture. Intercultural translations may succeed in communicating the manifest content of another people's humor, but they so frequently miss its intent that the result is either perplexity or disappointment ("Yes, and what happens then?").

The dangers of trying to share humor interculturally were perhaps never brought home better than when I tried to get the villagers' reaction to a story that received most subtle expression is in the marvelous word games that the villagers play. What is striking about these games from an analytic viewpoint is not so much that they are funny, but that villagers are continually attentive to opportunities for playing them, and actively try to structure situations along such lines. In a sense, they are not "games" at all but verbal asides that emerge spontaneously from the discourse of everyday contact, and which serve to make such contacts enjoyable. One form of word play is particularly popular. For the lack of a better term, it could be called "silent stinky pinky." [9] Here two persons are chatting, and person A works into the conversation a statement that sounds completely innocuous. (A man, for example, says to a woman, *hen mii*, meaning "see the bear.") Person B, forever attentive, knows that words are deceptive: although A *said* one thing, he was really *thinking* of, and expects B to be *thinking* of, its rhymed phonemic inversion, which is vulgar or insulting. (Although the man said to her, *hen mii*, he was really thinking of *men hii*, meaning "your vulva smells.") Person B picks up the cue and responds with a statement that sounds equally innocuous but which when mentally inverted is just as scatological. The game continues until one of the parties gives up, whereupon the conversation returns with laughter to its original concerns. It must be emphasized that although this game is phrased in terms of a verbal contest, its purpose is not to best the other person but to work out with him or her a dialogue entertaining to both.

Sometimes these games arise and die out so quickly that it is difficult even for other, nonparticipating Siamese to spot them. The particular example cited here is one that has become almost part of the folklore of conversational gambits. However, what delights many of the villagers is the unpredictability of these patterns. On one occasion, I unwittingly juxtaposed a few English phonemes that had two informants and my assistant literally rolling on the floor with laughter. We were talking about the

---

wide currency in Bangkok newspapers during 1956. It seemed that a husband was waiting outside a brothel to escort his wife, one of the prostitutes, home. She was busy with a customer. The husband called to her, telling her to hurry. She called back, saying that she would be through shortly. A few minutes later, he called again, and once more she said that she would be coming along. Finally, the husband went in and shot both his wife and her customer "because I lost my patience." When I told this story to several villagers, I was the only one who chortled. Most of them either commented on the sadness of the story or said the husband was stupid for killing the family breadwinner.

[9] In American stinky-pinky, people try to guess the rhymed equivalents of abstract definitions. Thus, if person A says, "I am thinking of a 'cadaverous Marxist,'" person B might say, "a dead red." The Thai version differs from its American cousin in that it is not only unspoken but is not really a parlor game. The tonal, monosyllabic nature of the Thai language probably is an important preconditioning factor here. (See also Haas 1951 and 1957 for illustrations of other kinds of verbal play.)

various kinds of ants living in Thailand and the United States. (Such are the topics that interest villagers.) The villagers wanted to know the English names for small red ants, normal black ones, and the large, rusty colored variety that are indigenous to the tropics. I named the first two with no difficulty. For the third, I said simply, "a giant ant." The assistant, turning to one of the informants, first gave the literal Thai equivalent of "giant," and then, as if this were the funniest thing he had heard that week, began to repeat, "giant, gi-ant, gi-ant." In a few seconds, they were all bursting with laughter.

Different, yet part of the same psychological constellation, is the whole complex of behaviors associated with the term, *sanug*. *Sanug* is usually translated into English simply as "fun." However, this translation conveys little of the motivational significance of the term. Essentially, *sanug* is a quality inherent in all situations which are not only fun but also emotionally worthwhile. In fact, these two states are often thought of as reciprocals of one another. An activity that is novel, diverting, or that can be done comfortably, is *sanug dii* (good fun); one that is tedious, over-demanding, that lacks the opportunity for frivolity, is not *sanug* and should be avoided. Harvesting rice in coöperative work groups, attending a ceremonial, participating in an election (see Phillips 1958: 45–46), or even taking something as outlandish as a Sentence Completion Test are all *sanug*. (The unifying elements of these diverse activities are either their novelty or the fact that they involve the presence of relatively large numbers of people but require no genuine interchange with them.) On the other hand, going into the army or working for a demanding superior are not *sanug*.

The importance of *sanug* is that it provides the villagers with a standard of value, a measure of how much they wish to commit themselves to a particular activity. The role of this standard should not be underestimated. Villagers who have taken a job in the city, often involving a time-bound daily routine or continuous, sustained attention to a task (work in a small factory, for example) frequently return to the village explaining that they quit "because it wasn't *sanug*. How can you work on a job if there is never any time for fun?" Foreign employers, with their greater concern for the job than with the person who does it and with their annoying tendency to be *cuu cii* (compulsive, fussy, exacting) are a particular target for this indictment, although this is usually based on hearsay rather than personal experience. On the other hand, villagers will often take on free of charge a major job (for example, helping a neighbor build a house) precisely because it is *sanug*. Although there are other considerations operating here—creating or repaying a personal obligation, doing a *bunkhun* ("a goodness") for a neighbor—the "sanug-ful" aspects of the task are always salient: the free food, drink, and chitchat at the end of a hard day's work; the fun of working together with several other individuals. Notice that in this kind of situation there is no overseer demanding the person's effort. His labor is freely given and may be freely withdrawn.

In describing *sanug* as a measure of how much villagers wish to commit themselves to a particular activity, I mean to communicate a point and not merely to turn a phrase. The word "commit," which appears often in this book, is used to convey the idea that coöperative, mutually expectable interaction as we know it in the West does not "simply take place" in Bang Chan. Rather, there is always the intervening factor of whether individuals want it to take place. Siamese are, first and foremost, free and independent souls. Much of the time they fulfill each other's expectations, but this is only because they want to, not because others expect it of them or because the situation demands it. It is the individual that is primary, not the social relationship. The strength of this principle is demonstrated by the fact that one is almost never surprised when one's expectations about another are not fulfilled. The assumption is: "If he did not do it, he must have had his own good reason."

The potentialities for interpersonal frustration that are inherent in such a system are minimized largely by the hesitation on the part of individuals to build up strong expectations about people or events. In general, the Thai are a people who do not live at, and rarely reach, a high emotional pitch. Witness, for example, the specifications of "sanug-ful activities," those which afford the greatest pleasure: they are novel, diverting, comfortable, and frivolous, but there is no Faustian intensity about these joys. They are all rather muted emotional experiences. The point here is simply that in this kind of psychological environment, people rarely permit themselves to become *so* committed to an activity or to another person that the frustration of that commitment will be overly disturbing to them. They proceed from a premise which says in effect: "Well, it is really not that important that he did not do what I expected of him. I will simply have to make do."

There are a few aspects of the villagers' concern with *sanug* that warrant underscoring. First, from an analytic point of view, *sanug* seems to reflect an attempt on the part of the villagers to lead a psychologically integrated life, wherein the time and energy one gives to an activity is rewarded immediately and directly with pleasure. This low-keyed pleasure should be an inextricable part of the total situation in which one finds oneself (or more accurately, into which one places oneself), not something to be deferred until a later, "more appropriate" time when it becomes an isolated segment of experience. Essentially, *sanug* should be—it not always is—a concurrent aspect of almost everything that one does. At the same time, however, these conditions are also the source of an inevitable paradox. Since "sanug-ful" activities are, by definition, novel and diverting, and since even the most novel activities eventually become routine or stale, it is obviously impossible for all one's hours to be animated with *sanug*. From a total time perspective, many of the villagers' activities are of course either "sanug-fully" fallow or "sanug-fully" short-lived. To a large extent, this paradox is resolved *subjectively* by the short-term time perspective of the villagers. This is the second major point to be noted about *sanug*, that is, *sanug* reflects a more generalized tendency on the part of the villagers to concern themselves with activities that require only brief time commitments or whose effects are immediately forthcoming. Bang Chaners are not an impatient people in an active, negative sense, but they do have difficulty in attending to tasks that demand from them a sense of compulsiveness or staying power. They will often drop demanding tasks right in the middle once they have recognized that the work is taking longer than originally expected. What is striking is that they will do this with apparently no sense of frustration over not having fulfilled their aims and with no regret over having wasted their time. It is as if their original purposes had simply become irrelevant, and they had gone on to other things. This is precisely the attitude, for example, surrounding the construction of the unusable road referred to earlier leading from the Minburi Highway to the Bang Chan school. After devoting considerable labor to building the high mound that would form the foundation of the road, villagers lost interest when they were unable to obtain funds for its surfacing. Since no one was ever interested in maintaining it, the road now lies in the middle of a rice field, rutted and pitted; much of the foundation has sunk back to the level of the adjacent fields. However, no villager has ever considered the road a fiasco or "folly"; it was just something done in the past and has since been forgotten. The road project might be revived in the future, but from the villagers' point of view that too is irrelevant. The point is that *sanug*, with its emphasis on novelty and diversion, is expressive of this same underlying time orientation. In the villagers' way of thinking, no activity is really worth doing unless it has the potentiality for fun.

Another expression of the villagers' concern with play, related in some respects to what will be discussed in the next section, is their preoccupation with humorous *topics* of conversation. For the most part, they enjoy hearing and telling stories with a "banana peel" twist: of a husband who is caught by his wife sleeping with another woman; of an individual who, through his failure to take heed, is cheated out of his money. Such stories of course always concern other people, not those immediately present. Too, stories that combine whimsy and the supernatural—for example, of a "super-dog" that can find buried treasure or foretell the future—elicit laughter, although often with a tinge of apprehension that the stories may be true. However, what is most impressive about these and similar stories is the amount of time given to them.

The sociological context of a story-telling is probably what is most important here. Bang Chan is a community where other than cultivating the single rice crop and attending to daily household chores and religious activities, the villagers realistically have little else to do but talk to each other. This is clearly not an inevitable attribute of the peasant condition, but it is true of Bang Chan where little attention is given to such creative leisure activities as craftsmanship, music, and art, and where there is little occupational specialization. In fact, probably more time is given to gossiping than to any other single waking activity except daydreaming. Bang Chaners talk of many things, serious as well as lighthearted: the price of rice, religion, gambling, the doings of "big people," family disputes, and the like. However, by far one of the largest segments of their total conversational repertoire is given over to "funny" stories. Of course, no story is ever *exclusively* humorous in nature; all communication is inherently multidimensional, and even the funniest story has a substantive, non-humorous message. However, if stories may be judged by their behavioral effects (laughter) irrespective of their intellectual content, then the function of a major part of Bang Chan gossip is amusement.[10]

The motivations for the selection of banana peel type stories are more complex. In part, the choice seems prompted by a "there but for the grace of God go I . . . " mentality. As suggested earlier, Bang Chaners have a keenly developed sense of the possible: to them, this is a world where anything, not only the probable or the predictable, can happen. The banana peel story, with its emphasis on the painfully ludicrous and extreme, is a perfect representation of such an uncertain world. Its beauty is

---

[10] During the early stage of field work, I attempted to do systematic naturalistic observations of these gossip groups. The purpose was simply to identify the kinds of topics uppermost in the villagers' minds and the modes of interaction that most frequently developed during the sessions; it was hoped that the latter information might be related to the psychological test materials of the discussants. As a precisely designed and executed project, the effort, however, was dropped after a short time. For one thing, it was too difficult for two observers to record the *simultaneous* verbal and kinesthetic interaction of *several* people without the aid of a self-powered tape recorder and with the added burden of having to strain the material through the translation process. The task was further complicated by the fact that the membership of these groups continually changed as people would leave and enter the conversations. Also the groups would often break down into smaller sub-groups. Most important was the sheer multidimensionality of the conversation: any one utterance could simultaneously be funny, aggressive, boastful, carry practical information, etc. However, enough information was culled from these early attempts and later less ambitious ones to prompt the statements presented here. It is this writer's observation that one of the reasons behind the success of so much of the "small group" research conducted in the United States is that the groups studied have been *problem solving* or *task-oriented*, rather than simple gossip groups. The highly functional nature of the former has provided built-in constraints on the freedom of action permitted the discussants, and has made observational problems comparatively easier to deal with.

that it is simply a "story," a description of the plight of other people, not the self. The story-teller or listener has the pleasure of a vicarious experience, but none of the pain of the real life situation. He can laugh over his good fortune in not being the person who was cheated out of his money or who was caught philandering by his wife. On the negative side, these stories also serve as a means by which the participants can express, through identification and projection, some of their own hostilities. The veil of humor provides in fact the ideal dress for hostility: one can be completely unabashed about expressing one's feelings (of wanting to steal, say, or wanting to humiliate), since what is expressed, in a form so exaggerated as to be acceptable, is simply the feeling and not the act itself. The hostility is made even more acceptable by the fact that it is projected onto the person in the story rather than referred to ego himself. In these terms, the telling of these stories probably does have something of the cathartic function cited earlier in the chapter: aggressions and hostilities that are otherwise kept under careful control are here permitted to emerge not only painlessly, but with a bit of relish. Finally, some of the laughter at these stories is probably also based on the feelings of embarrassment evoked in listeners. This is similar to the "there but for the grace of God . . ." motive but is different in that it is not based on personal identification with the person who suffers but rather on a diffuse feeling of discomfort over the expression of aggression—aggression toward anybody. There is embarrassment over things not being as they should be, over one's moral universe being temporarily out of joint. Also, the laughter is probably symptomatic of the listener's uneasiness as he becomes aware that the hostilities portrayed in the story are strikingly similar to those he himself harbors toward others. Embarrassed about his own aggressive impulses, he assuages them with laughter.

The motives for focusing on whimsical topics of conversation are less recondite and defensive than the above. Stories of the type describing "super-dogs" who find buried treasure are told because they are at the same time such outrageous and yet gentle distortions of reality. It is the juxtaposition of incongruous elements that is so appealing here. In ordinary Thai thought, for example, the dog is generally considered to be one of the most inconsequential and worthless of creatures. He is tolerated for his ability to warn of strangers and dispose of refuse, but nothing remotely approximating the feeling of "man's best friend" is associated with him. For such a lowly creature to be the sudden possessor of miraculous power is just too foolish. An elephant, monkey, or cobra perhaps, but not a dog.[11] Only "uncivilized" forest people would accept such a story. Yet, because the dog is such a familiar part of one's environment and also a living creature

---

[11] Doubt would exist for these creatures too, but because of their mythological and historical significance it would be somewhat tempered.

("Who knows what he was in earlier lives and what powers he brought
with him into this one?"), there is enough reality about the tale to make
people want to listen. Moreover, it is wish-fulfilling fantasy; people laugh
because reality has been outraged, but with a lingering desire that it really
could be.

The kinds of stories outlined above do not exhaust the villagers' stock of
conversational humor. There are also tall stories without the supernatural
touch, broad burlesques, "dirty" jokes,[12] and the countless epigrams that
work their way into almost any conversation; the last are not so much topics
of conversation as they are means of punctuating a point. However, enough
has been said to indicate that in its cognitive stylization and social psychological purposes, Bang Chan humor is not too different from Western
humor. It is rather the content, frequency, and evaluation of the humor
that is so distinctive. That the content should be distinctive is of course
self-evident, since all humor is rooted in the implicit and familiar premises
of workaday, cultural life. In fact the very essence of a joke is seeing the
culturally familiar in an entirely new light. This may help to explain,
incidentally, why it is always so painfully self-defeating to try "to explain"
the content of a joke: its entire effect is dependent on the listener's implicit

---

[12] Sexual and scatological humor in Bang Chan pose some special problems. On the
one hand, because villagers take such a matter-of-fact approach to sex, there are
actually few jokes and stories that aim explicitly at being titillating or risqué. For
most Bang Chaners, sex is something to be experienced and enjoyed in private, not
snickered about barracks-style; there is no *sanug* in *talking* about sex (although there
may be in playing with tabooed words, especially if cleverly done). Also, villagers
seem to lack any interest in lewdness for its own sake. Not only Bang Chan, but Thai
culture in general, is striking for its relative absence of attempts to edify sex: there is
nothing in Thai literature or art, for example, approximating the exaggerated bawdi-
ness of Rabelais or the graphic sensuality of the kind of sculpture found at Khajuraho
and Konarak in India.

On the other hand, sexual situations are very often used as vehicles for portraying
the foibles and stupidities of people. Villagers particularly enjoy stories of individuals
of either sex who devise ways for seducing the unsuspecting, or of individuals who
manage to outwit their spouses while philandering with their lovers; the more complex
their machinations, the more amusing the stories. However, it is the social psychological, not the sexual, dimensions of these tales that form the major bases of
their appeal.

Finally, it should be noted that villagers tend to distinguish between what could
be called "genital" and "anal" modes of humor. The latter type has considerably
fewer taboos associated with it. Thus, whereas most villagers would avoid going into
descriptive detail in reporting the physical aspects of a tale of sexual conquest, they
would have few qualms about discussing (and often with acoustical detail) such things
as people who pass air in public or who otherwise get themselves into compromising
anal situations. (Interestingly, J. Marvin Brown in his linguistic work with Thai
informants, often including female university students, reports in a personal communication that he encountered difficulty in obtaining the various Thai terms for sexual
organs and acts, but that the terms for anal and excretory behavior were given with
little hesitation.)

recognition of the incongruity being portrayed; to have to explicate the way the familiar has been violated is to miss the whole point. Yet the very problem with which the anthropological investigator is characteristically faced is his unfamiliarity with the culturally implicit. His major intellectual task in fact is to make explicit that which is implicitly held by his informants. The only way to deal with this paradox is either to consider humor a special case of anthropological investigation, leave the content alone, and focus principally on forms and functions, or do a humorless exegesis and be prepared for disappointments. As indicated earlier, this writer greatly prefers the former alternative.

Why the frequency and value of the humor should be so different is difficult to say. That the villagers devote considerably more time to this mode of play and place considerably higher value on it than do most Occidentals is clear, especially from the pejorative comments of Westerners who are so disturbed by it. One possible reason may be the simple lack (compared to Occidentals) of time-consuming, functional tasks in the village; that is, given the villagers' definitions of things that have to be done during the cycle of daily activity, there is just more time available to them to be "frittered away" in amusing conversation. However, this negative explanation is at best only a partial solution since many people who have "little to do" manage to make busy work for themselves (in a diagnostic, not deprecating, sense); also, granted the fact that Bang Chaners have time to talk of many things, it does not explain why such a large portion of this time should be given over to humor. Another possible reason was indicated earlier: comedy provides an outlet for certain feelings that otherwise are denied direct expression or are a source of anxiety in the culture. The higher frequency of humor is a function of the degree of prohibition or anxiety, which in the case of some feelings—aggression, for example—is very high indeed. Since, as has probably been detected, much of the villagers' humor does revolve around aggressive situations, there is clearly some cogency to this approach. There is a third possible reason for the villagers' greater concern with humor. Humor, with its emphasis on the exaggerated, the incongruous, and unpredictable is, from a psychological point of view, essentially a form of new experience. In fact, it, and the real life situations to which it refers, are "invention" in the purest meaning of the terms: the breaking through of tried and established patterns of expectation. But people in different cultures look for their new experience, or express their inventiveness, in different ways. There is no inherent necessity (a consideration often overlooked by scholars concerned with culture change) for inventiveness to be expressed primarily through technological, economic, or sociological forms. It might well be, as Keesing has suggested (1960), that in many cultures the favoured modes for expressing the innovative impulses are recreative or aesthetic, either in content or form. Simply stated, the reason Bang Chaners may spend more time than Westerners in telling amusing stories to each other is because they feel they are gaining something new and worthwhile from the experience.

Politeness: A Social Cosmetic

It has been previously noted that the villagers' ubiquitous politeness appears in several different forms: sometimes it is associated with a genial interest in others or a concern over their welfare and comfort; at other times it is used as a means of handling one's anxiety over the intentions of others or one's uncertainty over the nature and purpose of the relationship; and at other times, it is used as a means of impressing others or getting in their good graces. The term "social cosmetic" is used here because it embraces at one time all these varying usages. A cosmetic not only makes one appear more attractive and conceals one's blemishes, real or imagined, but permits one to deal with others more easily and comfortably. The last consideration is in part a direct consequence of the first two, that is, a person who feels he is attractive to others will in all likelihood be more relaxed in his relationships with them. However, it is probably also a product of the conventionalized, relatively explicit interactional "frame" [13] that the very wearing of the cosmetic creates. The cosmetic indicates that regardless of his basic intentions, the person will conduct himself properly and agreeably; it defines the presence of and prompts conformity to certain behavioral rituals which simplify for the participants the kinds of behavior they may express. In a sense, the cosmetic of politeness represents one of the most "civilized" modes of social interaction: it is based on a fundamental concern with structuring one's behavior (again, irrespective of intentions) so as least to disturb others and thus permit them to act in socially easy, uncomplicated ways. Further, it stresses respect for the dignity and psychological integrity of others. The actual topic of conversation or non-verbal ritual that links the participating individuals together may be either meaningful or inconsequential, but that is essentially irrelevant when compared to the fact that the respect the participants feel for each other is being communicated. In

---

[13] This term is somewhat akin to what Goffman (1959: 22–24), in his attempt to analyze behavior in a dramaturgical framework, calls the "setting" or the "scenic aspects" of the interactional situation. However, Goffman's terms refer explicitly to the physical layout—the furniture, decor, and the like—of the behavioral situation rather than to the psychological "setting" that is created by the behavior of the participating individuals. On the other hand, his term, "personal front," refers exclusively to the attributes of individuals, rather than to the situational definitions that they create. The term "frame" used here refers to the psychological setting which is created by the behavior of individuals and which defines for all participants the nature of the situation.

essence, much of the villagers' interaction is based on certain formal, rather than substantive, considerations,[14] the net effect of which is to minimize the impact that they might have upon each other but to maximize each person's sense of psychic independence and integrity.

Our phrasing here is principally in analytic not evaluative terms. However, it should be clear that from an evaluative point of view, there are both "positive" and "negative" consequences to the continuing use of this interactive mode. On the positive side, the villagers' politeness contributes to their extraordinary tolerance for nonconformity, personal deviance, failure, or the inability of individuals to live up to standards. In effect, the villagers seem to be saying that if another person is poor, weak, stupid, or naïve, that is essentially his own business (or problem), not cause for ridicule or even amelioration. People are publicly accepted and respected for what they are, despite their shortcomings. The sense of psychological security that such treatment affords is clear: it means that no matter what an individual's status or personal qualities may be, he can generally expect to be treated well by others. The canons of courtesy require this. On the other hand, to have to be continually sensitive to one's effect on others is, from ego's point of view, not without its psychic costs. Thus, although politeness is aimed at keeping social relationships smooth and uncomplicated, it frequently results in a lack of spontaneity and in the inhibition of genuine feelings. A cosmetic is supposed to enhance one's natural qualities, but inevitably it also conceals them.

To what extent this concealment "troubles" the villagers is most difficult to determine. There clearly are circumstances in which certain negative consequences follow directly from such concealment. But whether villagers are generally unhappy because they cannot express what they feel is problematic. Their admiration for individuals who "speak their feelings from their hearts" is occasionally unmitigated; but far more frequently, they speak of the "kindness" and "good hearts" of those who hide their feelings "so as not to hurt others." [15]

---

[14] All interaction is of course based on *both* formal and substantive considerations. The issue here is the relative emphasis given to one over the other, and how one may even be used as a substitute for the other when presenting the self.

[15] The case of Dang (Hanks and Phillips 1961) referred to earlier is an excellent example of the kinds of difficulty that may follow from the concealment of one's real sentiments. Dang's story is a somewhat plaintive tale: how, because of his anxiety about revealing his true feelings to his father, uncle, and aunt (his social superiors) he lost a house, some land, and married a girl he "did not quite want to." Yet at all times he maintained courteous relationships with all concerned. What is most significant about Dang's case, however, is the position of psychic isolation to which politeness brought him. Basically, Dang substituted in his relationships with his relatives the *form* of politeness for the more enduring *substance* of love, loyalty, and obligation. Rather than trust to the strength of such sentiments to help resolve his

Of the various forms politeness takes, its most relaxed, least contrived form in the cordiality that villagers extend to newcomers. Strangers to Bang Chan are hardly swept off their feet, but once contact has been established, they are welcomed with a degree of attention far exceeding simple tolerance of their presence. People express a curious interest in them as individuals, as if somehow their presence were adding a new dimension to the lives of their hosts. In the case of many Bang Chaners, this is probably true: the lives of these villagers are sufficiently routine and insular that the appearance of a new face is identified also with the advent of a significant and new experience. Still other villagers approach the newcomer with an attitude that says in effect: "One should try to meet and know as many persons as possible. Who knows what good may come of it?" The implied meaning here is that the cursory contact may in time develop into a firm relationship of reciprocal rights and obligations, whereby person A could turn to B to borrow money, ask his help in finding a job, help sponsor his son's ordination, and vice versa. There is in this attitude a sense of gentle optimism combined with opportunism. And still other villagers, probably the majority, approach the newcomer with no self reference at all, but with the simple intention of trying to make him feel comfortable. Whatever the intention in each case, however, the dominant behavior exhibited to the newcomer is openness, amiability, and curiosity.

The actual expressions of conviviality are at all times simple and straightforward. They involve asking the person such questions as his age, place of birth, whether he is married, or whether he has yet served in the monkhood. (Notice the phrasing of this last question. The polite Thai form is never whether a person has been a monk or not, but rather whether he has already been a monk or not *yet* become one. The syntax of the interrogative form assumes the good intentions of the other person.) If the individual is identified as coming from a locale with special or distinguishing characteristics, the conversation will often involve humorous allusions to the place. For example, if he is from the North, there will most likely be joking references to the beautiful women of Chiengmai; if he is from the Northeast, to the funny accent of the people of that area. If the relative statuses of visitor and host can be quickly identified (based upon age, clothes, speech patterns, and occasionally surname), the conversation may turn to topics whose very purpose is to emphasize status considerations and thus make the participants more comfortable with one another. If they

---

difficulties (ask his father to save the family land for him; tell the aunt he did not want to marry the girl she had chosen—which he could have done had he felt secure about his relatives' love for him), he politely said nothing. The net result of all of this, as indicated in the text, was a deep sense of personal inadequacy and resentment that loved ones cannot be depended on. Further, Dang had begun to treat others as he felt others had treated him.

are social peers, the Bang Chaners would easily turn the conversation to a discussion of the technical aspects of rice farming or even gambling. The latter would likely be discussed with a social superior only after some acquaintance. On the other hand, if one were clearly the other's superior, the superior would probably talk not about the methods of rice farming but, more generally and benignly, inquire, "Is all going well with you? Is there any way I might help you?" He might even proffer some unsolicited advice or aid. The tone and theme of the conversation would be expressive largely of the superior's concern with the welfare of his new-found friend, which the latter would typically accept.

All this is usually accompanied by gentle laughter and careful attention to appropriate pronominal forms. The good host will also serve his guest rain water, and if possible, scented rain water. If opportunity and finances permit, he may even offer him a warm Coca-Cola. The youngster who will actually serve the refreshment will make sure that it is on a coaster and that his hands are in the proper ritual position when he offers the drink to the guest. Such are the ingredients from which potential friendships are made.

Although the particulars of the kind of politeness found among family and friends are different from the above, the forms are essentially the same. Villagers do not talk about the funny accents of the people who live next door to them, nor do they rush to serve scented water when a brother comes to call. But they do take pains to express respect for each other by using proper honorific and pronominal forms, by looking to the oldest competent family member for advice, by talking of subjects that are pleasant and amusing, but never threatening or embarrassing.

The avoidance of embarrassing topics—even when the airing of such topics may be crucially important or beneficial to one of the parties concerned—is one of the most pronounced facets of village social life. To a Westerner accustomed to outspokenness, the types of situations that villagers define as embarrassing and the lengths to which they will go to avoid them sometimes appear to border on the sado-masochistic. Detailed interviews with two women whose husbands had taken second wives, for example, indicate that although at the time they were deeply disturbed by their husbands' actions (primarily for economic reasons; secondarily for emotional-sexual ones) they never once even brought the subject up with their husbands. They explained that they were too ?aaj (embarrassed) to do so. In neither case was this embarrassment expressive of any feeling of inadequacy on their parts (the fear of hearing their husbands say, "I took a second wife because you are not adequate"). It was prompted rather by the desire to avoid an awkward and potentially rancorous confrontation. They did not want to put anybody on the spot. (Whether such a confrontation would *actually* lead to overt rancor is almost impossible to ascertain because it in fact so rarely takes place. In fact, the "hypotheses" of these women are perfect manifestations of what, in the technical sense, is *anxiety* rather than *fear* about what might occur.) The marital situations of both these women have since been routinized so that they have come to accept the second wives as part of their normal domestic lives. However, the vehemence with which they report these incidents indicates that at the time they paid for their wish to avoid embarrassment with considerable psychic distress. In terms of the basic attitudes involved, these situations were not too unlike that which obtained for Dang: to avoid a potentially sticky social situation, politeness and complete silence were maintained.

Somewhat different order from the above are the numerous instances where "good friends" will avoid reporting to each other unhappy or distressing information although it is clearly to the other's advantage to have such information in order better to cope with the difficulty. In one case, a villager had been working for weeks on a land sale deal which would have netted him a brokerage fee of two thousand *baht* (approximately one hundred dollars, a considerable sum in a community where the average annual family income is, before expenses, only eighty-five hundred *baht*). A friend had meanwhile learned that another villager, with whom he was not at all close, had sweet-talked the customer into permitting him to handle the sale, much to the detriment of his own friend, the original broker. However, rather than warn the friend of what was happening, he simply said nothing. When asked to explain why he kept his silence, he said that he was just too ʔ*aaj* to speak up. Although the consequences of "ʔaaj-ness" were in this case more extreme than usual, the situation itself was not. In another, less dramatic instance a villager mentioned to us that in coming across the rice fields that afternoon he had noticed that his neighbor's windmill had broken down. The belt connecting the windmill to the irrigating machine used in raising water into the fields had slipped from the drive shaft. However, despite the obvious importance of this fact to his neighbor—the planting of his rice seedlings was completely dependent on the noria raising a sufficient amount of water into the field at the right time—the friend failed to tell his neighbor what had happened. When asked why, he said that he was ʔ*aaj* about making his friend unhappy.

What is important about the above illustrations is not so much their typicality—one can cite instances where friends are considerably more realistic and helpful—but rather the legitimacy of the rationalizations of the inactive friends. All Bang Chaners can understand and accept the reluctance of a villager to be the person who actually triggers off another individual's discomfort. There is a genuine (albeit misplaced) sense of responsibility about not making another unhappy. What is important is the immediate, face-to-face situation. If a person must ultimately suffer, that is his own problem; but at least the friend can say, "I did not 'cause' it."

Villagers also recognize the reluctance of an individual to become involved in another person's problems on the grounds of avoiding the accusation of *actually* having caused them. They say (but again, empirical instances of this type are very hard to find) that frequently the person with good intentions is turned on by the very friend he is trying to help, for example, "Since you know so much about the broken windmill perhaps you were the one who broke it!" Both these attitudes result from a rather overinflated view of one's importance to the friend, as if the friend would be more concerned with the agent of information than with the information itself. This is not so much a confusion of means and ends as a re-identification of them. Finally, some of the villagers' reluctance is probably also due to simple indifference or laziness regarding the plight of the friend.

Other expressions of the "ʔaaj-ness" complex are more clearly altruistic than the above. Villagers explain, for example, that the reason there is never any more than one candidate for the post of hamlet or commune headman, on the rare occasions when such elections are held, is to avoid embarrassing the individuals involved. The eventual headman would be embarrassed because the presence of a competitor would suggest doubt about his competence; the candidate who lost would be embarrassed by the very fact that he lost. To avoid hurt feelings, only one candidate is presented, voted on, and elected.

We have been talking above about politeness primarily in a negative sense, that is, about the lengths to which villagers will go to *avoid* discomforting others or upsetting peaceful relationships. This aspect was stressed because its expressions represent a somewhat unique form of patterned social interaction. However, the many positive forms of the villagers' politeness to friends and kin should not be minimized: their concern with choosing topics of conversation they think will interest or entertain others; their search for opportunities to flatter them, sometimes in pseudo-mocking fashion, but more often to make them feel good; their attention to providing others with a pleasing audience—being silent, attentive, and eager when others are declaiming on a favorite subject. Of course, many times the villagers are not listening, but they try to behave as if they were. The aim here is to make others feel that what they are saying is worthwhile. An important part of this is that one almost never directly challenges the veracity or logic of the speaker's statements. If disbelief is the only appropriate response, it should be done silently. Nothing except personal pain and interpersonal tension would be gained from a direct challenge. If one feels strongly enough about the issue, which is very rare,[16] the presentation of an *alternative* view would not be inappropriate. But one

---

[16] The rarity of strong feelings is due to the fact that so often the very purpose of such conversations is to convey politeness and nothing more. The actual topic of conversation is simply a medium of contact, not a matter to be seriously discussed.

must be extremely careful not to phrase it as a direct refutation of the speaker. Again, there is present in this approach the Thai assumption that the most important aspect of a social relationship is the psychic comfort and welfare of the persons involved, not the truth or validity of the matter under discussion. The overriding ethic is that each person not only has a right to be heard, but should be made to feel comfortable as well.

Related to the above, but distinctive enough to require a category of its own, is the form of politeness expressed in the villagers' nervous laughter and in their preoccupation with inconsequential topics of conversation. Laughter and smiling is such a universal attribute of Thai demeanor (an early volume on Siam by W. A. R. Wood was in fact entitled *Land of Smiles*) that it is not always easy to distinguish precisely between this particular form and other more relaxed expressions of lightheartedness. From the point of view of social intention—to be appealing and inoffensive to others—they are probably not distinguishable. What sets this form apart is mainly the situation in which it is found: a villager is apt to laugh nervously when talking about unhappy or unfortunate experiences. Likewise he will laugh or resort to inconsequential topics when trying to get something from another person or knowing that someone is trying to get something from him, in either case being unsure of how the other person will react; when meeting a person, often of higher status, for the first time and feeling compelled to relate to him, but not knowing quite how. Again, this mode of interaction is clearly not unique to Bang Chan. However, villagers resort to it so frequently, or define so many situations as the kind necessitating its use, that it emerges as one of the most salient modalities of Thai interaction. In a sense, the nervousness that is betrayed indicates some of the internal strain that villagers undergo in maintaining a constant front of politeness.

It should be noted, however, that they are well aware of their uneasiness: they will often admit it to you in more relaxed moments. Also, other villagers in attendance can immediately spot it, and will tell you that the person was nervous. What is so characteristically nice about the villagers, however, is that they will almost never take advantage of a person's nervousness to score a point for themselves. Uneasiness is defined simply as a neutral personality trait, part of the way in which an individual presents himself and not a symptom of psychic weakness. In fact, from the point of view of influencing the purpose or direction of an interaction, it is usually ignored. What is *socially* important is that a person act nicely, not how he feels about the way he acts; the latter is his own business. It might further be noted that the recognition of one's own uneasiness, without at the same time feeling threatened by its exposure, is symptomatic of the villager's relatively strong ego structure. A Bang Chaner can maintain a certain front, know that it actually elicits and betrays his anxiety, but have such implicit trust in his own resources that he feels no need to alter his behavior. Simply stated: uneasiness when it occurs is accepted as a social psychological fact of life; it is not felt as a threat to the integrity of the personality.

The actual expressions of nervousness and inconsequential conversation vary considerably. Perhaps their most obvious (and justifiable) expression is when a villager, who wants to get something from another person, for example, a job, a loan, higher rent on land, is uncertain about the other's reaction and approaches him by hedging around the issue with giggles and light, irrelevant comments. This mode of behavior typically occurs when there is no history of reciprocal benefits between the parties or when a middleman cannot be used.[17] Although villagers themselves do not consider such comments "irrelevant" (probably because from a ritualistic point of view they are not), it is hard to define a detailed discussion of a person's buttons or belt buckle as anything but a kind of phatic communion. Sometimes conversations of this type will go on for twenty and thirty minutes, often branching off to include more topical interests such as the size of eggs or the calls of birds, before reaching the point. Frequently they never reach the point, since somewhere along the line the individual recognizes from the tone of the conversation that the other person is not in the proper mood to entertain his request; in this case, the individual will explain that he came simply "to chat." Sometimes the friend will begin to giggle uneasily (particularly if the protagonist's references to him contain an excess of flattery) as he becomes aware of the purpose of the conversation and wishes to evade facing the ultimate issue. Very often, even when the final request comes out, he can avoid it simply by giggling. Under such circumstances a giggle is crucially communicative: it is the person's polite substitute for "No," or "Let us bring this particular topic of conversation to an end." Giggling is a wonderfully effective way of carrying on a "conversation" (for those who can read its "vocabulary") because one can so readily convey his refusal, wariness, and even hostility while at all times maintaining the illusion of friendliness. It is precisely because the villagers' giggling frequently rests on such devious attitudes that it appears

---

[17] The *quid pro quo* basis of the former would permit a considerably more direct approach. It is not difficult to be frank with a person when both you and he realize that you are asking for an earlier obligation to be repaid or that you are creating a new one which may be called upon later when needed. Villagers are highly responsive to such obligations, often going to considerable effort and personal discomfort to meet them. A middleman, on the other hand, is used precisely to avoid the kind of delicate encounter described here. As a disinterested third party, he can be completely candid in his requests. However, for reasons of secrecy (usually when the request involves some potential competition or envy of other villagers, or perhaps some sharp-dealing) the use of a middleman may be inappropriate.

to be somewhat nervous. Like the conversational topics mentioned above, its purpose is to maintain social contact, but at a minimal substantive level.

Other uses of giggling are less consciously purposeful than the above. Perhaps the most frequent instance of this is when villagers are talking about or responding directly to an unfortunate situation: a flood destroying the rice crop, a friend or relative dying or being beaten up, a person committing suicide. Giggling under these circumstances seems to represent several related sentiments. On the one hand, it indicates a slight feeling of embarrassment over having discovered something or talked about something which would have been better left undiscovered and undiscussed. At the same time, it is an attempt to make light of the misfortune by suggesting that the speaker and those present should not be overly pained by what they are encountering. Giggling here serves very much the same kind of function as the phrase *maj pen raj* ("it is nothing") referred to earlier; it is a means of shrugging off and denying a feeling of distress. Finally, giggling often is also a kind of ironic commentary on the human situation—not in any abstract philosophical way, but in the sense that a tragedy is so often actually felt to be a comic exposure of human hopes and intentions. A little exchange between the writer and an elderly villager perhaps best illustrates this. During one of the two rainy seasons I spent in Thailand, the rains were especially heavy in the Central Plain and destroyed the rice crop of many Bang Chan farms. As might be expected, it was a topic of considerable discussion. Paddling down the canal one morning, we met a villager who was returning from inspecting his fields, and we stopped to chat. The discussion inevitably turned to the flood, and he told us, in a completely matter-of-fact way, that he had already lost about 50 percent of his crop. He then giggled nervously over what he had said, and followed it up with, "But that person over there has lost everything." His giggles then turned into laughter as he nodded his head in an attitude of pain. Months later, when things were considerably more comfortable for the villager (as it turned out, he had lost only about 5 percent of his crop) I recalled our meeting and asked him what he thought was so funny about the flood. He did not remember, but volunteered in a nice, didactic way: "When something like a flood happens, all you can do is laugh."

Giggling is also a favored mode of dealing with the countless situations that arise in daily life that are perceived by the villagers as potentially, or imminently, embarrassing. Here giggling is a substitute for an explanation of one's actions, particularly those that are considered annoying to others. Villagers who have missed an *important* appointment (lesser ones are missed with few qualms) will tend to giggle when they finally meet the person and there is the slightest indication of the latter's displeasure.

Giggling is very often used in the marketplace when an item must be bargained over. Similarly, a villager who wants to quit working for another will usually preface his request with some giggling, although equally often he will just leave—saying absolutely nothing—and will later send a middleman to collect his wages and make the severance official. The latter alternative is prompted by the desire to avoid *all* awkwardness.

The third major form of the villagers' politeness—that associated with making a good impression on others—has to a certain extent been covered by the materials already presented. Thus, in terms of the actual manifestations, there is really little difference between flattering another person, for example, because it will make him feel good, because it will make getting something out of him much easier, or because it will make one appear much more attractive in his eyes. However, it is clear that the motivations in these three cases are all quite different. It is for this reason that this last category has been introduced. When villagers meet another person whom they regard as significant (and this by no means includes all their contacts) they do put forth considerable effort to make a good impression on him. And being polite—courteous, helpful, flattering—is one of the most suitable means for achieving this effect.

Discussion of this interactive mode would perhaps not be necessary were villagers themselves not so keenly aware of it. Village children are continually and consciously taught, by word and deed, the necessity always to put their best foot forward (cf. the earlier illustrations in *Characteristics of a Good Person*). Bang Chaners assess themselves and others in terms of their capacity to make themselves appealing: both the "good" and the "competent" person is one who can make himself attractive by speaking softly, gently, and if possible, beautifully and cleverly. Often villagers take offense at an individual who refuses to do this because his very refusal suggests that he does not feel respect for others. Again, it should be emphasized that we are talking here about the form of behavior, not the substance or commitment behind it.

What the ultimate psychological roots of this behavior are is unclear. It is apparent—largely because of the great attention given to formal considerations such as manners, proper speech, and the like—that this concern is not prompted primarily by the desire to be loved by others. Love would require a more substantial medium. Gaining the respect and approval of others is clearly an important component of the attitude, but one wonders why a people otherwise so self-loving and self-accepting should need their self-esteem repeatedly validated by others. Perhaps the most important reason behind the villagers' concern with impressing others really has little to do with the others themselves, although obviously at the behavioral level it implicates them—that is, I would suggest that the major factor behind the

villagers' concern is essentially self-referring in nature: it is both a manifestation and validation *to the self* that one is a fine, proper, and upstand-
ing person; that to treat others well is to perform one's role as a civilized,
meritorious person. This last term, "meritorious," was intentionally selected. It is meant to suggest that much of the villagers' politeness is
consciously (although perhaps not explicitly) related to the notion of
accumulating Buddhist merit, and that in being nice to others Bang
Chaners are managing to fulfill, a little bit, what is to most of them the
raison d'être of the human experience.

The Dynamics of Loose Structure

The foregoing discussion was concerned with the nature of some of the
most frequently occurring forms of face-to-face contact in Bang Chan. It
focused on manifestations of, and motives for, behavior when people
actually meet and interact. However, human relationships involve considerably more than the forms and rituals of face-to-face interaction. They
also include feelings, attitudes and behavior toward others once the interactive situation has been left behind; a readiness to become involved with
others in the first instance; and a sense of social linkage, functional or
sentimental, that ties people to one another over time. This last has
reference to the system of rights, obligations, and responsibilities that form
the substance of enduring relationships.

These latter considerations are perhaps the most difficult to talk about
in Bang Chan because their most conspicuous expressions tend to be
negative in nature; that is, empirically it often is considerably easier to
point to cases where there are no enduring ties between individuals or
where there is hesitation to become closely involved with others than it is
to identify what links them together. There are a few relatively explicit
means of linkage: the "dyadic contract" (to be discussed below); kinship
ties, in many respects a special case of the dyadic contract; and on some
occasions, certain cosmological considerations ("I owe him this because we
were friends in earlier lives," "We love each other because we were born on
the same day"). However, even these modes of linkage require continuous
behavioral validation and are recognized as ultimately unreliable. A Bang
Chaner who fails to fulfill his "contract" by refusing to return a favor
would at very worst be considered selfish. Most villagers would not even
bother to assess his actions, assuming that he must have had a good reason
for them.

To a large extent, the descriptive problem encountered here is the result
of certain methodological conventions. An investigator concerned with
how human beings relate to each other inevitably, and not unreasonably,

tries to identify the bases of their contact. Having once identified these, he then tends to assume that not only the bases but the relationships themselves are relatively constant and reliable.[18] The relationship between Bang Chan employer and employee is an excellent example of the problem. An investigator concerned with specifying the bases of their relationship could readily point to two factors; contractual (in the strict meaning of the term) and sentimental. The former involves the exchange of a sum of money for labor fulfilled. The latter involves an array of behaviors expressive of the employer's concern for his retainer: feeding him well, not making him work too hard, treating him like a younger sibling or "adopted" child, recognizing his birthday, or buying him small gifts if possible. Interestingly, the subordinate's obligations to his superior are considerably less explicit and social psychologically less demanding: he must simply respect and obey him. However, as accurate as these specifications are, they say nothing about the reliability of the relationship. It may be broken off over matters that have nothing to do with how well each is fulfilling his interactive responsibilities. The employee may become bored; he may have a sudden desire to take a trip or go to Bangkok; if he is from a distant village, he may suddenly become homesick and just as suddenly leave. As indicated earlier, he will frequently do this without saying a word to the employer; his absence is sufficient to indicate the termination of the relationship.

Very often the breakdown of the relationship is short-lived. I recall my exasperation during the early stages of field work when right in the middle of an important interview, my field assistant would tell me—with absolutely no forewarning—that he had to be in Bangkok in an hour and a half, and would have to leave now. When I suggested that the interview first be completed, the reply, the first time this happened, was "No, I promised a friend I would meet him at the movies, and I have to go now." When asked why he made a movie date during working hours, he answered: "Well, this was the only time my friend could go." The straightforwardness of his response indicated that it was both futile and dangerous (he might never return from the movies) to ask why the friend could not go alone, what the real reason was for his sudden departure, or why he did not tell me beforehand so I could have made different plans. Pursuing such queries would have served only to annoy my assistant, rather than hold him; and from his own point of view, they were really not my business. This kind of behavior was neither idiosyncratic to this individual nor limited to movies. Later on, when other assistants asked for intermissions, the explanations

---

[18] Certain relationships are of course explicitly recognized as inconstant and unreliable. The relationship between appliance owner and repairman in our society, for example, has come to have these special attributes—not without strain and exasperation, but as part of the reality of the relationship.

given were equally oblique. Although I never really overcame my feeling of helplessness in dealing with such situations, I did manage over a period of time to communicate to those in my employ the appropriateness (at least regarding our own particular relationship) of giving me fair warning, e.g., "Europeans are different in this way."

Again, there is nothing extraordinary or unique about personal desires and inclinations intruding on the stability of an interpersonal relationship. However, what is unique to Bang Chan and Thai culture in general is the frequency of such intrusions, the extent to which they take precedence over the responsibilities of the established relationship, and perhaps most important, their general expectability. No Bang Chaner is ever taken aback when another does not fulfill his assumptions about how that other will behave. Note that these intrusions may have little effect on the face-to-face contacts existing between people. My assistant's declaration that he was going to the movies was presented in a most affable way and in the other examples cited, where people were left in the lurch, there need not have been any contact whatsoever between the parties involved.

Reference was made to these modes of relationship in the section on Bang Chan social organization and kinship. However, they received their first formal, and perhaps most elegant, formulation in a now famous article entitled "Thailand—A Loosely Structured Social System," by the late John F. Embree (1950). Embree's application of the notion of "loose structure" was mainly descriptive rather than analytic; it was used to summarize a wide variety of empirical materials. Thus (182): "The first characteristic of Thai culture to strike an observer from the West, or from Japan or Vietnam is the individualistic behavior of the people. The longer one resides in Thailand the more one is struck by the almost determined lack of regularity, discipline, and regimentation in Thai life. In contrast to Japan, Thailand lacks neatness and discipline; in contrast to Americans, the Thai lack respect for administrative regularity and have no industrial time sense." After providing an extensive series of examples—on the lack of binding filial piety, on the tendency to permit a thief to steal from a neighbor's house without raising an alarm or attempting to stop him, on the capacity to delay and double-talk those with whom one has business dealings, Embree concludes (184): "The point here once more is that . . . while obligations are recognized, they are not allowed to burden one unduly. Such as are sanctioned are observed freely by the individual—he acts of his own will, not as a result of social pressure."

While Embree's formulation is by definition phrased in social structural terms, it inevitably directs our attention to an underlying motivational issue: the nature of the villagers' dispositions to conformity. Conformity to the expectations of others—whether such expectations are shared, complementary, or emergent—is of course a basic requisite of all effective [19] social action. It is perfectly clear, as was demonstrated in the earlier discussion, that Bang Chaners are highly motivated to conform while in the direct presence of others. Often there is over-conformity when in such situations villagers become overly solicitous to what they think are the needs of others. However, the hallmark of Thai social relations is that there never is any certainty that such face-to-face contacts will take place, or if they do take place, that the conformity which exists during the direct encounter will be sustained once the contact has ended. The overriding inclination of the Bang Chaner is to separate the encounter itself from that which precedes or follows it; psychologically, they are independent and unrelated experiences. The typical Bang Chaner excels at the art of indicating agreement with people—responsiveness, coöperativeness, and compliance with their verbal requests and orders—and then once the situation has been concluded, doing precisely what he wants, often the exact opposite of that to which he had agreed.[20]

Ordinarily, this is not intended as a form of duplicity. Villagers are quite sincere (and probably correct) when they say: "People are much happier when you agree with them and tell them what they want to hear." Too, the behavior is explained in part by the fact that most villagers feel they can change their plans and intentions with impunity at the slightest provocation. Unfortunately, the other persons involved may not be informed of the change until it actually occurs. A Bang Chan employee who

---

[19] The term "effective" is inserted here to acknowledge that social action is just as likely to be characterized by ambiguity, confusion, and misunderstanding—the absence of clear expectations—and that in some cases (for example, greeting rituals) it is oriented mainly to *discovering* patterns of expectations. Further, insofar as such action occurs through time, it is never completely free of a minimum of both ambiguity and certainty: the ambiguity of not being able to anticipate what might *next* occur; the certainty of knowing that what does emerge has *some* relationship to what has gone before.

[20] Bang Chan and Thai culture in general evidently are not the only places in Southeast Asia where one finds these modes of response. Addressing himself to a rather different issue, Geertz (1956: 155), writing about the social attitudes of Javanese peasants, notes: "Now, as in the past, the central government and the *prijaji* [aristocratic, learned, upper class] outlook which justifies it sits uneasily in the general social context of Javanese peasant society, with much less actual control over the behavior of the villager than it would seem at first glance to have. Without the intricate ties between the rural and urban gentry one finds, for example, in China, or without the deeply rooted clearly defined, land-rights-linked social code of reciprocal obligations of feudal Europe, the *prijaji* has always found outward submission, exaggerated respect, and placating excuses easier to obtain from the *abangan* [traditionally oriented peasants] than actual obedience." This passage, of course, was concerned with the nature of the Javanese authority system rather then with more generalized patterns of interpersonal response. Whether Javanese respond in the same way to fellow villagers and to other social equals is unclear. However, the stylistic similarities between Thai and Javanese peasants are striking.

walks out on his superior because he does not like the food he is served or a villager who agrees to lend a person money and then is not at home when the person calls for the loan can easily account for his actions by saying that circumstances had changed.

It must be noted, and this is crucial, that there is generally no animosity felt toward the employer with the unpalatable food, toward the fleeing [21] employee, or toward the unreliable creditor. Villagers are thoroughly conditioned to the possibility of such events and accept them simply as part of the inauspicious nature of life. That they are in fact considered inauspicious rather than results of the willful or malevolent intentions of others is not accidental. Bang Chaners faced with a breakdown in the fulfillment of commitments can of course point to the individual who directly caused it. But there is no satisfaction to be gained from this. The person who broke his obligation must have had his own good reason, and beyond this, there were probably other factors, unknown to both parties, that caused the breakdown. For most Bang Chaners, all human intentions are forever set within a framework of cosmic, and particularly moral, unpredictabilities.[22] If things do not work out the way one expects, it is most likely due to the inauspiciousness of the time, place, and persons involved. The proper time is particularly important. It is precisely for these reasons that the more important events in a person's life—marriage, trying to win a lottery or a maiden's heart, taking an important trip—are so often preceded by ceremonial attempts to decide the cosmologically auspicious conditions for effecting the event. These involve consultations with monks, shamans, and other religious practitioners, and highly ritualized forms are followed to select the appropriate conditions. (See Textor 1960 and 1962 for systematic discussions of the various kinds of problems and practices associated with this complex.) The kind of occurrences discussed above are not of this order of significance, but they do partake of the same cognitive assumptions that lead to such highly institutionalized practices. Thus, whereas most Occidentals would point exclusively to the actions of the other person as being both the necessary and sufficient cause of the interactional breakdown, Bang Chaners, who have considerably less confidence in human capacities, would really not be sure. To them, human volition represents only one of several indeterminate and uncontrollable factors giving rise to events. Who knows what accident, change of heart, sudden windfall— particularly one occasioned by something done by one of the parties several lives earlier—might intervene to alter what had originally been planned and agreed upon?

---

[21] This is just the term that villagers, with their wonderful sense of hyperbole, apply to such cases. The original Thai word is *nii*.

[22] I am indebted to L. M. Hanks, Jr., for suggesting this line of thought.

These assumptions about the indeterminate nature of the universe and human actions are so integral to the villagers' cognitive orientations that Bang Chaners often hesitate to make even the most elementary kinds of prediction. Thus, in asking a village lad how he felt about his older brother's forthcoming ordination, I was told, "I don't know." The tone of his reply indicated that he was not evading the question, so I pursued the matter further: "Well, do you feel happy about it? Do you wish you were being ordained together with him?" He answered: "The ordination is not for another three days. I do not know how I will feel at that time. But when that time comes I will know." In another case, I was going up the canal with a villager to attend a "Kathin" being held at the monastery. (A "Kathin" is a fiesta-like merit making ceremony sponsored by a person or group of persons from outside the village at which new robes are presented to the monastery monks. It involves the sponsors, their local hosts, and all villagers who wish to attend.) Although not necessarily an annual event, "Kathins" are held often enough at Monastery Bang Chan so that this villager, who was also a member of the monastery lay committee, was thoroughly familiar with every aspect of them. Simply to make conversation, I asked him: "What is the 'Kathin' going to be like today?" to which he replied, "I do not know. I have not been to the monastery yet today." Assuming that his past experience with "Kathins" provided him with some knowledge of the goings-on, I went on: "Well, do you think there will be many people?" His answer: "I do not know. You never know what a situation is like until you meet it. I have not met this one yet today."

The point of these various illustrations is that they represent a psychological universe of uncertainty and unpredictability. And in this kind of universe—where one hesitates to build up sharply defined expectations and where one is forever aware of the mutability and frailty of the environment—it is not unusual that there should also be a high tolerance for interpersonal nonconformity. What the actual limits are, theoretical or empirical, to this tendency to nonconformity are uncertain. Much of the nonconformity is undoubtedly made possible, in the first instance, by the sociologically simple and relatively undifferentiated nature of Bang Chan society; that is, the actual number of functionally specific tasks and roles— those that require special competencies—are few, and any number of different individuals can perform them. Thus, when a Bang Chan employee walks out on his boss or when a wife walks out on her husband, their actions do not from a functional point of view disable the system. Since the requirements of the role of house servant or farmhand are characteristically simple and understood by all, the departing employee can usually be replaced by another individual. Similarly, since any adult—aunt, grandparents, older sibling—can and often does rear another's children, and since there is always sufficient fish in the canal for an abandoned spouse to feed himself,[23] the departure of a wife or husband need not, from a functional point of view and the point of view of most villagers, work any great hardship on the individuals involved. This suggests that not all social systems are equally demanding in their functional requirements for people to conform. The importance of this point is taken up in the final chapter.

It is recognized, of course, that the sociological simplicity of Bang Chan represents a necessary, but not sufficient, condition for the nonconformity found in the community. There undoubtedly are many cultures which are functionally and sociologically less complex than Bang Chan but where culturally defined requirements for interpersonal conformity are considerably greater. I would suggest that the loosely structured nature of relationships in Bang Chan is due primarily to psychological and philosophical ("world view") factors and is *permitted* expression by the relatively undifferentiated social system. A more complex, highly differentiated social system, one whose functioning is completely dependent on the technical competencies of its members and on their meeting each other's expectations (a factory system, for example) obviously could not afford this luxury.

It might be noted that, in the example cited earlier regarding the movie-going field assistants, one of the reasons for my consternation (over and above my being an American) was the fact that these persons were highly trained individuals who could not be easily replaced. Their temporary departures were strain enough; had the departures been permanent, it would at that point have paralyzed the research. In this respect, their behavior was typically Thai, but the situation in which they found themselves was not.[24]

The ultimate psychological sources of the villagers' tendency toward loosely structured relationships are not easily determined. (The indeterminacy here is inevitable. It derives from the impossibility of ever being certain whether the loose relationships are actually consequences or causes of these other factors, or whether both are expressions of a single, under-

---

[23] This is just what one informant, a female, said when her husband left her. The sociological simplicity of Bang Chan is also supported by the slight differentiation that villagers make between the adult roles of the two sexes. In contrast to all other known cultures, in Thailand both men and women may serve as midwives and do plowing. They both own and operate farms, inherit property equally, share equally in the property brought to a marriage and divide it equally in case of divorce. It is not uncommon to find men tending babies while women are off on a business deal; nor is it unusual, as indicated earlier, to see women paddling right along with men as crew members in a boat race. (See Sharp *et al.* 1953 for an amplification of this point.)

[24] In fact, this event is a perfect illustration in microcosm of what was referred to in the introduction, following Inkeles and Levinson, as "personality-institutional noncongruence."

lying configuration.) However, from the point of view of their etiology in the individual, it is clear that the villagers' tendencies toward loose relationships are related to early childhood experiences. A second source is their philosophical notions concerning the nature of the individual. These notions are largely cultural derivatives of Buddhist doctrine, although at the behavioral level they function simply as unstated premises which guide and tacitly define behavior.[25]

Reference was made earlier to the basic assumptions governing the socialization of the Bang Chan child. When the child enters the world of human beings, he is already a partially formed and psychologically independent individual, with his own *?upanidsaj* (ingrained character) and *khwaan* (soul-stuff), not to mention his stock of accumulated merit and demerit from countless previous lives which predetermines his character. The effect of these definitions is not only to award to the child a sense of psychic individuality that is partially [26] independent of any social environment to which he is exposed, but to assign to him a fundamental sense of psychological equality. We are not speaking here of *social* equality. The

---

[25] From a strict analytic point of view, it would probably be best to consider Buddhist doctrine as an abstract, codified representation of these premises rather than consider the premises as explicit, logically coherent deductions from Buddhist doctrine. To be sure, many Bang Chaners often explain and justify their actions by pointing directly to Buddhist doctrine, sometimes applying its tenets correctly, and sometimes not. But for most, Buddhism is a diffuse, ubiquitous *Weltanschauung*, the precise effects and applications of which the villagers are typically unconscious. It would probably not be incorrect to think of most religious "traditions," particularly the "Great" codified ones, as functioning in this way.

[26] The term "partially" is inserted here to indicate that despite these ontological notions, few villagers, as J. R. Hanks (1959) points out, ever consider "any human child so marvelously endowed . . . from previous existences that training is unnecessary." The child's *?upanidsaj*, *khwaan*, merit and demerit, as well as his *winjaan* (psychological motive power), *caj* (heart), and *phroomli?khid* ("the lines of his destiny as established by Brahma") are all crucial predeterminants of his character. But few Bang Chaners ever think of a person's character as due solely to the uncontrolled emergence of these pre-natal forces. Rather, they represent the basic psychological raw material with which parents and other socializing agents must work, and set the limits of these agents' enculturating efforts. What is important is that the limits—the "degrees of freedom" permitted the parents—tend to be narrowly defined. Intensive probing of informants indicates that there is no general agreement on whether these cosmological forces are more or less influential than parental training in shaping a child, although they tend to be invoked more frequently as explanations of negative characteristics and of unusual happenings, positive as well as negative, in the lives of individuals. Also, villagers are inclined to think of them as the reasons behind *particular* characteristics and events, assigning to parental training a more diffuse influence in the development of the child. Thus, when asked why a particular individual grew up to be a *nagkleeng* (an aggressive, daring, sometimes bullying type of person) and how one of their fellow Bang Chaners had grown up to become an admiral in the Thai Navy, informants attributed the character and success of these individuals respectively to their *?upanidsaj* and *kam*. (*Kam*, the Thai derivative of *karma*, is the proportion of merit to demerit that a person may have at any particular moment in

child is clearly a social inferior, and is due all the prerogatives of his position: he is to be dealt with gently, kindly, and benevolently, with sympathetic regard for his incompetence; correlatively, he must be taught to express deference and obedience to superiors. Rather, the equality awarded the child results from the recognition that in the workings of the cosmic scale it is impossible to ascertain what the child could once have been or eventually will become, and he, like any soul, is always *potentially* of the same value as any other person. It is precisely for this reason that most Bang Chaners, if they mention it at all, are only mildly pleased rather than particularly proud that one of their own grew up to become an admiral in the Thai Navy. It comes as no great surprise that such a thing can happen. To them, it is no more unusual than that the prime minister himself should be a person who was born and reared in a village. (By the same token, the peasant background of these two individuals creates no special sense of personal identification with them on the part of the villagers. They are perceived simply as two unique *individuals,* their peasant roots being viewed as only one of the literally countless factors that made them what they are today.) [27] To a large extent, the equality of the child derives from the premise that he is not so much a child as he is a human being who happens to be at a particular stage in his ontological

---

time). When probed further and asked if their parents' training may have had any influence on these individuals, they replied "yes" and "maybe" in the case of the admiral, but disavowed all parental influence in the case of the *nagkleeng.* A few said that the *nagkleeng* became that way because of bad friends.

One villager, phrasing his comment as a personal conjecture, volunteered that the notion of parents being the major influence on a child's character is a "modern" idea. Another informant, the wife of a school teacher and well versed in her husband's teaching training manual (prepared in Bangkok by Western-trained educators) argued that a person's character is dependent "mostly on the influence of the home and school." However, since on other occasions she complained to me that one of her sons "does not have an *ʔupanidsaj* for studying, and there is nothing a parent can do but let the child have his own way," it would suggest that her commitment to the pronouncements of her husband's mentors was not too well internalized.

To avoid confusion, it might be added that from a historical point of view only one of the above cosmological forces (*kam*) is strictly Buddhistic in origin. The others are either Brahmanic (*khwaan* and *phroomliʔkhid*) or traditionally Thai (*ʔupanidsaj, winjaan,* and *caj*). Of all the terms, *kam* and *ʔupanidsaj* are the ones most frequently referred to when discussing an individual's character.

[27] It is precisely for this reason, as I indicated in an earlier writing on Thai social structure (see Sharp *et al.* 1956: 163) that Thai society "cannot be said to have a class system in the classical European sense of the term." People identify with others as individuals, not as representatives of social classes.

The very fact that individual peasant boys can climb the social ladder to attain some of the highest social positions of the land, without it even being considered particularly noteworthy, attests to the fundamental equalitarian nature of the ideas underlying the Thai social system despite the obvious emphasis given to status and hierarchy in individual face-to-face relationships.

career. From an epistemological point of view, there is of course nothing strange about such an approach. What is perhaps somewhat unique, however, is that the villagers actually use it as the point of departure in their treatment of the child.

The practical consequences of these equalitarian notions are manifold. For one thing, with the child defined as a separate and equal soul, the relationship between parent and child takes on a highly instrumental flavor; that is, rather than expressing love toward the child as an end in itself or otherwise treating him in ways that require no further justification (it is assumed that love is characteristically an absolute sentiment, not a means to any other satisfaction) villagers explicitly see the relationship between parent and child in contractual terms. Thus villagers say that they "are going to the trouble" of bringing up their children and "doing good things for them" (just as their own parents "went to the trouble" of bringing them up and "doing good things" for them) so that they will have someone to care for them in their old age and make merit for them when they die. Similarly, they say they love their parents because they are indebted to them for bringing them into the world. The language of the "contract" is poignantly explicit: "When I think of my mother, I think of the debt I owe her for bringing me into the world and feeding me so I would survive"; "Parents who do not teach their children how to *waj* [exhibit respect to the parents] get nothing from them. I did many *bunkhuns* [good things requiring reciprocation] for my daughter, so now she gives me everything"; "When I was three my father gave me to my uncle who fed me and trained me, so I loved my uncle more" (cf. pp. 64–66, L. M. Hanks 1959c, and Phillips 1959 for further documentation of this point).

In and of themselves there is nothing strange about these "contractual" criteria. However, they do reflect a fundamental recognition of the independence of parent and child and of the fact that parent and child have the *option* of fulfilling each other's needs. More specifically, they are expressions of the assumption that there is nothing intrinsic to the parent-child relationship that requires the two persons to be linked together. The relationship clearly is not fortuitous, but neither is it absolute. It functions primarily for the instrumental and symbiotic satisfactions that its participants can gain from it.[28] Lacking the absolute elements of an ultimate

---

[28] In his paper on "Changes in Family Life" in Bang Chan (1959c) L. M. Hanks notes: "At birth a parent ceremonially formally accepts obligations to an unknown infant soul lightly bound to its body; to this point the new-born one without relation to its parent has been under the protection of a spirit mother. This phrasing contrasts sharply with the Occidental concept of 'flesh and blood.'" In another place in the manuscript, Hanks also comments: ". . . but every case [every kinship tie] is reducible, if one presses the question, to benefits of an older or richer or stronger for the

relationship (*disinterested* appreciation or admiration of the other individual; loving the child or parent in his own right, rather than in terms of his effect on the self) [29] it has a strong undercurrent of unreliability. Since the maintenance of the relationship is always dependent on what the participants can gain from it, *i.e.*, from the other person, and since the participants are essentially free to break the relationship once they feel that such rewards are not forthcoming, it is inevitable that there will be many instances when just that will happen. The crucial point is that there is nothing over and above the instrumental nature of the relationship to keep the individuals tied to one another. The only possible exception, an important one, is that which goes with the realization that by treating one's child or parent nicely, one is behaving in a moral way and is thus accumulating Buddhist merit; but even this purpose is avowedly self-referring in nature. In this regard, it might be noted that other than the marriage ceremony, which is ignored by half of Bang Chan newlyweds, there are no institutionalized attempts to sanctify the solidarity of the family, or for that matter the solidarity of almost any social group. That is, unlike China and the West, there is nothing in traditional Thai folk belief and ritual, or in the literature of the indigenous "Great Tradition," that alludes to the sacredness of the family as a social unit. All moral aphorisms concerning family relationships are phrased in terms of the dyadic relations between individuals, not in terms of affiliation with the family unit as such.

The looseness of the ties that result from the instrumental nature of the parent-child relationship are perhaps best revealed in the villagers' responses to the Sentence Completion stimuli, "*We want to give our child to him because* . . . (This is the English translation of the best Thai translation of the original English item, "*He wanted to give his child away because* . . ."). The reasons behind the use of this somewhat uniquely worded item are important. (The reader might imagine American responses to such a query.) The item was selected for inclusion in the SCT battery only after it became apparent that there might be a pattern to what

---

services of a younger, poorer, or weaker. This includes parent and child, sibling and sibling, or husband and wife, and all kinship relations are reducible to these terms."

[29] The responses to the Sentence Completion stimuli, "*When I think of my mother, I think of* . . ." and "*When I think of my father, I think of* . . ." are particularly revealing on this point. The vast majority of the responses on both these stimuli are in terms of the parents' effect on the self rather than in terms of what the parents are in their own right. Careful checking of the cues indicates that there is nothing in their grammatical or semantic structure that would predispose informants to produce such completions, *i.e.*, it is just as easy and feasible for informants to say ". . . how beautiful she is" or ". . . how clever she is" as it is for them to say ". . . the good things she has done for me." See chapter v for the actual responses.

were at first a series of unrelated incidents—that is, the possible tenuousness of the links between parent and child first came to my attention with the occasional, but wholly unselfconscious, reports from informants on what to my Western ears seemed like rather turbulent childhoods: their frequent movement from family to family while they were still children and their own care, as adults, of friends' or relatives' children. (This suspicion was reinforced and partially verified later while recording life histories). Later it was noticed that, in sharp contrast to the West, villagers tend to be less concerned about the illness of children than the illness of adults; informants with whom this observation was discussed said either that they had not noticed or explained it by saying that since children recover so quickly from sickness there is less need to worry about them. Finally and perhaps most important, it became clear that the request of the villager who stopped me and asked me to take and rear her child was by no means idiosyncratic; the request was made on four separate occasions by different individuals, both within and without Bang Chan. The intent of these requests were difficult to ascertain. Since the requests tended to come up rather suddenly, in the presence of the child, and were always accompanied by laughter, they may well have been said in "jest" or as a threat to the child. On a few occasions the parent took pains to be sure the child understood what was being said, in which case the child responded with screaming. Also, Europeans have traditionally been used as bogey men in the disciplining of children. (I myself have occasionally been addressed as a malevolent spirit by young-sters.) On the other hand, because children of poor families have been known to be given to individuals of high status, and because Occidentals are automatically assigned such status, it is not altogether unlikely that the parent was sounding me out as a potential patron of the child.

The problem with all the above, however, is that it was unknown to what extent they represented typical or deviant attitudes and responses. The Sentence Completion item, *"We want to give our child to him because . . ."* was selected for use in the SCT administered to a larger, representative sample of villagers because, being an extreme phrasing of these attitudes, it might shed light on the villagers' general readiness to accept them as well as their justifications for them. Of the fifty-six inform-ants who responded to the item, 79 percent accepted the premise and 21 percent rejected it, *i.e.,* "I do not want to give my child to anybody." Of the forty-five individuals who accepted the premise, nineteen said it was good for either the child or the parent, *i.e.,* "that person was good, and he wanted that person to teach his child to be good"; "I would get some money by giving it away"; "I could not stand the child anymore." And eighteen said it was justifiable, *i.e.,* "because of poverty"; "I did not have the means to rear the child."

None of the above is meant to imply that 79 percent of the adults of Bang Chan would in fact give away their children. But the relatively high frequency of agreement they exhibited in admitting to such a possibility and the fact that as many as 65 percent agreed that it was either good or justifiable reveals something of the psychological environment within which the Bang Chan child is reared and where he learns his basic orientations toward other persons. The responses to this single stimulus must of course be seen in the context of the more naturalistic, behavioral materials presented earlier. The point of all these illustrations, however, is that they indicate there is nothing sacrosanct about any human tie in Bang Chan, even that which exists between parent and child. If necessity or personal predilection requires, then this tie too may be broken. What is perhaps most significant here, from a developmental point of view, is that the breaking of the tie always exists as a realistic potentiality in the life of the child. Reared in an environment where he learns that no human tie need be permanent or sustaining, the developing child inevitably takes on some of these same patterns of expectation in his own dealings with others. Thus the villager who abandons his spouse or the employee who with little warning leaves his employer are acting in terms of patterns the prototypes of which they either actually experienced as children or came to expect as part of the realities of interpersonal relations in Bang Chan.

The second major source of the villagers' loose relationships lacks the developmental reference of the above. To a certain extent it is not even social relational in nature, although our concern with it stems from its having crucial consequences to the social orientations of individuals. I am referring here to the Buddhist emphasis on the primacy of individual action and individual responsibility. Without going into a lengthy discussion of the subtleties of Buddhist doctrine, it is imperative to point out that the principal tenet of Hinayana Buddhism is the complete psychological freedom, isolation, and responsibility of every person. This is not the Occidental idea of "free will," but rather the notion that every person is a free agent, responsible only to and for himself, and that he inevitably reaps the fruits of his own conduct. Buddhist canonical literature is replete with references stressing the centrality of this doctrine. The last words of the Lord Buddha before he left this world to achieve the sublime state of *nibphaan* (nirvana) are said to have been: "Work out your own salvation with diligence." A frequently quoted passage of the *Dhamapada* reads: "By oneself is evil done; By oneself one suffers; By oneself evil is left undone; By oneself one is purified." The whole complex cosmology relating to the accumulation of merit and demerit is phrased in terms of the individual's lonely journey through cycles of interminable existences working out his own moral destiny. Who his progenitors were, what kind of environment he was born and reared in, what social advantages or disadvantages he was exposed to, are considered all secondary, and in some cases even insignificant, in influencing what he is and what he does. The life and career of Gautama himself is perfect testament to the essential irrelevance of these factors. (On the other hand, the attention given to these considerations in Western ontology is a perfect expression of our "sociological bias." In our system, even our original moral state is determined by what someone else—Adam and Eve—did.) In Therevada Buddhism, an individual's worldly and cosmológical condition—the former essentially a temporary, special case of the latter—is for the most part self-generative, although because one never knows *when* the effects of one's *kam* may emerge it is also unpredictable.

These formulations translate and function on the level of workaday behavior in an extremely subtle manner. Every time a Bang Chaner is about to do something he does not ask himself whether it is in his own best moral interest. Similarly, every time he ignores another's expectations about how he will behave he does not justify his actions in terms of the Buddhist doctrine of enlightened self-interest. However, these formulations do impart a fundamental legitimacy to the pursuit of individualistic self-concern. More important, they establish—in a diffuse, unreflective, but nonetheless highly meaningful way—a definition of social reality that assumes the ultimate reference of every person's act is himself. In these terms, social relationships become defined as either artifacts of, or media for, the attainment of one's own ends. People need and use each other to satisfy their own purposes. (This is not to say that social relationships do not have many other functions. Our concern here is with the way *villagers* view the aims of their social relations.) What keeps the social system running relatively smoothly is the assumption that every person is acting on precisely the same bases, and the realization that one's own purposes are best served by acts of reciprocation. The basis of the system, however, is the continuous satisfaction of each participant's individual needs, for should such satisfactions not be forthcoming, there is always complete freedom and sanction to withdraw. Villagers typically define benefits gained from reciprocal acts to be materialistic (the food or gifts a parent gives a child or an employer gives an employee); psychological (the respect a subordinate awards to a superordinate or the security the latter provides the former); and spiritual (the merit parents gain when their son enters the monkhood, the merit being repayment for their having gone to the trouble of rearing him).

Translated into theoretical terms, Buddhist doctrine functions here in two ways. First, it represents a codification of certain *assumptions* about the nature of human responsibilities, an articulation of what Wallace (1961b: 94) calls "primitive predicates," or the frames of reference that provide the primitive categories into which people code their experience. From a psychodynamic point of view, the predicates do not *require* codification; people think and act in terms of "primitive" (tacit, axiomatic) categories many of which are never explicated in the propositions of their formal religious, ethnophilosophical, or mythological systems. Why certain categories are selected for codification and others are not is beyond the scope of this book. However, it is clear that a major function of Buddhist thought—like that of any articulate symbolic or ideological system—is to *objectify* and *clarify* some of the more important experiential assumptions of its adherents. This is the cognitive essence of all belief systems. As a belief system, Buddhist doctrine also takes on a special value of its own. This is in fact its second major function; that is, the tenets of Buddhism not only serve to objectify through philosophical elaboration that which is already accepted but also to act as standards in assessing the value, propriety, and significance of human actions. In this sense, Buddhism (again like any coherent ideological system) provides a corpus of knowledge for rationalizing and *sanctioning* certain types of behavior and for disapproving of others. The very belief system that codifies aspects of reality for its adherents assumes the normative function of reinforcing and promoting those activities that are in conformity with it. This is the motivational essence of all belief systems. Needless to say, we are speaking here of activities that are subjectively felt to be valuable and proper, irrespective of the social psychological dysfunctions that may follow from them. Thus, returning to our major theme, most villagers would agree that the Bang Chaner who without saying a word leaves his spouse in order to avoid an embarrassing or rancorous confrontation over some difficulty is behaving in a manner thoroughly consonant with "doing evil by himself; suffering by himself; leaving evil undone by himself; and becoming purified by himself." How the wife responds to his actions is her problem. Her *kam* may well have been the reason for this happening to her. (Note that I say ". . . for this happening to her," *not* ". . . for his doing this to her." This is the typical village way of perceiving such events. Again, the interactional dimension is secondary: it is what happens *to* individuals, not what happens *between* them, that counts.) How *explicitly* villagers would apply Buddhist doctrine to this particular situation is problematic. Applications of Buddhist thought usually emerge only after villagers have been asked to think actively about and articulate justifications for the actions of people. Their comments are typically *post hoc* explanations that appear only when there is a necessity either to understand or ethically evaluate an individual's actions.

The above discussion was concerned with detailing some of the sources and supports of the loosely structured relationships that are found in Bang

Chan. However, there remains the crucial question of how villagers man-age to develop the long-term relationships that they do have, for despite the inevitable unpredictability of all human contacts, most Bang Chaners do live together in family units for more or less sustained periods of time, fathers do save for years in order to give their sons respectable ordinations into the monkhood, relatives and friends who have not seen each other since childhood do assemble for the cremation of a late kinsman or mutual friend, and mature adults do continue to feel a profound sense of respect and obligation to individuals who were their teachers when they were young-sters. What are the bases and rewards for these enduring interpersonal commitments?

The immediate rewards for these commitments are, on the one hand, quite apparent. They involve such things as the simple, unrationalized kind of love found among any group of kin or close friends. In the case of the ordination and cremation, there is the reward of making merit, not only for the son and the departed soul, but for all those who sponsor and participate in the ceremonials. The satisfactions gained from increasing one's social prestige by putting on an ostentatious ceremonial are not to be overlooked either. At a more subtle level in the case of the respectful student, the reward is gained from knowing that one is behaving in a proper and courteous way toward one's *aacaan* (in its social psychological connotations, similar to the Indian term *guru*) and is thus upholding established normative patterns. The rewards of maintaining the rituals of the moral order are not to be glossed over for Bang Chaners, like most Siamese, are a deeply ethical people. This is not meant as an evaluation of their behavior or as a statement of their capacity to conform to their ethical prescriptions, but simply as a statement of their preoccupation with ethical concerns. The rewards of *feeling* (genuinely or self-deceptively) that one has behaved in an ethically and ritualistically prescribed way are among the most satisfying of sentiments, although as indicated in the discussion of "social cosmetics," villagers often use the rituals of ethical behavior as substitutes for more demanding interpersonal involvements. Indeed, the great emphasis given to the performance of ethical rituals (speaking in soft and gentle words, honoring one's mentors) helps perpetuate the loosely structured relationships found in the community in that conformity to these rituals is perceived by many as comprising the fulfillment of their interpersonal obligations. Beyond this they are free to pursue their own interests. To a large extent the ritualistic forms serve as a comforting psychological justification for the pursuit of individualistic concerns, *i.e.,* "But I otherwise treat others so nicely." [30] This is not the result of conscious

---

[30] In one of his more recent and typically penetrating works, Goffman (1963) coins the terms "Involvement Shields," "Main Involvements," and "Subordinate

psychological manipulation. The frequency with which villagers evaluate themselves and others in terms of the performance of these rituals and the high frequency of rituals in actual behavior attests to the seriousness which Bang Chaners attach to them. Their compensatory nature in no way detracts from their importance to the individual. In fact, the precise opposite seems to be the case. Bang Chaners are a highly ethical people irrespective of the social psychological functions such ethics may serve.

Less apparent than the above immediate rewards for fulfilling interpersonal commitments but perhaps the very factor that is common to most of them is the sense of reciprocity that is at the basis of all enduring relationships in Bang Chan. Reference was made to the *quid pro quo* nature of Thai social relationships at several points in the text. However, the importance of this consideration cannot be fully appreciated without realizing that the functioning of the entire Thai social system is ultimately dependent on it. Individuals become involved with others and do things for them because they consciously expect others to respond in kind. This applies to the relationships existing between family members who live together *because* such an arrangement is most advantageous to each; to the father who gives his son an ordination *in order that* the latter will make merit for him and feel obligated to care for him when he becomes old; to the friends and relatives who make merit for the departed soul *because* of the good things he had done for them during his lifetime; to the adults who feel obligated to their childhood teacher *because* of the knowledge, and thus power, he imparted to them. It might well be, as Mauss (1954 [originally

---

Involvements" to describe in theoretical terms what has been analyzed here empirically. The major point of Goffman's concepts, and of his entire book, is that human behavior is typically polyphasic (people act one way and simultaneously think or feel another); that there are types and degrees of involvement with people, situations, and self; that situational behavior typically entails patterns of "deception" as ways of implementing disinvolvement (or, as he says, as ways "to conceal improper involvement and to affect appropriate involvement"); and most important that such patterns of "deception" are culturally—and not as heretofore assumed, idiosyncratically—phrased. His definition of "Involvement Shields" (p. 41) is particularly apposite to the discussion above: ". . . we think of involvement shields as one means by which the individual can maintain the impression of proper involvement while he is actually delinquent in his situational obligations."

Dealing mostly with American culture, Goffman does not of course analyze ethical rituals as a particular kind of "Involvement Shield." Americans favor other, more culturally distinctive patterns of deception. Also, he uses the term "involvement" in the same way that I have been using the term "commitment." Unfortunately, neither Goffman nor I say very much about the conditions, cultural or psychological, which determine whether a person is fully ("properly and appropriately") involved or committed in any particular situation or is simply shielding himself. However, I would argue on theoretical grounds that the *decision* is almost always idiosyncratic, the *actual behavior* almost always cultural.

1923–1924], translated by Cunnison) and Homans (1961) have argued, that human relationships everywhere are based on just such a consideration, usually concealed by ethically palatable amenities (such as in American culture, from which most of Homans' empirical materials come). However, what is so intriguing about the Thai case is that *quid pro quo* factors are forever in mind as justifications and explanations of why people relate to one another. Although villagers, because they are such polite people, rarely say to others, "I am helping you because I know the day will come when I need your help," or "Do this for me because you owe me a favor," they do use such arguments *to explain* the basis of their ties: "Of all my friends I love Lek the most because she has done me the most favors (*bunkhuns*)"; "The purpose of marriage is to have a companion who will take care of you when you get sick"; "Of all my daughters, the one who gives me the greatest pleasure is the one who sells things. . . . When she gets money she gives it to me"; "Friends are very useful because it means that you have people who will do you favors. And when they need help, you will take care of them. This is love." [31]

One of the finest discussions of the nature of reciprocal obligations appears in a recent paper by George M. Foster (1961) that deals not with a Thai community, but with the Mexican village of Tzintzuntzan. Foster outlines in his paper the notion of the "dyadic contract" which he presents as a model for the social structure of Tzintzuntzan. Or, more precisely: "Specifically, I suggest a model . . . to reconcile the institutionalized roles which can be recognized and described in the community with the underlying principle which gives the social system coherence." Foster's focus thus differs somewhat from our psychological emphasis. However, his abstract statement of the "dyadic contract" provides such an excellent summation of the major factor making for enduring social relationships in Bang Chan that it merits quoting in detail here. There are of course inevitable differences in cultural content between the two communities and the fact that

---

[31] Such explanations are not unique to Bang Chan. In his description of the Thai–Lue village of Ban Phaed in Northern Thailand, Moerman (1962) observes: "The society of Ban Phaed operates in terms of something got for every something given. This is not merely an analytic device which permits a predictive, if crass, view of any human society. It is the way in which villagers explain and evaluate their own behavior. Favor for favor, visit for visit, meal for meal, one should return what he receives. 'We help our kinsmen because they help us. If a kinsman however close didn't help me, I wouldn't help him.' 'We care for our children when they are young; they will care for us when we are old.' Actions which we would justify in terms of compassion, generosity, public-spirit, patriotism, pride in a job well done, the Lue villager speaks of in terms of reciprocal, short-term self-interest. Their actions are no more selfish than ours. Far from it. But the moral rhetoric of a Lue villager is different from our own. In politics, economics, family life, and religion it focuses on something got for something given."

status differences and the looseness of social ties loom considerably in Bang Chan probably makes for some other structural variations.[32] However, as stated below, Foster's formulation applies almost perfectly to Bang Chan (1173–1176):

The model appears to account for the nature of interaction between people of the same socio-economic status, between people of different statuses, between fellow villagers, between villagers and outsiders, and perhaps between man and supernatural beings as well. Although my analysis deals only with Tzintzuntzan, I think the model will prove useful for other societies with similar structural features . . .

Briefly it is hypothesized that every adult organizes his social contacts . . . by means of a special form of contractual relationship. These contracts are informal, or implicit, since they lack ritual or legal basis. [This is not completely true for Bang Chan. There is, for example, a special "Teachers' Day," sanctioned by the national government, set aside for honoring teachers, and thus providing ritualistic reinforcement to the contract.] They are not based on any idea of law, and they are unenforceable through authority; *they exist only at the pleasure of the contractants.* The contracts are dyadic in that they occur only between two people; three or more individuals are not brought together. The contracts are noncorporate, since social units such as villages, *barrios,* or extended families cannot truly be said to enter contractual relations with other families, although spouses often honor the obligations inherent in each other's contracts.

The implicit dyadic contract is made between members of a family as close as siblings [and in Bang Chan, as close as husband and wife, and parents and children] . . . ; and it unites neighbors and friends. Contracts are found between social and economic equals within Tzintzuntzan or with similar people in other communities. And they are found between people (or beings) of different status and category, as on those few occasions when outside political leaders or economic patrons have ties with villagers and when a villager invokes the aid of the Virgin Mary or a saint. [In Bang Chan, a functional equivalent of the latter would be when villagers propitiate the *caw,* or Spirit Lord, who resides in the *San Phra Phuum,* or house of the Guardian Spirit of the home. This is a replica of a house, about the size of a bird cage, located in every house lot in Bang Chan. The offering of rice and flowers to the *caw* is explicitly a form of payment to him for the use

---

[32] A second paper on Tzintzuntzan (Foster 1963) indicates that there are some crucial motivational differences as well, viz., Bang Chaners enter into dyadic contracts with a much greater sense of freedom than do Tzintzuntzeños. Their attitude is both more cavalier and cold-blooded than the Mexican peasant who feels that if he is to exist, he has no choice but to enter into these contracts. The Bang Chaner is animated by a sense of personal advantage; the Tzintzuntzeño by a sense of passive participation in a system he cannot change.

of the land upon which the human home is built. In effect, humans have temporarily "rented" the land from him.]

. . . [The] contract implies and is validated by reciprocal obligations . . . [In] its totality the system of complementary reciprocity validates, maintains, and gives substance to the implicit contractual networks. The symbolic meaning of exchanges (as contrasted to economic and other functions) is accepted without question by all villagers: as long as a person continues to give to and receive from a partner, he is assured that the particular relationship is in good order. *When an exchange pattern between two people terminates, it is overt evidence to both that the contract is dead,* regardless of the formal institutional ties or the religious validation which may, in theory, continue to bind the participants. [Italics added.]

In anthropological analysis it is customary first to seek and attempt to identify the factors which link human beings together rather than those which keep them apart. This is so much a part of our professional tradition—in effect, one of our "primitive predicates"—that we tend to gloss over ·the question of the extent to which people must have enduring interpersonal commitments. This question has not been pursued in precise detail in our discussion. However, the realities of Bang Chan social behavior are so weighted in the direction of atomistic and essentially non-relational considerations that any coherent discussion of them should be organized in approximately equivalent terms. It is for this reason that the bulk of our presentation has focused on the individualistic nature of the villagers and that the factors accounting for interpersonal linkage were left to the end. It is hoped that such an organization has accurately reflected the tone and quality of Bang Chan social life as it is encountered and felt by an outside observer trying to understand its meaning to those who experience it.

III

Methodology in the Field

The discussion until now has been concerned with describing and interpreting aspects of the villagers' psychological life with little mention made of how these materials or those which follow were actually obtained. Since one of the larger aims of this study is methodological (to present a method for dealing with some of the problems involved in designing cross-cultural personality research) and since the balance of the presentation depends directly on technical procedures, it is necessary to examine the nature of the data collection process itself. I will focus on three aspects of the research process: (1) the human beings involved (the villagers, the anthropologist and his assistants, and their interrelations); (2) the development and use of the Sentence Completion Technique in the field, including a discussion of translation procedures; and (3) the selection and nature of the sample.

Most of the foregoing discussion was not the result of a pre-planned methodological effort. Since I was dealing with data that emerge naturalistically from life's daily round, it seemed reasonable to impose few *a priori* methodological constraints on the investigation. My method was simply to try to be sensitive to *repetitive* and *culturally different* modes of behavior manifested by the villagers. Knowledge of the available literature and general knowledge of Thai culture may have helped, particularly with regard to the interpretations that were made. However, because both the observations and interpretations were made by a human being, it is inevitable that several of the factors discussed below should enter into my deliberations.

Field Research As a Social Event

Despite the entry into anthropological field work of what Kroeber (1955a: 307) called the "social science" tradition, the field situation remains a fundamentally human one where the kinds of data obtained, the willingness to provide information or to hold back, the types of interpretations that are made are all influenced by the personalities of the parties involved and how they perceive and deal with one another. The data that appear in most field studies are in part distillations of these complex interpersonal and intrapsychic forces, tempered by the investigator's capacity to see through them. Exactly what role they play in the fashioning of the final research product can probably never be fully determined since informants may not know or will not tell you what they "think" of you; and they are likely to be even less aware of how their thoughts have influenced their responses. Similarly, despite his training in self-consciousness, the investigator never has complete command over all the factors that prompted him to pursue a particular course of action in the field or an interpretive bent during the write-up. The problem is further complicated because there are numerous things which occur in the field that have little to do with the research as such, but which often impinge upon it, for example, an informant becoming markedly more aggressive during an interview when he learns that you have just returned from seeing a villager whom he dislikes. (This kind of information when it is available is not without interest. But no field worker is so omniscient as to have such complete knowledge of the likes, dislikes, and psychodynamics of every informant and thereby comprehend every turn in his behavior.) Yet, despite these ultimate limitations, the investigator can try to make as explicit as possible those human factors that he perceives as influencing the nature of the research experience. We will proceed from the relatively obvious to the more subtle considerations that bear on the materials being presented.

Villagers' Attitudes Toward the Investigators

Perhaps the major factor conditioning the villagers' attitude toward the research was the fact that other Cornell University investigators had worked in the community prior to my arrival. This meant several things: that precedents had been set for asking villagers personal and impersonal questions; that friendly, but generally not intimate, relationships had been established with several key villagers, notably those recognized as informal community leaders; that the villagers had come to accept the presence of Europeans as a normal part of their lives; and that our presence was seen as essentially a good thing. Not only were the *farang* (the Thai term for Occidentals) a source of novelty with their strange interests and long noses, as well as a source of prestige (for having singled out Bang Chan as the community being studied by "American professors"), but they were also a source of considerable practical help. Earlier Cornell workers had given funds to the Bang Chan monastery and school, had helped obtain vaccine to prevent a diphtheria epidemic, and had contributed added income to a few families in the form of rent for the "Cornell office" or salaries for the boys serving as the research team's boatmen. Perhaps the most important contribution the members of the research team made to the community, as perceived by the Bang Chaners themselves, was to act as a source of advice and practical knowledge. The kinds of counsel villagers sought from the field workers varied considerably. Some wanted help in deciding whether it was more profitable to raise chickens or turkeys; another wanted us to obtain information for him on the laws governing land ownership. However, some of their requests simply could not be met, *i.e.*, "Tell me some of the modern, scientific ways to get a woman to fall in love with you"; "Can you get me one of those 'machines' that prevents children?"

Not all villagers of course viewed the Cornell activities in these terms; the vast majority in fact accepted our presence with no marked sense of involvement of any sort. The *farang* and their Thai associates were perceived by this majority group simply as people with their own interests whose presence might prove beneficial, and toward whom one should behave tolerantly and coöperatively. Interestingly enough, during all the time I worked in the community I encountered only two cases in which villagers actively expressed disapproval or annoyance at "Cornell." In one case, a villager was deeply affronted because he felt that a Thai research associate whom he knew in the village had snubbed him during a chance meeting in Bangkok. In the other case, involving my own research, a villager complained that we had wasted his time asking him to take the Sentence Completion Test: "The questions they asked me had no use at all. They did not ask about food, or making a living, or anything important. I have more important things to do with my time." There may have been other villagers whose feelings were not too unlike those of this individual. However, this was the only case that came to my attention of a villager actually articulating his displeasure toward the research, despite my active search for any indication of negative attitudes on the part of respondents. In this connection, it might be noted that of the 123 villagers who were approached to take the Sentence Completion Test, only two gave us outright refusals. One, the Chinese tailor, said he could not handle Thai well enough (he was right) and did not like to talk to people; the other, a girl of twenty, would out of embarrassment run out the rear door of her house every time she saw us paddling up to the front. The generally open and accepting attitude of other villagers toward my research requests, however, was very similar to that given to earlier researchers, and was undoubtedly conditioned by the precedents they had established.

Given the above considerations, my entry into the community did not elicit any kind of special response from the villagers. For most, I was simply another representative of "Cornell" who had come to study their "way of life"—a friendly, interesting, and harmless soul who, if the need arose, might be of some help. If and when I came to visit them, they would find out precisely what I came to study and what I was like. But they clearly were not waiting for my visits with any keen sense of anticipation. The dominant attitude was one of conditional acceptance which could easily turn to active, amiable interest once a face-to-face encounter had been initiated. In general, they expected me to initiate the contact. This somewhat passive attitude was in part a result of the feelings of *kreeŋcaj* (humbleness and self-effacement) that they had toward social superiors, a role they automatically assigned to me. In part it was probably also a legacy from the role of respondent (a person who reacts, rather than initiates) that they had developed with earlier field workers and which had become part of their normal expectations toward Cornell personnel. There were of course villagers who from the very beginning actively sought me out and tried to develop special kinds of relationships. The person who tried to sell me the idea of building on his land a newer, more expensive "Cornell Office" was one such individual. Less business-minded was the villager who occasionally would stop by at the office to tell me not to see any informants that day: he knew of a special ritual being performed that he thought I would be interested to see instead. Still another villager approached me with the proposition that he knew more about what was happening in Bang Chan than anyone else and that I should not believe what people told me until I had checked with him; I was never able to discover what this person's motives were, other than to satisfy his own self-image.

Several relationships developed that had little to do with the services we could perform for each other or even with the research itself but which seemed based simply on the mutual regard we felt toward one another. This area of "friendship" is perhaps the most difficult to talk about because its limits were always set, in some latent and undefinable way, by the facts of cultural differences. No matter how relaxed and enjoyable a relationship might be, it was always colored by awareness of the possibility that the other person might not understand. Potential lack of understanding, however, was not always detrimental: sometimes it helped to underscore the fact that *despite* possible miscommunication, we could enjoy and respect each other. Here "friendship" was based in part on the willingness to appreciate each other's differences.

What qualities of the author these villagers considered attractive—over and above the social and service characteristics he shared with other Cornell people—can only be surmised. It is clear that despite the fact that for most purposes villagers lumped all Cornell personnel into the general category of *farang*, many Bang Chaners made sharp personal distinctions among us. My field assistant, partly for his own amusement and partly at my request, asked a number of villagers for their opinions of the different *farang*. Included among his informants were some of the same people toward whom I felt especially close. (It should be noted that these "close friends" never numbered more than eight or ten people, out of a total population of 1,771.) Although their opinions differed in detail and covered a considerable range, they seemed to agree that I had a *good heart*. One villager said that he knew I had a good heart because children like me, "and children are only attracted to people who have good hearts." On the other hand, another more critical person said that my personality was just like that of a child, "because he always shows his feelings. He does not know how to be cool." The contrasts the villagers saw between myself and other researchers were particularly instructive. Of another field worker, an informant said: "he is not a kind person like *Aacaan* Herb, but he knows how to treat people in the Thai way. *Aacaan* Herb does not know how. He laughs too loud and does not use flattering words. He does not help me as much as the other person either." Yet, in contrast, another villager said: "I like *Aacaan* Herb because he likes me. He tells funny stories. He is not like some of the other *farang* who leave as soon as they get information from you."

The ultimate importance of these personal assessments are not easily determined. One villager perceptively noted, for example, that although the "boss" of the Cornell team was a "good person," it really did not make any difference whether he was good or bad "because he is the 'boss' and bosses have to be respected." Of more direct relevance to the research was the fact that those individuals whom I counted among my warmest friends were not necessarily my best informants; in fact, some became inordinately anxious and evasive while taking the Sentence Completion Test and TAT. On the other hand, some villagers whom I had never seen before responded to these tasks with obvious enthusiasm. Even the villager who complained about my having wasted his time was a good informant, in the sense of appearing stimulated by and genuinely involved in responding to the sentence cues. It is clear, however, that villagers who liked me were the most approachable of informants, and were more ready, at least initially, to acquiesce to interview requests. The crucial factor here may well be the difference between responding to the field worker versus responding to the research; that is, even though all the respondents were originally induced into being interviewed as a favor to me—and their willingness was in part a function of how much they liked me—such favors did not necessarily carry over to the substantive purposes of the interview: reacting to my queries in a concerned and committed way. Thus, some informants went through the entire interview experience carefully fulfilling the interpersonal "obligation" but all but ignoring its content; others were so stimulated by the content that their initial attitudes toward me, positive or negative, became largely irrelevant. The vast majority of informants of course fell between these two extremes; and in no case were either the interpersonal or substantive considerations completely ignored. In this regard, it must be remembered that for much of the research I was dealing with informants who were selected not for their readiness to give revealing information but for their social psychological representativeness as adult Bang Chaners. Under such conditions, it was inevitable that there should be people who cared little about me or my purposes, just as there should be people who felt the precise opposite.

One aspect of the villagers' attitudes deserves special mention. This concerns their perception of me as an *aacaan*, or "teacher." This perception had significant effects, both positive and negative, on their behavior during the interviews. On the positive side, many informants were genuinely flattered by being asked for information that would contribute to "knowledge." Precisely how their thoughts and opinions might contribute to "knowledge"—or as I sometimes told them, "science"—was not too clear in their minds. But the fact that I was a "teacher" who had crossed the seas and would spend months asking them questions clearly indicated the seriousness of my business. This definition had a marked influence on their whole orientation to the interviewing situation in that they generally approached it with an attitude of earnestness, and on occasion, even solemnity. In fact, my "rapport time" with informants was very often spent in trying to mitigate their expectations about the interview so that they would respond to the substantive questions in a relaxed and easy manner. Usually these efforts were successful and the interview proceeded as a well-balanced combination of seriousness and *sanug*. The most frequent comment of informants after the Sentence Completion interviews was, "It was much easier than I thought it would be." On the negative side, however, informants would sometimes use their solemn definition of the interview as a means of resisting participation in it. Their resistances would take the general form of pleading that they were only ignorant peasants who did not know much about anything; that if I wanted a "true" picture of the way peasants "think," I ought to see more intelligent informants; that their information would "spoil" my results, and the like. Again, I was usually able to allay such protestations by emphasizing the simplicity and "sanug-fulness" of the experience. However, sometimes informants took me literally and produced responses which were "simply" literal restatements of what I had asked them or which had no intelligible relationship to the questions. Once, when I stopped an interview to clarify my purposes, an informant asserted, "But I am giving you simple answers"; in another instance the informant smiled wryly and said, "But I told you I was not very intelligent." A few informants were genuinely interested in the interview but simply lacked the wherewithal to deal with the material. If asked, however, to make a judgment on whether the villagers' perception of me as a "serious-minded teacher" generally worked to the advantage or disadvantage of the research, I would definitely answer, "the former."

Perhaps even more important than the villagers' attitudes toward the author were their attitudes toward the Thai field assistants who worked with me at various times. It was through the field assistant that many villagers had their actual contact with the research and through him (or her) that I obtained a large part of my data.[1] Because the role of field assistant requires such distinctive qualities—"competence" in a foreign language, willingness to work with peasants and an appreciation of them, a desire to learn the way "other people" live—it was not easy to obtain or retain individuals to work with in Bang Chan. In a country such as Thailand where the term "social science" was virtually unknown until a few years ago, the position of "research assistant" simply offers no occupational future. Consequently, I had six different assistants working for me at different times during almost two years in the field. Two of these individuals were with me for less than three weeks. (One left the rice fields of Bang Chan for a position at the Thai Embassy in Rome; the other just did not like peasants.) Two were extremely able female graduate students in Education who worked only on Sundays and holidays, primarily with the younger village women. Out of both loyalty to me and a genuine interest in, almost love for, the villagers, they stayed on until the research was completed. The fifth, my major assistant, took three months to find, but he remained with me for fourteen months. When he left to work in Burma ("because I have never been to Burma") his place was taken by a very competent and sophisticated assistant district officer whom I "borrowed" from the Ministry of Interior. This last chap saw me through the life histories. Although he was excellent in the highly personalized setting of the life history interviews, his polished urban manner would have been too overbearing for the majority of informants during the earlier, more sensitive stages of the research. While this coming and going of field assistants,

---

[1] During the early stages of field work I was completely dependent on my assistant-translators, despite six months language training prior to leaving for the field. Later, I gained enough control over Thai to participate actively in the interviews. In order to minimize translation errors, however, it was decided to conduct and record all *formal* interviews (those involving the Sentence Completion Method, TAT, and life histories) completely in Thai, and translate later. The reasons for this are more fully discussed below. In effect, this meant training the assistant to carry the burden of the Sentence Completion interviews, the first large block of the research. By the time we reached the life histories, the interviews were taking the form of the informant replying directly to both myself and the assistant. All formal interviews were based on carefully prepared schedules, including even such matters as instructing on seating arrangements. Only a portion of the total data of course came from these formal interviews. All the preceding materials, for example, were based directly on my own observations, or on the small but crucial verbal events that occurred outside the interviews and which actually comprised the interactive substance of day-to-day life.

particularly that of the one who went to Burma, had considerable effect on me and on the continuity of the research, it appeared to affect the villagers not at all. In their less predictable world, such movement was quite customary.

Because three of the assistants were with me for substantial periods of time, a few words should be said about them as individuals and their role in the community.

My principal assistant was an individual whose own life history, although not unusual for Thailand, describes one of the most important and least known psychological types emerging in the newly developing countries of the world today. Born and reared in a Northeastern village, he came to Bangkok in his bare feet at the age of sixteen to fulfill a childhood dream of becoming a newspaperman. (He once said to me that "if the first *farang* who came to Thailand in the sixteenth century had wanted to study a village, they would have had to pick a village just like the one in which I was born.") After working on a road construction gang during the day and going to school at night, he accumulated enough money to support himself and to enter Thammasart University. While working as a newspaperman, he became ill, had to leave Bangkok, and took a job as a forest ranger in the North, which gave him considerable free time for writing. It was while he was in the North that I heard about him, and asked him to come down and work with me. While working in Bang Chan, he was able to reëstablish some of his old Bangkok ties so that after my departure, he and a wealthier associate established a publishing company, one purpose of which was to have an outlet for their own writings. He has since published a volume of short stories, and has undertaken with his colleague and others a field survey of Thai peasant oral literature. His ultimate aspiration at the time was to start the first newspaper in the Northeast, one addressed especially to the interests of Northeastern peasants. When we first met he had just turned twenty-five.

Despite his worldly experience, his primary reference remains that of a peasant, albeit a well-educated one. I have seen him discussing the beauty of a field of fresh growing rice with a group of Bang Chaners exactly as if he were one of them. Similarly, his spontaneous use of peasant idioms, fictive kin terms, and body gestures were indistinguishable from those of almost any Bang Chaner. He "knew" precisely when to take a villager by the hand or to place his own hand upon the villager's leg as a sign of affection. Even his wisecracks to the girls were perfectly delivered: cute enough to raise a titter but never broad enough to be considered offensive. Although some of these actions were prompted by his desire to get on good terms with the villagers, most of them were quite spontaneous.

None of this of course was lost on a people as socially perceptive as the villagers of Bang Chan. Although in their eyes he probably never ceased being identified in some ways with the *farang,* he was defined primarily as "one of us." He helped reinforce this definition by referring to himself and the villagers as "we Thai" or "we Thai farmers," as contrasted with the *farang.* Often, not out of any enmity but simply because he had a ready foil, he would make fun of my *farang* ways for the benefit of the villagers. It was conduct like this, repeatedly expressed, that permitted him later to ask the villagers their opinions of the *farang* without raising any eyebrows. On the other hand, when the need arose, he readily assumed the role of the gentle, guiding, probing representative of the research who, in his efforts to get the villagers to participate, would appeal to everything from pride in country ("Don't you want the *farang* to know the true way we Thai people think") to the principle of reciprocity ("We do a favor for *Aacaan* Herb by helping him pass his examination, and he helps us by bringing us fame").

The two female graduate students who worked part-time were not as distinctive as their male counterpart, but in their own way, were equally as effective in the research. One was the daughter of a high-ranking Army Officer School teacher; the other was the daughter of a low-level bureaucrat. In their early twenties, they had been closest friends during college and graduate studies. To a certain extent, they were prototypes of the upper-middle-class, college educated Thai female.[2] Confident about their professional abilities and aware of how much they are needed, they are caught in the conflict of whether to participate in "worldly affairs" and thus become independent and admired social leaders, or to become wives and mothers, and thus live in the shadows of their husbands. Their problem, unlike the case in the United States, is that both alternatives are equally valued and equally available and that because the social need is so great, they can actually become leaders with not too much effort. The conflict is further aggravated by the fact that they come from the social class that emphasizes a double sexual standard. At the same time as they are expected to be assertive and competent in their jobs, they are also expected to be sweet, docile, and compliant females. They resolve this conflict to a large

---

[2] The daughter of the lower-level bureaucrat had this status by virtue of her own accomplishment, not her father's. In fact, one of the most touching scenes I ever observed in Thailand was when the girl's entire family assembled at Don Muang Airport to see her off to the United States where she had won a graduate fellowship. She had become the hope and pride of her family. Her mother, in the traditional cropped hair style of the Thai female and her mouth stained with betel juice, was trying to stand on the pair of oversized high heels that she had bought especially for the occasion. Tears were flowing down her eyes, both in pride over her daughter and because she could hardly walk on her first pair of "modern" shoes. My male assistant, in his inimitable way, turned to me and whispered: "Khun Maeae [the honored mother] wants to be just like her successful daughter."

extent by becoming succoring females—taking care of the less fortunate, seeking opportunities where they can help others, and the like.

The relevance of these remarks to the work of the assistants in Bang Chan is that they represent the attitudes the girls brought into play in their relationships with the villagers. In the eyes of Bang Chaners, they were well-educated, high status city girls who combined the finest qualities of the Thai woman. They were not only clever because they carried clipboards and spoke two languages but they were "good" girls who used "sweet words" and proper terms of address and "brought us medicine when we were ill. They knew how to help farmers." In contrast to my own practice—which was to give villagers aspirin only if they explicitly asked for help, or if the problem was more serious to plead incompetence—their actions were entirely spontaneous. In the same way, villagers would often wonder why after working all week at the university, these girls would spend their Sundays and holidays in Bang Chan. The answer was not hard for them to find: "These girls have much progress. They want to help the nation and themselves. So they come here and work for *Aacaan* Herb. This will help them go to America. And then they will have more progress." Although this motive may have entered into the assistants' decisions, a more important reason was the simple pleasure they derived from listening to villagers bare their problems and preoccupations. By giving of their time and interest they were fulfilling their own best image of themselves.

A final word should be said about the various relationships existing among the assistants and myself. The relationships that developed among the assistants themselves was perhaps the ideal Thai adjustment to the unique situation in which these three young, unmarried people found themselves: they began to treat each other like brothers and sisters. Theirs was not a perfect sibling relationship—not even in the fictive sense, for they were keenly aware of their differences in background and of the desirability of keeping romantic considerations out of the relationship. However, their very differences in background helped form a bond of mutual respect.

Their attitudes toward the author were more complicated. Although in many ways they treated me too as a sibling, their attitudes were forever colored by the fact that I was a *farang*. On the positive side, this meant that they respected me for my technical training and knowledge, and for my obvious concern about learning as much as I could about the villagers. By the same token, however, they would frequently become annoyed by my inability to see things which in Thai terms were obvious, or by my insistence on probing matters that in their terms were either unanswerable or better left unexamined. Their attitudes toward me were not too different from those of the villagers, except that because our relationship was considerably more sustained and intellectually stimulating (they wanted to know about the village almost as much as I did), it was more intimate and unguarded. My closest friend in Thailand was not a villager but my male field assistant.

Investigator's Attitudes Toward the Villagers

Anthropological field work has been referred to variously as "a period of stepped-up socialization," "the ultimate test of the value and limitations of empathy," and more simply "the most rewarding part of the anthropological endeavor." It is all these things. However, perhaps its most distinctive characteristic is that it is a period of intensified self-control. It involves the willingness to suspend one's normal and familiar patterns of behavior in deference to patterns which are appropriate to the culture being studied, or at least not too incongruent, and which are aimed at one's overriding purpose in being there: to obtain data.[3] The rewards of field work are of course immediately apparent: to encounter directly a different arrangement of the human experience. But field work also involves the psychological price of being temporarily willing not "to be oneself." There are of course numerous instances within one's own culture when one does not behave like "oneself," but simply assumes the pose associated with one's role. What is distinctive of field work is the highly *sustained* quality of one's "acting"; the researcher must be *continuously* concerned with tailoring his actions to suit others' preferences. The problem is complicated further by the fact that in field work the preferences of others are usually only slightly known; in fact, the discovery of such preferences is part and parcel of the very process of field work. Thus, the researcher tends to be even more hesitant and concerned with keeping himself under rein. It should be noted that "not being oneself" is not identical with "not being true to oneself." Indeed, the ideal adaptation to the psychic requirements of the field situation may be to feel any way one wants to *feel* toward one's informants, but to be sure to *act* properly toward them.

My overt behavior toward the villagers involved assuming something of a social pose, but a relatively straightforward and simple one. I attempted to present myself as an interested, uncritical, and mildly bewildered young

[3] I am not speaking here simply of functioning comfortably in an alien culture. Cultures differ radically in the degree of conformity to or deviance from prevailing patterns that is permitted individuals; and in this respect, Thai culture is extraordinarily tolerant of personal deviance. However, this is not the same as living in a foreign culture when one's *raison d'être* is to induce members of that culture to coöperate, provide information, and confide in oneself. Here it is incumbent upon the outsider to make some adjustments in his normal behavioral responses.

man who wanted their help for the sake of "knowledge." I came to Thailand because a very wealthy American who manufactured automobiles (The Ford Foundation) had decided to make merit by giving money to universities as well as to monasteries and hospitals; I had applied for a fellowship, and he had given me the money.[4]

In my actual contacts with villagers, I tended to be much more docile and unassertive than is my wont, often to the extent of appearing diffident. Although in the relationships with my assistants I did not hesitate to express my opinions and evaluations of things—often in an excitable and seemingly aggressive way, which is one of my "natural" and extremely non-Thai modes of expression—I tried to keep my comments to villagers free of any evaluation. The only time I really let myself go was in laughter, which villagers liked but which they sometimes thought was undignified. To the countless little frustrations that occur in the field—spending an hour with an informant "making rapport" only to be told that he was too tired to take the TAT; seeing an informant get up at the high point of an interview, say "I must go," and simply leave—I responded either with giggling or stoicism, never anger. This latter posture was particularly difficult to maintain. When the owner of the "Cornell Office" asked me for three times the agreed upon cost of rent and board, I answered first by giggling and then by changing the subject, although neither was in any way representative of my genuine feelings. I later paid the original amount through a go-between, and nothing further was said.

Not all my behavior was oriented toward controlling such feelings, and not all of it was by any means intended as a disguise. In fact, the role of being an "interested, uncritical, and mildly bewildered young man" was not only the best way to present myself to the villagers from the point of view of effective research, but was often the way I felt. (The bewilderment was effective to the extent that it often elicited clarifications and specifications from informants who wanted to be sure I understood.) Similarly, my expressions of laughter were quite consistent with village patterns, and they could not easily be feigned. Perhaps one of the most enjoyable aspects of the pose was when I provided villagers with accurate and truthful answers to questions they might ask, but in an idiom that I thought would be most meaningful to them, e.g., Henry Ford's merit-making activities.

---

[4] The source of my funds was of never-ending interest to the villagers. One Bang Chaner said he understood what the source of my funds was, but did not quite understand how I actually obtained them. "How does the money get into your wallet?" I explained that prior to my departure from the United States, I made arrangements with my benefactor's secretary to have the money deposited in a bank in Bangkok. And whenever I needed money, I would write a check and obtain the baht equivalent of the amount I had written. At this explanation, the villager broke out into a broad smile and said: "That's wonderful. It sounds just like Communism!"

My attitude here was not patronizing, any more than was theirs when faced with a culturally complicated question from me. Such rephrasings were simply easy and "sanug-ful" ways of communicating our points.

An investigator's feelings toward the people whom he is studying, as distinguished from his overt behavior, are significant only to the extent that they might affect the nature and interpretation of his data. It is the writer's belief that except where indicated, my feelings toward the villagers did not influence my description of them in any significant way. However, because I am dealing here with rather subtle materials and because, irrespective of intentions, personal feelings can be insidious in their intrusion, a few words should be said about my sentiments toward the villagers.

My dominant feeling toward them was shaped by the intellectual challenge they presented me. There were things they did that I simply did not understand, that I struggled with for months, and only some of which resulted in solutions coherent enough to be presented here. There were other things they did that I never managed to comprehend, but which I just came to respect as their way of functioning, e.g., a villager stopping himself in the middle of a conversation and, without a *single* word of explanation, leaving. What was "incomprehensible" was not only that he did this, but that the other villagers in attendance accepted his behavior as thoroughly normal. When asked how they felt about his leave-taking, the answer was almost invariably, "*Chəəj-chəəj*" (cool, indifferent). When asked more precisely, "Well, weren't you surprised by his suddenness; that he just turned his back and left?", they answered, "No, he must have had somewhere to go." What was "challenging" here and in the literally hundreds of other events of the same order was that the act was contrary to one of my most fundamental *assumptions* about the nature of human contact: in this case, that there should be some cue indicating the imminent termination of the relationship. Perhaps there was a cue, but one so subtle as to be impossible for me to spot. However, it was events of this kind, occurring week after week, that made the research the intellectually exciting experience it was.

On the less cerebral level, my feelings toward the villagers were more ambivalent. On the negative side, I was annoyed by their unabashed self-seeking, their manipulation of each other as well as myself, their ambiguity, and the relative lack of trust that many of them had in others, even those who were supposedly closest to them. Much of this was explicable in terms of their life histories and, to a lesser extent, in terms of their poverty; nonetheless, they were realities which I as a human being (as distinguished from an anthropologist) reacted to subjectively. On the positive side, I admired them for their easy acceptance of themselves, for their down-to-earth quality, for their tolerance of others, and for their use of social forms, which, although often lacking in depth, emphasized the dignity of each person. Particularly attractive were the older villagers who, having made their peace with life, would freely articulate their thoughts and feelings about themselves and their world.

Again, the relevance of these personal, subjective considerations to the research results is problematic and I would hope inconsequential. They have been presented here because despite its avowed purpose, field work is always both a human experience and a research experience.

Fashioning an SCT For Bang Chan

In this section we shift our attention from the human and interpersonal dimensions of field work to the more technical area of the development and application of the Sentence Completion Technique in Bang Chan.[5]

To begin, it is well to keep in mind a few important historical considerations. The Sentence Completion Technique (hereafter referred to as the SCT) comes out of an intellectual tradition whose premises and intellectual style the author is familiar with but does not necessarily share; that is, the SCT was developed and has been used almost exclusively in the context of the "testing and measurement" tradition of clinical and educational psychology. This was a tradition, beginning with the work of Galton during the latter part of the nineteenth century, that appropriately emphasized the precise and objective measurement of human capacities and traits but which, as it developed through the years, tended to make "the test"—a shorthand, simplistic, preferably quick and self-administered summary of the traits or persons being studied—an end in itself. The I.Q. test, with its single numerical summary of a person's mental capacities, is perhaps the ultimate expression of this tradition.

The individuals who developed and refined the SCT (originally Payne 1928 and Tendler 1930; in more recent years, Rotter 1951, Sacks and Levy 1952, Levy 1952, Holsopple and Miale 1954, Burwen, Campbell and Kidd 1956, Trites 1956, Zimmer 1956, Benton, Windler and Erdice 1957, and Rohde 1957) have all operated in terms of this intellectual orientation. Reading their work and other SCT literature reveals a recurrent concern with how the SCT should be administered and coded, with whether short items are better than longer ones, with what other tests and measures the instrument should be correlated, and the like. However, *nowhere* can one find a statement of why the test works (to my knowledge, the discussion in this book is the first to be addressed to this question) and no one, except Hanfmann and Getzels (1953) and Davids (1955) raises the crucial issue

---

[5] The basic *theory* behind the Sentence Completion Technique and the rationale for the analysis of the research *results* are presented in the next chapter. Our concern at this point is more empirical and focuses on the actual construction of the instrument for use in Bang Chan and on some of the problems and resolutions encountered in its application.

of whether the test—or *any* test—is really the best way of investigating what the researcher wants to know.

I raise these questions because my use of the instrument does not presuppose that the major value of the SCT derives from its being a "test" in the sense of providing a neat, easily administered, and easily scored synopsis of the villagers' predispositions to behavior. (Of course, some psychological testers would point out that because the instrument lacks norms it should not be considered a "test" at all.) Rather, I have used the instrument because it possesses certain characteristics that enabled me to obtain a kind of data that I could not have obtained as efficiently by other means, *viz.*, the villagers' internal views and definitions of a series of relatively unstructured but highly realistic psychological situations, presented in a manner that created a minimum of anxiety and resistance. Beyond this general consideration, and the fact that it uses "suggested" rather than direct questions, the SCT is essentially no different from other interview procedures. Perhaps the only thing that it has in common with a "test" is that all the "questions" are asked at the same sitting.

Construction of the SCT

There were three major stages in the construction of the SCT. The first stage involved the specification of the various problem areas to be covered by the technique. On the basis of the available literature on Thai personality, it was apparent that three areas—aggression, dependency, and attitudes toward authority—loomed particularly large in the psychic lives of most Thai, and that items descriptive of these areas should be included in my version of the SCT. Too, during my early months in the field, there were several facets of the villagers' behavior that were mystifying—for example, the mechanisms they used in orienting themselves to other people—and it was decided to include items which would tap such areas. Most of these items were derived from the events and conversations of the workaday world: the villagers' repeated use of the phrase *maj daj* (I cannot do it; I am not able; I do not know how); their ambivalent attitudes toward *nagkleengs* (the aggressive, daring, sometimes bullying individuals who speak their feelings from their hearts). It should be noted that although these items were derived directly from Bang Chan culture, a concerted effort was made to phrase them for the SCT schedule in more universal, non-culturally specific terms. In addition there were several specific items which were standard fare on most versions of the SCT, but which seemed to represent universal psychological issues or problem areas, that is, "He is most afraid of . . ." (anxiety); "He often daydreams of . . ." (psychological isolation).

When the final version of the instrument was ready for informants, there were thirteen general categories, although not all were of equal significance in the lives of the villagers, and were not equally productive of meaningful data. These thirteen categories were:

Aggression: Causes and Reactions	Attitudes Toward Authority
Achievement-Failure	Dependency
Reactions to Crises	Self-Image
Dominant Drives and Aspirations	Anxiety: Causes and Ways of
Kinship Relations	Handling
Psychological Isolation	Orienting Toward Others
Notions of Good and Evil	Love, Sex, and Marriage

Because not all categories were equally revealing (the "Notions of Good and Evil" category, for example, was singularly unrevealing, perhaps because it is such a ritualized area of Bang Chan life) and because some categories can be merged with others (for example, "Reactions to Crises" fitting with "Anxiety") the final analyses will focus only on seven major categories.

The second and most time-consuming stage involved the assembling, ordering, and translation of the actual SCT items. In research of this type, there are always more questions to ask than there is time to ask them. My first draft of potential material, for example, included as many as 350 items. After considerable pruning, the number of questions was reduced to 144. However, 144 items were still far in excess of what our otherwise coöperative Bang Chaners would be asked to bear; ideally, no more than an hour should be spent on the formal portion of any interview, and for some "sanug-fully"-oriented villagers, even this was too long a stint. It was decided therefore to divide the 144 items into two schedules of 72 items each. Although the number of individuals responding to identical stimuli was consequently reduced, it provided broader coverage from all informants on each of the areas covered by the SCT, and increased the certainty of the interpretations and judgments. Because the items on the two forms are different in specific intent, they cannot be considered "reliability" checks of each other, in the strict meaning of the term. This would require the two forms to be precisely analogous.[6] However, because they cover

---

[6] Actually, any attempt to apply the notion of "split-half," "inter-item," or "inter-form" reliability to an open-ended technique such as the SCT creates more methodological problems than it solves. This is because even the slightest change in an item —for example, the difference between the articles "a" and "the"—can change the semantic and psychological value of the sentence fragment. Notice, for example, the difference between the following three items: "He wants his son to be . . ."; "He wants his son to be a . . ."; "He wants his son to be the. . . ."

From the point of view of methodological theory, a "test-retest" reliability check would probably be the more sensible form to apply in the case of the SCT, although

different facets and dimensions of the *same* problem areas, they do serve as useful checks on one another at a more general level of interpretation. The assigning of specific items to Form A or Form B was largely arbitrary.

One of the most important and, as it turned out, intriguing tasks of the SCT construction involved the arrangement of the various items into an interview schedule.[7] I wanted the interview to be an interesting, non-threatening, and not overly difficult experience for informants. Thus, it was necessary to motivate them to "take" the interview, in the sense of

---

this procedure too has its disadvantages. I tried to implement such a check in Bang Chan, but was unable to carry it out because of suspicion on the part of informants. That is, I selected a dozen items from each form, and approached informants who had responded to the same items when they took the complete form at least two months earlier. Three of the first four informants we spoke to replied: "Didn't you like the answers I gave you the first time?"; "I gave you true answers before. Now I can only lie"; "The answers I gave you the first time were right; do you want me to give you wrong answers now?" Since these informants all but told us that they would aim for qualitatively different responses, the reliability value that such a retest might have seemed minimal. When we tried a different tack and explained to an informant that we had "lost" the responses on these twelve items from his first test, and wanted to be sure we had a complete record of that interview, he guffawed and commented: "But that was three months ago. I cannot remember what I told you then. The answers I give you now will have to be different." This individual did acquiesce to our request for a retest, and in perfect fulfillment of his own prophecy gave responses that were strikingly different from his earlier version.

On the other hand, a genuine error on our part did reveal something of the stability of informant responses over time. During the final weeks of field work I was checking all my protocols and discovered that the protocol of a particularly interesting villager was missing from the SCT file. This was approximately thirteen months after he had first taken the SCT. The informant was especially friendly with us and unlike the individual above, acquiesced to our request for a retest with obvious pleasure. Later, when I was packing my field notes, I discovered his original SCT; it had been mistakenly filed with some other materials. Considering that more than a year had gone by, his responses on the two protocols were amazingly similar. Following, for example, are the "before" and "after" responses to the first three sentence fragments, all "aggression" items:

"*He is most annoyed when . . .*": his peace of mind is disturbed and when distasteful feelings pass across his mind, *versus,* he wants to concentrate, but some other feelings disturb him and don't let him concentrate.

"*When he gets angry, he wants to . . .*": let off his anger in a suitable way; maybe it is bad or maybe it isn't bad to let off one's anger, *versus,* do something to let off his anger.

"*When he insulted me, I . . .*": felt displeased, as it was natural, and wondered why he insulted me, *versus,* I was displeased and annoyed with the person who had insulted me.

[7] All the SCT's were administered orally, rather than in written form. This was necessary not only because 40 percent of our potential informants were illiterate, but because among the 60 percent who could "write," the very process of writing creates additional psychological obligations: the necessity to write in a beautiful hand; to phrase one's thoughts in an appealing, and even poetic, manner; to be sure that one's spelling is correct and that one does not smudge the paper. Many villagers perceive written messages as having a reality and value of their own, as contrasted with speech, which dissipates itself almost immediately after it is articulated. (See Sjoberg 1960: 285–293 for an excellent discussion of the social psychological significance of writing in peasant societies in general.)

becoming psychologically involved with it; having accomplished this, it was necessary to sustain their interest; and should they become tired or bored toward the end, it was necessary to rekindle their attention to see them through to the finish. With these ends in mind, I had my assistant divide each form of the SCT into two equal groups of "easy" items and "difficult" items. The 72 items were then ordered so that the easiest item became item number 1; the next less easy, item number 72; the next less easy item number 2; and so on. The most difficult item in the schedule was number 36. Thus, the final interview took the form of following a progression from easy items to difficult ones back to easy ones. The position of an item was occasionally changed if the answer to it could conceivably affect the answer to an item which came later.

What was perhaps most surprising about this entire procedure was my assistant's perception of "easy" and "difficult" items. He had selected as the opening item of Form A, "*He was most afraid of . . . ,*" and as the opening item of Form B, "*When he insulted me, I. . . .*" When I pointed out to him that the opening items of the interviews should interest and relax informants, not threaten them, he answered that all the Thai peasants he ever knew, which were considerably more than I knew, think about being afraid and insulted "all the time," and that it was very "easy" for them to express their feelings of fear and their response to insult: "these are things that happen to them everyday." I then pointed out to him some of the items I would have selected as "easy" items, if I had ordered the schedule myself. I immediately chose, "*He wishes he were. . . .*" The assistant smiled, and pointed out that this was perhaps one of the most difficult items—he had placed it in the 47th position—because Thai villagers find it very difficult to think about the future or about being something other than who they are. He agreed that many of them want to be something other than who they are, but they cannot think about it too long because it worries them "and gives them a headache." Assuming that at the time he knew the subjective side of his culture considerably better than I did, I went along with his selections.

Very early in the research it became apparent that language was the lifeblood of much of the project, and that considerable attention would have to be devoted to translation procedures.[8] However, the significance of the translation process in affecting the quality of my data did not really strike home until I actually began the task of translating the pretest SCT items from English into Thai. This was only half the task: the informants' *responses* would also have to be translated later from Thai into English.

At first glance, there was nothing seemingly complex about the transla-

---

[8] An expanded version of the following discussion on translation originally appeared in Phillips 1959–1960.

tion assignment. Since the SCT items described very basic human experiences, and since I had tried to select items which would be appropriate in any culture, I expected the job to go relatively quickly. It soon became clear, however, that even "very basic human experiences" resist quick translation. Using two translators, I first tried the usual technique of "back-translating": one person translated the items from English into Thai, his Thai version was then translated back into English by the other person, and the two versions were compared. The results of this procedure, however, were so dismal that it was abandoned after a dozen items. It was obvious that the majority of the translations were not coming through accurately, but the source of error could be discovered only after prolonged discussion. Items that originally read *"He often daydreams of . . ."* or *"Sometimes a good quarrel is necessary because . . ."* appeared in the retranslated versions as *"When he sleeps during the day he dreams of . . ."* or *"Sometimes a quarrel brings good results because. . . ."* (This last item later proved to be utterly untranslatable. After much discussion the translators decided that although it was conceivable that an American might enjoy a quarrel for its cathartic effects, the notion would be incomprehensible to a Thai.)

In order to save discussion time and to profit from the accuracy of a consensus, the following procedure was substituted. Both translators, working independently, translated the remaining items into Thai. All items which were identical in every respect were set aside. The assistants then discussed among themselves the balance of the items: what their English intent and meanings were and how these could be best communicated in simple Thai. If after fifteen minutes they could not reach agreement on a particular item, they were to put it aside for later discussion with me. By combining my limited Thai with what I hoped were proper probes and with the translators' explanations of why they originally disagreed and now agreed, I decided on the acceptability of the items; in effect, this step substituted for the English retranslations of "back-translating." The whole procedure took approximately a week and a half.

The items on which they could not agree were considerably more difficult to handle. For one thing, they required more than three weeks' discussion. The differences between the translators were always small, but crucial. For example, in the item, *"His most attractive quality is . . . ,"* there is no Thai equivalent for "quality." There are terms for "inborn personality traits," "behavior," "manners" (politeness, etc.), and "physical characteristics." One translator was sure I meant "behavior," the other, "manners," and during their disagreement the other alternatives did not even occur to them. It took a half-hour to tease them out. Sometimes the translators could not come to any decision: there is no way to say in Thai, at least in a half-sentence, "*He feels frustrated when.* . . ." This item, along with three others, was eventually rejected.

Before the items were finalized, they were all reviewed by an American linguist thoroughly conversant in Thai. Despite all our previous efforts, he suggested lexical changes in approximately thirty items and pointed out a basic but easily remedied grammatical flaw (with semantic implications) which ran through almost the entire test.

For the more time-consuming task of translating the villagers' protocols back into English, I managed to obtain the services of two urban Thai translators, both graduates of British universities. The only contact these translators had with informants was through the SCT responses. The theory and method of the test was explained to them as was a list of twenty instructions which were to be used as translation guides. (These are described in Phillips 1959–1960.) After each test was translated (the translator working independently of his colleague and the author), it was checked by me for ambiguities, multiple meanings, and statements that simply did not make sense. These questionable items, which averaged approximately one-third of each test, were then analyzed and discussed by the author and a third person and when necessary, changed or qualified. Thus, responses that were originally translated as "*Most high government officials are* . . . kind people. They speak nicely, but some of them don't" or "*People have to help each other because* . . . of humanity's sake" became, after analysis, "kind people. They speak nicely (use nice-sounding words), but some of them don't" and "of humanity's sake (because it is in the nature of human beings, because they are human, to help each other)," respectively. Each test took an average of seven hours: three hours for the translation, one hour to check, and three hours to clarify questionable points. After about eighty of the tests had been completed, the translations started to become very sloppy and their clarifications more difficult, so that toward the end it took a minimum of ten hours per test.

One of the more important and perplexing decisions that had to be made during the translation process was how to label the hypothetical individuals referred to in the various SCT items. The decision was important because of the controversy surrounding the question of whether the SCT is truly a "projective technique"; that is, a technique which not only induces individuals to reveal their needs and wishes, but which induces them to do this unknowingly. It is argued that materials obtained projectively are less guarded and less censored than those derived from more direct techniques. The identity of the hypothetical individual described in the sentence fragment enters into the controversy in that the informant's identification of him directly affects the "projectability" of the item. Thus, it is asserted that if the individual described in the item is referred to in the first person singular—*e.g.*, "When he insulted *me*, I . . ."—the informant will realize that he is describing himself, and the projective advantage of the item will be lost. On the other hand, if the individual described in the item is referred to as "John," "him," "people," or some other hypothetical soul, the informant will be less aware that he is describing himself, and the projectability of the item will be maintained.

In my own work, I never became convinced that the SCT would operate as a "projective technique" in the terms just outlined. I would argue that the data elicited by the technique is indeed less guarded and less censored than data obtained by more direct investigative methods, but this is a result of the linguistic structure of the SCT, not of its projective capacity, if what is meant by "projective" is that informants are unaware that they are talking about themselves. This conclusion about the SCT is based primarily on theoretical considerations, but it is also heavily influenced by the distinctive nature of my own research medium, the Thai language.

In fact, the "special" nature of Thai almost precluded the SCT operating projectively in the terms described above. That is, in ordinary Thai usage, pronouns and proper nouns are often not used. In linguistic terms, they represent "optional" rather than "obligatory" grammatical categories, with the semantic context accounting for any seeming confusion. When they are used, however, they function as specifying and explicating devices: to single out the person or persons referred to from a larger, ambiguous social "field," and thus *distinguish* him or them semantically. This specification function is further enhanced by the fact that all Thai pronouns have associated with them an attribute of social status, and some are associated with an attribute of group membership, *e.g.*, *khon raw*, which may mean either its literal English translation, "we people" or "I who am a member of an unspecified group as distinguished from you, who are a member of another unspecified group." The significance of all this is that when pronouns and proper nouns are used, Thai are considerably more attentive to their referents than are English speakers to theirs, and they tend to take them more literally.

Because of this Siamese sensitivity to "active" pronoun usage, I decided not to use the Thai equivalent of the hypothetical "John" or "Mary" (villagers would wonder precisely which "John" or "Mary"), or the first person singular forms, *phom* (used by males) and *chan* (used primarily by females, but often by males). These last two would not only reduce the supposed projective quality of the item to nothing, but would appear excessively awkward in an SCT item; using them would be akin to saying in English, "When he insulted me myself, I myself. . . ." Of the remaining Thai pronouns, those most frequently used in the SCT items were *raw* ("we" or "generalized I") [9] and *khon raw* ("we people"). However, I used two other terms, *khon* ("people") and *khaw* ("he," "she," or "they") in those items most descriptive of the expression of ego-alien sentiments: that is, those sentiments which, on the basis of my knowledge of the villagers, I expected to be most readily denied as being self-referring. Thus, an aggression item read: *"Khon most often get angry when . . . ,"* instead of *"Raw most often get angry when. . . ."* To simplify matters for the reader, later SCT materials which list both the original English language item and the English translation of the Thai translation will also include the Thai pronouns that were used in the various items.

The third stage of the SCT construction involved the pre-testing of the SCT schedule with ten villagers. A major aim of these trial interviews was to examine the quality of all the items. I was particularly concerned with how well informants understood the items and with identifying those items which interested them, those which required revision, those which brought forth revealing material, and those which elicited useless information.

The second purpose of the pre-test was to train my assistant in how to conduct the SCT interviews. Of principal concern was to try to minimize the effects of the interpersonal situation on the informant. Such effects can never be fully cancelled out, but they can be controlled to the extent of insuring that the data obtained represent the informant's product, not the product of ideas the interviewer might introduce into the situation. The major task of the training period, therefore, was instructing of the assistant in elementary interviewing techniques.[10]

The instructions also included such considerations as seating arrangements: try to locate the informant so that the canal—where people paddle by and can be waved to—is in our line of sight, not his. Ideally, he should be able to observe only the interviewers. If interviews are to be conducted in boats (later, eight of them were) the boat should be pulled off into one of the canal tributaries to minimize the disturbance from canal traffic. In general, privacy can be obtained by telling informants that since we wanted

---

[9] *Raw* as a "generalized I" is not as ear-catching in Thai as it is in English. Thus, although *raw* can always mean "we," it is a perfect synonym, not a substitute, for "I" when the speaker wishes to indicate less self-reference. Another way of putting it is that when it is used to mean "I," the ordinary "we"-"I" contrast is psychologically inoperative; *raw* simply becomes an attenuated form of "I."

[10] The techniques which I had the most difficulty impressing on my assistants concerned such seemingly simple matters as the following: never afford the informant any hint of a response; if his first few responses are wild, repeat the instructions, and pick up the interview where it was left off, adding the items with the strange responses at the end; do not hesitate to encourage the informant with comments such as "that is fine"; if the informant gives funny responses, smile but do not laugh; if he is hesitating too long on an item, simply repeat the item as a prod; if he does not respond after three repeats, go on to the next item, and the like.

each person's own ideas, not those of other family members, it would be best to find somewhere we can be by ourselves.[11] Every informant in the sample eventually accepted our request for privacy with complete understanding. Also, it was usually easy to find an isolated spot: underneath the house, a buffalo shed, in a grove of trees, or if necessary in the boat. However, because Bang Chan notions of privacy do not apply to children, approximately one-third of the interviews were conducted with children in attendance at one point or another. The first time a child appeared, we made an attempt to shoo him away. This, however, was usually futile: he would leave and then return; only the boredom of our adult conversation would eventually drive him away. In the case of nursing children, we would always wait until the mother was free, although if the child wanted the breast during the interview we would simply continue and "ignore" his presence; his mother seemed to,.at least at the conscious level.

One of the more important administrative tasks of the pre-test was to try out various instructions that would be given to *informants* on how to take the SCT. During these trial interviews, we experimented with various versions of the "introductory remarks" and settled on the following as the version to be used with our final 111 informants.

After explaining to the informant that we had come to chat, and after having chatted (which varied from ten minutes to two hours, depending upon the subject matter and the mood of the informant) we reminded him that I had been sent to Bang Chan by Cornell University to study the life and thought of the Thai people: "My professor sent me, and when I return to America, he will examine me on the information that I have gathered. So I would like to ask you for your *personal* help. I know that you can help me and can give me a true picture of the life and thought of Thai farmers. And [with a giggle] I think you can help me pass my examination." At this point, during the regular interviews, I would remind the informant that a few weeks earlier the abbot of Monastery Bang Chan had, on a ceremonially auspicious day, supervised the lottery from which the names of my informants had been selected: [12]

Aacaan Phuang supervised the ceremony and your family was one of the families chosen in the lottery to be interviewed by me. Both *Aacaan* Phuang and I thought that this was the best way to select

[11] Informants were also asked, on the same grounds, not to reveal the items or their responses to other villagers. We are certain that there were several who ignored our request—not out of malice but simply because it was not that important to them. However, since there were so many items on the schedule, covering so many different areas, I doubt whether their reports to other potential informants biased our results in any substantial way.

[12] I am indebted to Robert B. Textor for having originally suggested this method of selecting part of my sample.

families if I am to obtain the true picture about the people of Bang Chan.

I have something here that is like a game or a puzzle. It is a list of sentences about things that happen every day in life; just plain, ordinary things. These sentences, however, are not complete sentences. They are only half sentences. I would like you to finish these sentences for me. For example, take the sentence: *"When it begins to rain, he. . . ."* I would appreciate your finishing this sentence with anything that comes to your mind. The only thing I ask is that your completion makes sense: that it fits with the first part of the sentence.

You can make your completions as long as you want; the length of a sentence is unimportant. I want to tell you that with these sentences there is no such thing as a right completion or a wrong completion. All I would like is your own idea on what the completion should be. I expect that different people will give different completions, so all I want is your personal opinion.

I am going to ask other people in this family—except the children, of course—to complete the sentences. But we would like to ask each person one at a time, individually and privately. So I wonder if we can go somewhere where we can have privacy. But before we begin, why don't we try a test sentence. Tell me the completion of the following sentence: *"A boy, crossing a bridge, was showing off to a girl, and he fell into the canal, so he. . . ."*

The Selection and Nature of the Sample

The 111 individuals comprising the SCT sample represent an 11 percent stratified sample of the adult population of Bang Chan (persons over twenty years of age, or 989 of the 1,771 villagers) on four major variables: age, sex, religion, and economic status. The sample is based on a village census gathered by earlier Cornell University researchers and brought up-to-date by me during my first few months in the field. The economic status variable is based on judgments made by the seven hamlet headmen and fourteen assistant hamlet headmen living in Bang Chan, and thus represents an "inside," nonobjective view of a family's economic position in the community.

Several factors entered into the decision to select the sample on a quota rather than random basis. Most important was my decision to select informants from only two of the seven Bang Chan hamlets. This in turn was based on the need to save time. During the period that I was working on the census and traveling through all seven hamlets, I noticed that I was actually spending twice as much time on travel than I was spending with informants. This was due to the widely dispersed nature of Bang Chan homesteads and to the fact that the headmen and assistant headmen for whom we were looking often were not in, requiring that we return a second and even a third or fourth time. (Appointments in the village can be made, but they are almost never kept.) There was no reason to suppose that regular informants would live any closer to the Cornell "Office," or would be any more homebound than these individuals. Since it was imperative to get on with the research, I decided to select the sample from the hamlet in which the "Office" was located and the one immediately adjacent to it. Although these two hamlets appeared similar to other Bang Chan hamlets in most respects, they contained a larger percentage of wealthier villagers, a smaller percentage of poorer ones, and more Moslems than did other hamlets. Since at the time I thought that wealth or religion might be crucial variables—for example, on such SCT items as "The most important thing in his life is . . ."—and since, if I had selected a completely random sample from these two hamlets I would probably have obtained too many Moslems or too few poor villagers, I decided to invoke quota considerations in the selection of informants. As it turned out later, after the data were gathered and examined, there were no notable differences in the responses of informants from different economic or religious categories to these and to most other items. This is one of the reasons that the data below are being handled in modal terms, rather than in terms of intra-sample differences. Also, my sample was much too small to consider such potential differences as anything more than heuristic. However, at the time I felt that it was necessary to have the representation on these particular variables absolutely correct.

Another factor pointing to a quota sample was the desirability of having some Buddhist monks as informants. Since on a random basis, the likelihood that any monks would have been in our sample was literally 1 in 296, it was decided simply to ignore chance considerations in order to include some of these individuals; seven of the SCT informants were monks. Similarly, there were other villagers with special attributes that I felt merited inclusion: the two male school teachers were two such individuals, as was the villager who had a reputation for being a *nagkleeng*. A young man who had been to Korea with the Thai army was also such a person.

To a certain extent, random factors did enter into the inclusion of a number of informants in the sample. This was one of the functions of the lottery, referred to earlier, conducted by the abbot of Monastery Bang Chan. However, the persons chosen by lot served mainly as a "core" group from which to select those individuals who would fulfill the criteria that had been established. When the persons in this group had been exhausted in terms of meeting these criteria, or when they were no longer available,[13] I went to other villagers. All told, 64 percent of the sample (72 of the 111 informants), equally divided between the two forms of the SCT, were chosen from this "core" or randomly selected group.

---

[13] During the SCT portion of the research, 20 percent of the households originally selected for interviewing in the lottery in effect dissolved. Note that the units of the lottery were households, not individuals. The reason for this was two-fold: (a) I had originally thought of the possibility of doing some intra-familial comparisons, and wanted to be sure I would have the data should such comparisons eventually appear worthwhile; (b) more important, because of the possibility that older members of families would feel affronted should I ask for their children rather than for them, it seemed advisable to have as many informants as possible from the same family unit. This consideration was not to be taken lightly. Some Bang Chaners, for their own peculiar reasons, felt honored to be interviewed by the *farang*. To enter their house, and then in effect ignore them because they were not members of the sample would have been an insult.

It should also be noted that although the purpose of the lottery was in part to select a portion of the sample, an even more important purpose was the religious sanction that it gave to the research in the eyes of some villagers.

IV

The Sentence Completion Technique

The following discussion details the logical considerations which underlie the analysis of the SCT responses and the procedures which have been devised for such analysis. At the same time it will serve as an introduction to the general nature of the SCT responses.

The analysis rests upon five premises.

How the SCT Works

First, despite its title and appearance, there is nothing particularly esoteric about the Sentence Completion Technique. It is primarily a useful and efficient way of asking questions about matters which are of central concern in personality research—feelings of rejection, failure, anxiety, and the like—but which might be considered sensitive or personal by our informants. That the questions are phrased as incomplete sentences rather than as direct interrogations is an attempt to get at these issues in a psychologically comfortable way. Concomitantly, it is an attempt to circumvent the tendency for individuals to set up resistances and blocks when queried on such matters.[1]

---

[1] Whether Bang Chan villagers consider feelings of rejection, failure, and so forth, to be sensitive or private topics is, at bottom, problematic, since we have little reason to assume that they or the members of any non-Western culture share our attitude in this regard. The writer suspects that in some areas Bang Chaners do share Western attitudes about what sentiments should be concealed from (or revealed to) others, and in other areas do not. For instance, Bang Chan men would no more discuss their sexual impulses toward their daughters than would American fathers—in contrast, for example, to Pilaga Indian men (Henry 1955: 265). In contrast, most Bang Chaners seem considerably more reticent than Americans about revealing their aggressive feelings, but are considerably freer in discussing feelings of personal failure. Such discussion, of course, always varies in terms of the degree of intimacy between people.

Two general considerations thus seem clear: (a) Bang Chan villagers are precisely like other human beings in that they have a tendency to conceal and reveal certain feelings, although the specific feelings concerned may or may not be the same as those of members of other cultures; and (b) since in the beginning of his research, an investigator really does not know in what areas or to what degree his informants are sensitive, it would seem prudent to use a technique which assumes sensitivity in all areas and attempts to get at these feelings in the least uncomfortable way.

An incomplete sentence (e.g., "When I realize other people do not like me, I feel . . .") has at least three advantages over a direct question (e.g., "How do you feel when you realize other people do not like you?"). These advantages are rooted in the use and structure of language.

First, the tendency to complete a half sentence is psychologically more compelling than the tendency to answer a direct question. A half sentence is both semantically and structurally an unfinished unit of thought which, because of the obligatory nature of grammatical patterns (Jakobson 1959: 144) requires completion. The necessity for grammatical completeness introduces a dimension of unconscious compulsion not found in a direct question. Without even thinking about it, we are aware that something is "wrong" with an incomplete sentence or with any syntactically irregular form, and we quickly move to make it "right." Thus, a person is motivated to complete an unfinished sentence not only to supply the information which is required by the sentence stem but because, unfinished, it sounds incorrect.

A direct question on the other hand is already a completed unit of thought. As such, it can be met not only with a direct answer but with a laugh, another question, a "don't know," and various other replies, all of which are structurally as well as semantically feasible. Such replies, however, cannot be used as full-fledged responses to an incomplete sentence, but only as asides or interjections. An unfinished sentence will normally accept only those statements which will fulfill its grammatical requirements. Because of the nature of language, these statements almost always have direct reference to the first half of the sentence; they usually cannot avoid the situation posed by the introductory phrase.

This condition also helps to account for the relatively unpremeditated nature of a sentence completion as compared to the answer of a direct question. By "unpremeditated" is meant that the completion is subject to less overt deliberation and decision than is an answer. Given a structurally induced incentive to complete a sentence, there is considerably less likelihood that much rumination will be exercised in selecting the phrase to fill out the sentence. Prolonged reflection of course encourages the introduction of resistances, evasions, and blocks.

None of the foregoing is meant to imply that people always speak in complete sentences or are totally constrained by the rules of grammar. In ordinary usage, human speech is infused with many free-floating thoughts and disconnected statements, e.g., "When I realize other people do not like me, I feel . . . feel . . . feel . . . well . . . gee . . . what did you think of the rain today?" However, if what human beings say did not conform most of the time to the elementary rules of syntax, communication would be impossible. Extreme or continuous indifference to the rules of syntax is in our culture—and except for certain ritual occasions, perhaps in all cultures—one of the basic symptoms of psychopathy. Witness the "word salads" of hebephrenic schizophrenics and the "mental lapses" of aphasics. (See White 1948: 527; Brown 1958: 293; Goldstein 1948; and Jakobson 1957.)

On occasion some of our Bang Chan informants would ignore syntactic considerations and use the sentence cues as triggering devices for their own unanchored thoughts and preoccupations: "When I realize other people do not like me, I feel . . . that's happened to me sometimes. When you see that other people don't like you, you should avoid them. The Lord Buddha says. . . ." And then the completion might develop into a brief lecture on morality. At other times, the cue would trigger off an autistic explosion: "His most unattractive quality is . . . don't have anything to do with him! He is a wicked person. I do not want to speak to him. He doesn't talk sense. One day while I was fishing, he came along and asked me to have intercourse with him. I cursed him!" (Other data on this informant indicate that she was referring to her estranged husband.) These types of "ungrammatical" responses seem to derive from the social aspects of the interviewing situation—the informant has a friendly listener with a willing ear and thus occasionally ignores the original definition of the SCT task to declaim on his favorite subject [2]—and also from the fact that in social discourse our Thai villagers seem to indulge more in, and have considerably greater tolerance for, autistic thought than do most Americans. That is, the villagers are more accustomed to making and hearing statements that have little apparent "objective" meaning (or in the language of psycholinguistics, "referential" meaning: Brown 1958: 315) but which are symptoms of inner states and preoccupations. The crucial point here is that a listener often does not know—or care—precisely what a speaker is talking about, but simply accepts the other person's utterances as expressions of inner, unknown concerns. Such expressions involve the leaping over of connective thought and syntactic constraints (as in the above example of the lecherous husband) or indifference to the logical currents of the discussion.[3]

---

[2] Sometimes his discussions are simply expressions of phatic communion—the desire to indulge in chitchat for its own sake. (See Malinowski 1923: 315; and Hockett 1958: 585.)

[3] It should be remembered that speech is not only a device for carrying on social interaction but also a mechanism for articulating one's inner preoccupations, whether or not other people understand. It is this latter use (which, incidentally, is ontogenetically the more basic: Piaget 1932; and Langer 1942: 35) about which Bang Chaners seem particularly tolerant. In general, a speaker in Bang Chan is not held very responsible for what he says. One rarely hears in the village—except from prying anthropologists—such charges as "I do not know what you are talking about. Explain yourself." For one thing, such a query would not be particularly polite; and in the villagers' scheme of things, what a person says is really his own business, re-

These various considerations are mentioned simply to note that our Thai informants, like all human beings, occasionally do break through the syntactic constraints of their own language, a condition which is probably aggravated here by the necessity for the SCT testing situation to be a dialogue. Nonetheless, as will be seen in examining the actual SCT responses, these lapses occur relatively infrequently. That they do occur so rarely undoubtedly attests to the power of grammatical patterns to bind human thought processes. By and large our informants are like most people in that they are habituated to think and speak in complete sentences.

The unconscious incentive to complete a sentence and the relatively unpremeditated nature of the completion both help to mitigate the potentially sensitive nature of the SCT "questions" and thus the tendency to resist answering them. However, the third and most important factor is our informants' familiarity with these sentences as declarative statements rather than as direct interrogations. All the items included in the SCT touch on experiences which although perhaps personally threatening, are quite commonplace. Certainly statements like "When I realize other people do not like me, I feel such and such," portray experiences which most informants have imagined if not actually encountered in daily life; they at least have certain expectations about how they would feel under such circumstances.

---

gardless of how unclear or irrelevant it might sound to others. A related factor may be the sense of the untrustworthiness of other people's statements that Textor (1959) has described as characteristic of Bang Chan discourse. However, untrustworthiness immediately implies a serious interpretation of the speaker's intent, an assumption that his statement is perceived primarily in terms of its truth or falsehood. Although this interpretation is undoubtedly appropriate for many situations, the point here is that the villagers have a considerably broader awareness and appreciation of the various uses of language: much of what people say is also viewed as a verbalization of unexplained fantasy, an articulation of a personal compulsion, or in some contexts, simply as a form of play or "nonsense."

Interpretations of fantasy or "nonsense" always depend of course upon the semantic and structural conventions of a particular language. And a common source of error is the foreign researcher who mistakes his own inability to understand the native language, especially implied meanings and assumptions, for autistic thought. The problem then reduces itself not to whether the anthropologist understands the native speaker but to whether other members of the culture do, and the matter should be checked and settled by the researcher's native assistant or interpreter.

This type of problem arose on occasion in my experience, and although I can recall instances when at my prodding the assistant could tease out into culturally meaningful terms the logic underlying an informant's statement, I can also remember cases when the assistant would concede: "I don't understand him either. A lot of people are like that. They say anything that comes into their minds, even if it doesn't make sense." From the assistant's Thai point of view, however, the latter state of affairs was quite normal and expectable.

It is this easy tolerance for the inexplicable in social discourse—or alternatively, a basic respect for the privacy of another person's thoughts—that seems to distinguish the Thai approach from our own, although we appear to share their attitude in our reaction to the autisms of children.

Yet because it is potentially offensive, it is doubtful that they have ever been faced with the straightforward question: "How do you feel when you realize other people do not like you?" When the problem however is couched in the familiar linguistic frame, "When I realize other people do not like me, I feel . . . ," informants can readily supply the response that they have been conditioned to associate with these words. The SCT is more comfortable than a series of direct questions because it taps the system of relatively unconscious expectations and conditionings which comprise the psychological essence of language and thought.

The SCT and Cross-Cultural Research

The second premise concerns the character of the SCT data and their analysis. It is important to make explicit that the research strategy here is one which places particular emphasis on abstracting from the kaleidoscope of the villagers' thoughts and feelings a series of descriptive and analytic types. Despite their commonplace appearance, the sentences are really brief verbal summations of how informants see themselves reacting in a wide variety of real-life situations. These summations are quite abstract, and much of the graphic detail of Thai personality—as can be had, for example, from the rich description of a life-history document—must be held in temporary abeyance.

As noted earlier, the writer is keenly aware that abstracting a series of analytic types is not the only way nor, in absolute terms, necessarily the best way (if there be such a way) to study personality. The limitations of the approach, particularly its lack of descriptive detail and naturalism, should be apparent. However, the method does have certain intrinsic advantages over other techniques.

First, it emphasizes the cross-cultural significance of our data. Although I can provide little empirical evidence to support this contention (other than what by implication might be found in the work of Schaffner 1948; Farber 1951; Roseborough and Phillips 1953; Fried 1953; Rychlak 1955; Rabin 1959; and Leichty and Rabin 1961—the entire body of cross-cultural SCT material to date) I would argue that *all* human beings, regardless of type or level of culture, must deal with the kinds of problems posed by such simple phrases as "When people annoy me, I . . ."; "When he was praised he . . ."; "He wishes he were. . . ." In our SCT batteries all but four items, designed specifically for Thai culture, have this pan-human emphasis. If this assertion is correct, it would have at least two important implications. On the one hand, from a long-range programmatic point of view, it would suggest that the SCT is an ideal technique for studying the range and variation of human personality. Here is an instrument the units of which seem to have true cross-cultural stimulus value and the responses to which seem genuinely comparable from one human group to another.[4] The only thing which might mitigate these advantages is the fact that both the stimuli and the responses must be mediated by the translation process. But as was indicated earlier, considerable attention has been given to controlling this factor.

The reader should be aware that I am talking about my particular version of the SCT, not the technique as such. Hanfmann and Getzels (1953) have noted that the common label, "Sentence Completion Tech-

---

[4] The claim of universal applicability that is made for the present SCT has also been made at various times for the TAT and Rorschach tests (Henry and Spiro 1953; Hallowell 1945 and 1955b; and Joseph and Murray 1951, among others). Without denying the TAT's and Rorschach's capacity to perform a number of important research functions—and to perform them well—the following points should be kept in mind with regard to this specific issue.

The familiar Murray–Morgan TAT cannot be used in every culture simply because not all people practice agriculture (as is depicted in card 2), use furniture (approximately one-quarter of the set), or even wear clothes (excepting 17BM, all cards portraying people). For such cultures, the stimulus value of the cards seems dubious. Some investigators (W. E. Henry 1947, Gladwin and Sarason 1953, and Lessa and Spiegelman 1954) have retained the principle of the TAT but have departed radically from the original cards by designing sets of pictures suitable only to the local and unique conditions of the cultures they were studying. Although this procedure satisfied their immediate research needs, it has contributed little to cross-cultural studies since the various sets have nothing in common. An alternative procedure, followed by the author in Thailand, DeVos in Japan, and Marshall in India, was to modify the flora, fauna, facial features, furniture, and clothes of the originals but retain the same social situations and aesthetic effects. This method permits cross-cultural comparisons, but only among peasant or more advanced societies —an extensive but incomplete ethnographic sample.

The Rorschach presents similar problems, but on a different level. The non-representational ink blots are clearly less culture-bound than the TAT pictures. However, their essentially pictorial quality creates difficulties in cultures where pictures are unfamiliar (Pilaga, for example; see Schachtel, Henry, and Henry 1942) or where graphic symbolism, particularly abstract graphic symbolism, has strong religious connotations (tribes of Central Australia, for example). In contrast to both the Rorschach and TAT, the SCT uses a medium which is truly universal—language.

Finally, assuming that the above difficulties may be resolved—Hallowell (1955a) calls them "administrative problems"—it should be remembered that the Rorschach, TAT, and SCT are not in competition with each other but serve different, although not mutually exclusive, research purposes. The Rorschach focuses on perceptual processes and the control and expression of inner promptings; the TAT on social needs, sentiments, and perceptions; and the SCT on reactions to realistic situational forces. In a sense, the three techniques emphasize different points of two underlying analytic dimensions: (a) inner determined as opposed to situationally determined behavior; and (b) unrealistic as opposed to realistic stimuli. The Rorschach falls on the inner determined and unrealistic sides of these continua; the SCT on the situationally determined and realistic sides; and the TAT in between. Again, without denying the importance of studying the inner determined and unrealistically stimulated aspects of personality, I would argue that the *primary* task of culture-personality research is to study personality in terms of realistically defined, albeit abstractly conceived, situations. A not too dissimilar point of view can be found in Linton (1945: 86–89).

nique," frequently makes one forget that variations in the context and form of sentence fragments actually make different versions of the SCT into entirely different "tests," leading to major differences in results and interpretations. Failure to recognize this obvious fact has led to some specious arguments (Lorge and Thorndike 1941 *vs.* Sacks and Levy 1952, for example) about the relative effectiveness of "the" instrument.

My point of view, of course, is that one can design an SCT to investigate *anything,* from cabbages to kings. The very nature of language—or more precisely, one of its defining characteristics, its "productivity" or "open-endedness"—permits this. (By "productivity" I mean, following Hockett 1959, that a speaker may say something that never before has been said or heard.) In this light, what is distinctive about the present work is not the fact that an SCT is being used but rather that the language of this particular SCT describes a number of universal social and psychological problems.

Second, the technique also helps to bring into focus an issue that is particularly crucial to cross-cultural personality studies. My primary task was of course to describe and analyze the villagers' predispositions in a number of areas of psychological concern: aggression, anxiety, dependency, and the like. There were originally thirteen such areas which, on the basis of prevailing ethno-psychological theory and practice, were presumed to be of major importance in the psychic lives of the informants. It should be recognized, therefore, that in selecting these areas I committed myself to the premise that there are in fact a number of analytic issues crosscutting all societies which are crucial to the psychosocial functioning of the members of these societies. This should not be taken lightly, because it is only on the basis of such a premise that a comparative science of personality may develop.

Such a science does not as yet exist, at least as a coherent, systematic corpus of theory and fact. Kroeber is absolutely right when he says (1955a: 303): "Culture and personality studies are being pursued with intensity and devotion, but one feels that they are popping off in diverse and unaccountable directions much like a string of fire-crackers. One inquirer is interested in tensions, another in Rorschachs, another wants to experiment on frustration; but in effect each starts off on his own—except when a string of them go in for a fad like toilet training. . . ."

Yet, there has been a steady flame setting off all these firecrackers: the search, at times undeniably ill-planned and unreflective, for a set of abstract, analytic categories by which the personalities of all peoples can be described and compared. Papers by Kluckhohn (1953, 1954a, 1954b), Hallowell (1950, 1953), Spiro (1954), Inkeles and Levinson (1954), and Kroeber himself (1955a, 1955b) on the psychological universals in human behavior suggest that there are now sufficiently solid theoretical and empirical grounds upon which to build such an undertaking. Inkeles and Levinson deal with the problem directly (1954: 989–990):

> One promising approach is to concentrate, for purposes of comparative analysis, on a limited number of psychological issues . . . that meet at least the following criteria. First, they should be found in adults universally, as a function of both maturational potentials common to man and of sociocultural characteristics common to human societies. Second, the manner in which they are handled should have functional significance for the individual personality as well as for the social system, in that their patterning in the individual will affect his readiness to establish, accept, maintain, or change a given sociocultural pattern. A further task, one that will take longer to carry out, is to develop a set of descriptive categories for the empirical analysis of each issue.[5]

Toward this end, Inkeles and Levinson present a provisional list of analytic issues, some of which are replicated in the Thai study: relation to authority, conception of self, bases for maintaining inner equilibrium, major forms of anxiety and ways of dealing with them, modes of cognitive functioning, styles of expressive behavior, and the handling of major dispositions such as aggression, dependency, and curiosity.

In formulating the various issues to be included in the SCT, I borrowed from Inkeles and Levinson and the other writers noted above. However, like them, I wish to note that this list of categories is neither exhaustive nor definitive. In fact, because of limitations of time and instrument design, some of the areas proposed above—cognitive functioning, for example—had to be ignored. Others were also ignored during the write-up because the materials elicited were not in my opinion sufficiently meaningful or revealing. The value of our list lies not in its formal completeness but rather in the fact that the issues which are included seem, on the basis of knowledge presently available, to be of universal psychological importance. This is a beginning.

A third attribute of the SCT, related to the above, deserves comment. This concerns the abstract nature of the SCT items.

A fundamental problem in all cross-cultural personality research is not

---

[5] In a later paper (1956), Inkeles qualified one of these criteria by noting that there are probably many personality complexes which are functionally significant to individuals, but which have little discernible relevance to the functioning of social systems. Much depends here on how one defines "social system" and "personality"—particularly "levels" of personality. Inkeles, for example, draws a clear theoretical distinction between "basic personality" and "social personality," the latter being comprised only of those traits which are necessary for the effective maintenance or change of the social system.

only the specification of a series of pan-human psychological issues as described above, but the selection of a research tool capable of obtaining empirical data that *accurately* reflect these issues in the various cultures studied. Aggression, anxiety, dependency, and the like may be universal human dispositions, but the causes and circumstances pertaining to them vary considerably from culture to culture. This is of course a basic anthropological truism (see particularly Whiting 1954 and Lewis 1955). Perhaps the best theoretical formulation of the problem from a research point of view can be found in an unpublished paper by Suchman (1955; see also Sears 1961) where the matter is framed in terms of what is called "concept equivalence" *vs.* "data or item equivalence." Or translated into our research operations: given the fact that the concept "anxiety" as applied to Thai culture is equivalent to the concept "anxiety" as applied to American culture, what kinds of items will bring forth *equivalent* empirical data from both cultures relevant to this concept?

My decision in dealing with this question was to design items which were sufficiently abstract so that they could be used in any culture with assurance that the empirical problems which they described were accurate and equivalent representations of the concepts.[6] In essence, statements such as *"He was most afraid of . . . ," "When something worried him, he usually . . ."* were derived directly from the concept of anxiety, by-passing culturally specific definitions of anxiety; the experiences portrayed by the items are in themselves descriptively universal rather than culture-bound. Cultural specificity—which is of course the central aim of this research—enters when informants react to these experiences in their completions. From an operational point of view, therefore, the requirements of concept and item equivalence were effectively merged.

A final aspect of the SCT, of an entirely different order from the above, merits attention. This concerns those general methodological advantages which the SCT enjoys as an organized, semi-structured research technique.

First, the SCT permits the field worker to present his research interests to his informants rather than wait for manifestations of these interests to emerge spontaneously from the behavior or remarks of the informants. Data collected by this method is by no means any better than that obtained, for example, by observational techniques, but it is more complete. If an investigator wants to know how an adult villager would react to being struck by another person or what the villager thinks about when he is

---

[6] Florence Kluckhohn (1960: 6–7) in her effort to develop a technique for the cross-cultural study of value orientations comes to a similar conclusion. She says that the "more highly generalized" an item was, the more readily it could be translated for use in another culture.

alone, he might have to wait months before an act of overt physical aggression actually occurred, or before an informant volunteered some of his reveries.[7] When these events do occur, it is exceedingly difficult for the analyst to assess how typical or deviant the event may be under the circumstances, whether it is characteristic of villagers of a particular age or sex and what other individuals may do or say in similar situations. Rather than depend upon what is essentially a "catch-as-catch-can" approach, the SCT brings the research problems to the informant and asks him to deal with them directly. It should be remembered that although the resulting data are not as naturalistic as observational materials, they are always the product of the villagers' own voluntaristic inclinations: their responses represent their own internal views of how to deal with the problems posed by the introductory phrases.

A corollary to the above is the fact that the SCT presents to a large number of individuals what are essentially the same stimulus situations. The primary advantage here is that it provides a solid empirical basis upon which to make statements about how typical or deviant a response may be.

The Selective Nature of the Responses

The third premise follows much of the preceding, but merits special consideration because of the cross-cultural phrasing of the study. In a sense, it is the basic methodological principle of all anthropological research.

In examining the SCT responses, it soon becomes apparent that the majority of our informants' statements make perfect sense and are the types of reactions that conceivably could be made by any human being. The word choice and style of many of the responses are of course inimitably Thai. For example, *"The most important thing in his life is . . . ohhh! . . .* having or not having something to eat. If you have something to eat: good. If you have nothing: trouble. We people are born in order to find things to fill our mouths and stomachs. Nobody can take his property and money with him when he dies." But the expressed meanings of the responses (in this case, practical survival) are not, despite perhaps anthropological expectations, alien or extraordinary.

The point to be emphasized is that although the villagers' SCT responses may not seem immediately familiar, they do fall well within the range of what is *objectively possible*. It is this element of objective possi-

---

[7] From an ethnographic point of view, the fact that such events do occur so rarely is not without significance. It is additional behavioral evidence of the amount of aggression control exercised by the villagers and of the fact that they prefer not to wear their hearts on their sleeves.

bility that lies at the heart of the SCT analysis. As Kluckhohn has said (1959: 247; see also 1951: 421–422):

The most specific quality of anthropological research arises from its preoccupation with culture. This concept (in the technical, anthropological sense) refers to those *selective* ways of feeling, thinking, and reacting that distinguish one group from another. . . . In the strict sense, we can speak of culture only when there are two or more objectively possible and functionally effective means or modes of meeting the same need, . . . and a given group exhibits a consistent and stylized preference for one path to the goal among a number of alternatives that are—from the observer's point of view—all open.

In this light, what is most significant about the responses is not that they are in themselves descriptively unusual, nor even that other cultural groups could not share some of them (the principle of "limited possibilities," supported by linguistic constraints, undoubtedly operates here), but rather that of all the objectively potential ways in which to deal with the SCT situations, the villagers select a few distinctive ways to the exclusion of others. In the example above, "the most important thing in his life" is *not* "his family" (the need for close social affiliation; being a source or recipient of succorance), his "love affair" (emotional-sexual need), "knowing himself" (realistic assessment of one's capacity for specific achievement), "passing his examination" (the need for status and accomplishment), or any other equally feasible response. Rather the response is "having or not having something to eat" (elemental subsistence). At bottom, it is the selective aspect of the SCT responses—in contrast to their strangeness or familiarity, which are secondary descriptive characteristics—that defines their essential "Thai-ness."

For readers who may be surprised by the interpretive labels given the above responses, it should be noted that we have touched here upon what is probably *the* crucial anthropological problem. I have tried briefly to suggest what these responses, if they were given, might mean—but in Thai, not American, terms. This compounds our interpretive problem considerably. The fact that such alternative responses are not typical is in itself, as we have just indicated, of extreme importance. However, if they were given, their meanings would not necessarily be the same to the villagers as they are to us. By way of illustration: it is hard to imagine any Bang Chaner completing the statement *"The most important thing in his life is . . ."* with the words "knowing himself." Few villagers are that introspective or self-objectifying. However, if by chance an informant did offer this completion, it would certainly not mean, as it does among some American sub-cultural groups, "the need for self-acceptance, personal identity, freedom from intra-psychic tensions," etc. (See Erikson 1950, 1954, 1959; Riesman

1950; and Wheelis 1958.) At best, it would suggest that the Thai informant was faced with a difficult problem external to himself—perhaps finding a job or a spouse, or thinking of his future—and was appraising his ability to deal with that problem. Also, such an appraisal would have a strong constraining element: the necessity to control one's hopes and desires (perhaps for the hypothetical job or spouse) in order to avoid potential pain or disappointment; in essence, "beware of your limitations; do not forget your station." This is in turn supported by certain Buddhist concepts, such as *ʔubeegkhaa*, or stoical indifference to the vicissitudes of life, among others.

Whether there is *any* way to express handily in Thai the Western notion of "the need for self-acceptance" is doubtful. Most villagers are too thoroughly narcissistic to require such a concept in their cognitive maps. Alternatively, there are other more direct ways of saying what "knowing myself" might mean in Thai, for example, "controlling my desires," "knowing whether I have the ability to do the job," or by referring directly to Buddhist doctrine. As such, these statements would be an expression of piety or the bolstering of one's self-confidence (or steeling oneself against failure) rather than psychic introspection.

A similar interpretive problem exists with the completion "his family." Because Thai kinship relations are so strongly influenced by concepts of benevolent superiority and dependent inferiority, most expressions of the need for affiliation with the family immediately imply the related need of succorance: security, support, protection, and sympathy, either as source or beneficiary.

The point of these comments is that the responses must always be first interpreted in the villagers' terms, not ours. Once made, precisely by explanatory notes such as these, these interpretations become part of the "data" and serve as a basis for our analysis. It should be recognized, however, that anthropological mythology (and these particular examples) to the contrary, not *all* the responses are interpretively dissimilar. When a villager says, "*When he hit me, I* . . . must hit him back," he means precisely the same thing we do. The point, therefore, is to be extremely sensitive to the possibility of differential meanings, underscore and explain it when it occurs, and use the native interpretation as a prerequisite and corrective to our own. For a brief but brilliant theoretical discussion of this problem see Bohannan 1959.

The Psychological Meaning of the Responses

The fourth premise concerns the psychological "meaning" of the responses. There are several aspects of this problem which require specification.

First, the informants' reactions to the imagined situations portrayed in the SCT items represent their *predispositions* to act in the manner indicated, rather than literal descriptions of how they would behave in real life.[8] They indicate a psychological readiness or propensity. Any overt behavior is the result of several determinants, only one of which is the individual's predispositions. Other factors include the nature and purpose of the reality situation; the individual's changing moods and skills; and in social situations, the expectations of the other person, his behavioral cues, and ego's perception of them, as well as the relative statuses of the participants (of extreme importance in Bang Chan). All these determinants—and probably others as well—come into play during any particular event, and the slightest change in one may result in different and unexpected forms of overt behavior. It is precisely because so many factors do lie behind the occurrence of an event that predictability in human affairs is so difficult. Yet, because to a large extent a person creates and structures for himself the situations in which he is involved, and because in these situations he is objectively free to respond in any number of different ways, his predisposition to act in a particular way is crucial in determining what actually does occur. Witness Rychlak's students. Basically it is the individual's organized system of predispositions, and their repeated—but not invariable—manifestation in action, which gives his overt behavior a certain consistency and unity, and which allows us to ascribe to him a particular "personality."

In real-life situations, however, the individual's predispositions are often obscured to the observer by more obvious factors such as those mentioned above, *e.g.*, the social climate and the expectations and status of others. A major advantage of an unstructured instrument like the SCT is

---

[8] Examination of the SCT literature on this point has been both time-consuming and intriguing. Despite the fact that there probably have been more than two hundred studies involving the use of the SCT—Levy (1952: 192) reports 135 studies between 1946 and 1951 alone—this writer has been able to discover only one, Rychlak's work on Japanese students in the United States (Rychlak 1955, and Rychlak, Mussen, and Bennett 1957), which concerns itself directly with the relationship between SCT responses and overt behavior. SCT responses have been correlated with other tests, attitude scales, psycho-galvanic skin responses, informants', psychiatrists', and teachers' reports, and measurements of "adjustment," but apparently only once with measures of overt behavior in the same areas covered by the items. Rychlak found that students who expressed a high degree of optimism and "sociality" on an SCT administered soon after their arrival in the United States (examples: *"To me the future looks . . . bright"*; *"To others I am . . . very sociable"*) were the same individuals who months later tended to participate in bull sessions and visit American homes; conversely, individuals who exhibited on the SCT an involvement with interpersonal conflicts (examples: *"My bosses are . . . intolerant"*; *"I failed because . . . others didn't understand me"*) later tended to use their leisure time in reading and avoided social clubs and parties. On the basis of these findings, Rychlak views the SCT as "a remarkably efficient predictor of the quality of the individual's social relationships."

that it gives the informant extraordinary latitude to express his predispositions with relative freedom from these social constraints. The social constraints which do exist are self-defined and self-imposed. Other than being required to make sense, the informant has complete freedom to structure the situation posed by the SCT fragment as he pleases. His predispositions emerge unobscured as he assumes all the roles of the real-life drama, defining the situation as he chooses, placing himself and the imagined others in context, and then reacting to the situation. Although the process is a subjective and imaginative one, it retains at all times its ties to reality by the highly realistic nature of the stimuli. The predispositions thus revealed are realistic and ostensive rather than deep-lying or hidden although, as was suggested earlier, their analytic significance derives not from the manifest meanings of the responses but from more general, underlying denotations.

A second aspect of the responses concerns their psychological primacy. It is a fundamental postulate of this work that the informants' reactions represent their primary or dominant responses to the situations portrayed in the SCT items. This by no means implies that the absence of another kind of response indicates the absence of the capacity to have that sentiment nor that such an alternative sentiment is potentially inexpressible; it does mean, however, that our informants are not predisposed to react in that way.

Earlier in this chapter it was argued that the responses are "relatively unpremeditated" and that an incomplete sentence "taps the relatively unconscious expectations and conditionings which comprise the psychological essence of language and thought." Although these assertions are valid—certainly as contrasted with the results of direct questions—the word "relatively" must not be glossed over. The actual process of constructing an utterance always involves a great deal of psychic editing, and few people ever say what they "really" want to say in the sense of being completely unpremeditative. This was of course one of Freud's earliest (1904) lessons. But somewhere in the process of split-second decision making that goes on within the mind (Freud hypothesized that most of it takes place in the pre-conscious) the individual must make a choice and we have to assume that this choice, as revealed by his articulated statement, is his principal response. The individual might well have said something else. But the point is that he did *not*. The proffered statement was in fact the dominant one.

This raises a question that has been the subject of some discussion in the anthropological literature and which is particularly germane to the present analysis. A cursory review of the SCT data immediately indicates that the villlagers phrase many, although not most, of their responses in terms of cultural ideals, that is, in terms of precepts to which behavior should conform. (For example: *"The best way to treat a subordinate is . . .* to speak to him with kind and agreeable words"; *"When he thinks of his father, he thinks of . . .* the goodness and kindness his father has done for him."*) This is not a universal pattern since definitions of the ideal are ambiguous, lacking, or inappropriate for many of the items; also, such definitions seem not to be applied to items which imply immediate action. However, they do appear with sufficient frequency to be noticeable.

None of this should be surprising, inasmuch as viewing behavior in terms of "the good" and "the proper" is a central characteristic of the villagers' thought and idiom. They tend, *considerably* more than Americans, to evaluate (in an ethical sense) people and events rather than describe them, and even to describe by evaluating. Ask most villagers: "What kind of a person is so-and-so?" and their replies will consistently be in terms of whether he is "bad" or "good," rather than in terms of non-evaluative description, *e.g.,* he is "funny," "passive," "interesting." The words, *khon maj dii* and *khon dii* ("a bad person" and "a good person") are two of the most frequently occurring items in the Thai lexicon. One might epigrammatically characterize much of the villagers' thought as "super-ego-dominated." That this mode of thought should be applied to many of the SCT situations is hardly unexpected.[9]

Having recognized this tendency, however, there is the problem of assessing its psychocultural meaning. Do such appeals to the ideal, especially as applied to the self, in any way weaken our definition of the responses as "predispositions to action?" Are many of the responses mere verbalisms that have little to do with real behavior?

A number of theorists, notably Murdock (1940 and 1954) and Kluckhohn (1943*b* and 1951) have taken the position that cultural behavior should be distinguished into two fundamentally different forms: ideal patterns and real patterns. The former are "those norms which are verbalized as the ideals to which behavior should conform" (Murdock 1954: 22); and the latter, patterns of actual, overt behavior. Opler has taken issue with the necessity for this distinction, and has argued (1948: 116):

> My own feeling is that the concern over precepts or ideal patterns which contrast with or stand apart from behavior is a pleasant distraction which will not get us very far. In my opinion the disparity between rule and behavior in society has been greatly exaggerated. Actually, behavior remains remarkably close to rules or precepts which are

---

[9] This same characteristic has been described in other contexts (Wilson and Phillips 1958, Phillips 1958, L. M. Hanks 1959*a* and 1959*b*) as the essentially moral nature of the villagers' universe: the tendency, largely implicit, for Bang Chaners to perceive events of the most diverse kinds within an ethical frame of reference. It might well be, as Redfield had argued for many years (1941, 1953, and 1956) that such a cognitive orientation is characteristic of all peasant peoples.

considered of moment by the group. I think that it can be demonstrated that when precept and activity draw too far apart, a modification of one or the other is likely to take place to close up the gap.

In assessing my psychological test materials, I take the following position with regard to this issue. The distinction between the ideal and the real is an analytic requirement because obviously there are some instances where the two patterns are not congruent. However, once such distinction has been made there is no inherent necessity to assume that there *must* be a gap between the two patterns or if there is a gap, to assume that it must be especially wide. One will inevitably encounter in Bang Chan cases where subordinates are not spoken to "with kind and agreeable words." But on the whole, the extent to which real behavior does accord with this precept is impressive. For the most part, it is not a mere verbalism but rather a viable guide to action: a subordinate who is not treated with kind and agreeable words will not (depending of course on other situational factors as well) long maintain his ties to his superior. This same reasoning applies to the majority of the cases in which informants couch their responses in terms of cultural ideals.

A third aspect of the responses concerns the psychological "level" at which they will be interpreted. Because of the highly realistic nature of the completions, the necessity to interpret them in Thai terms (which precludes "blind analyses"—see DuBois 1944) and the necessity to work with the pooled responses of many individuals, our interpretations will not go psychodynamically very "deep." On the other hand, neither will we remain at the level of the manifest meanings of the responses. Although an informant's completion may represent a precise description of the way he would behave in real life, and in many cases does, it is more sensible from an analytic standpoint to view the response as a symptom of an underlying, more generalized, psychological orientation. The reasons for this are twofold: first, many of the responses which are superficially different seem to express simply alternate facets of a single, underlying predisposition; second, and more important, we must remember that on theoretical grounds personality characteristics are not, as Inkeles and Levinson point out (1954: 981) "phenotypic, behavior-descriptive terms, but rather are higher level abstractions that refer to stable, generalized dispositions or modes of functioning and may take a great variety of concrete behavioral forms."

In these terms, a statement such as *"When he saw that others avoided him, he* . . . *also avoids them"* indicates not only a person's desire not to associate with those who avoid him but, more important, an underlying, more general disposition *to accept and maintain a breakdown in social relations.* Moreover, the latter interpretation also encompasses such varying responses as: ". . . must not speak to them because they are bad. They like to look down upon people" and ". . . probably was not generous with them, so they avoided him." The significance of this underlying interpretation becomes even more apparent when the three responses are contrasted with other possible but unoffered completions which belong to totally different interpretive categories, for example, ". . . tried to make up with them" or ". . . asked them why?" signifying *attempts to reintegrate or understand the interpersonal rupture* and ". . . felt terribly hurt," indicating *emotional pain or disturbance*.

A Working Conception of Modal Personality

Our fifth and final premise is concerned with developing a workable conception of modal personality despite the inevitable paradoxes which attend such an endeavor.

The fundamental problem here is that in abstracting out the psychological similarities which the villagers share with one another, we become unavoidably involved in the difficulties of working with "conjugate variables"; that is, the more we concern ourselves with the commonality of a personality trait, the less we simultaneously learn about the role of that trait in the functioning of the individual members of the sample. The significance of this is not so much that we sacrifice an understanding of individuals for an understanding of the group, but that in so doing we must also sacrifice some of the depth and perceptiveness of our analysis. A successful personality study is in large measure achieved by descriptive contrast: we learn more about human beings the less they appear like other people. When subtle individual differences must be submerged for purposes of group characterization, the resulting descriptions must necessarily be less sensitive and precise.

The root of the problem lies in the fact that our basic units of analyses are individuals who, despite all the similarities they share as members of Thai culture, are obviously different from one another in specifics. Moreover, as Wallace points out in a recent article (1961a: 147–148), from the point of view of culture-personality theory, they *must* have certain psychological differences:

> The problem of psychic unity is sometimes obscured by our tendency to regard human societies as populations and not as groups when we make psychological statements. A population of individuals may be described without references to their interrelationships; but a group cannot be considered apart from its organizational structure. Thus physical, demographic, or personality characteristics of the members of a population can be stated, explicitly or implicitly, as a statistical distribution on one or more dimensions, and to the extent that the data

permit, some measure or estimate of central tendency can be calculated which will allow the attribution of some value or range on one or more dimensions to all, or a specified sub-population, of the population itself. . . .

But such predicates, universally applicable to all members of a population, are inadequate for the psychological analysis of that population as a group, as an elementary consideration reveals: most culturally organized groups not merely permit but require that their members perform different roles in interaction. . . .

Although Wallace does not state it in so many words, it is apparent that he is referring to differences in age, sex, and occupational roles, or to any other roles that may be deemed important, and is assuming that the individuals who perform the roles have in some respects different personality types. (Whether the latter assumption is completely valid is still another problem. For a provocative discussion of the analytic complexity of the personality-role relationship, of the non-congruence which may occur, and of consequent psychological adjustments see Levinson 1959; Nadel 1957 also touches on the issue.) In any case, it is clear that whatever psychic unity informants have as members of the same culture, they are differentiated from each other on at least two counts: (1) their individual life experiences and genetic-constitutional backgrounds which ultimately give them each a unique personality; and (2) their performance of different social roles.

These differentiae are of course virtually self-evident. But what is not self-evident—nor easy to decide—is how much emphasis should be given to them in formulating or qualifying our conception of Thai peasant modal personality. Any decision that we make is from some point of view unsatisfactory. Should we treat our informants solely as individuals, and pursue our analysis with rigor, we would get an increasingly refined picture of the uniqueness of these individuals but, at the same time, a decreasingly clear picture of their cultural or shared characteristics. The analysis would undoubtedly be more precise but, in effect, we would be studying "idioverses"—idiosyncratic versions of culture (Mead 1958)—with little basis for determining what is culturally typical or deviant. In fact, questions of the normative or variant would become logically irrelevant. On the other hand, should we group the informants into age or sex groups and contrast the responses of these groups, it might well seem that the personality differences between men and women, for example, are greater than the similarities, or even that Thai women are more like Navaho or American women than they are like Thai men. Although I suspect that culture makes for greater psychological similarity than does sex and, as Sharp has pointed out (Sharp et al. 1953) Bang Chan culture is, from a cross-cultural point of view, impressive for its slight differentiation of the adult roles of the sexes, such findings are not empirically impossible. Finally, should we de-emphasize the distinctions between individuals and role-defined sub-groups, and consider all the responses as a whole, we would as suggested earlier be in the best possible position for determining the villagers' modal personality but would proportionately lack analytic precision. There would always be some intra-sample differences—as far down as the individual level—which the critic could point to as requiring discrimination, although such discrimination would obviously have to be achieved at the cost of group identification.

Given these various alternatives, each of which has its merits and shortcomings, what should the analyst do? I have decided to conform to the principal aim of this research and focus primarily on total group responses, that is, on those abstracted psychological similarities which all or, more realistically, large numbers of our individual informants share with one another. Operationally, this entails investigating the responses of all informants on each SCT item rather than those of each informant on all items, and explicating the major underlying psychological theme or themes of these responses.

The inclusion of both the singular "theme" and plural "themes" in the preceding sentence is not only intentional but crucial to our formulation of modal personality. Its significance will perhaps best be seen by contrasting our approach with the two prevailing points of view governing most modal personality formulations. On the one hand, the majority of the culture-personality and particularly "national character" studies of recent years have been characterized by an assumption of psychological *unimodality*; that is, an assumption that the culture being investigated has such a high degree of psychological homogeneity that it can be portrayed as having a *single* personality pattern, with perhaps a few deviant sub-types. The assumption is based partially on precedents established within the history of ethnographic method (Herskovits 1954); partially on unconscious aesthetic considerations involved in the presentation of data (Opler 1948 on Benedict); and partially on the apparent validity of the concept in some areas of psychocultural functioning in which, once established, it is tacitly extended to include all areas. Even Wallace's sophisticated study of the modal personality of the Tuscarora (1952) is based on the premise of unimodality, although his aim is to find out precisely how *unimodal* the Tuscarora actually are.

Whatever attractiveness the premise of unimodality may have, it is clearly an oversimplification of psycho-ethnographic facts. Human beings in any culture are simply too complex to be of the same psychological stamp in all respects. In his recent paper (1961a), Wallace points out that a research design for the study of modal personality which involves only twenty binary dimensions (which is considerably less than is actually employed in most Rorschach analyses) will yield up to 1,048,576 structural types, to which Wallace adds, "the uniformity of the population on each dimension must be impressive, or the types must be very crudely defined, before any one type is likely to acquire prevalence over any substantial proportion of the group. . . ."

Having recognized the oversimplification of the unimodal approach, however, there is no inherent necessity to go the the opposite extreme and posit a complete *multimodality*. Yet this seems to be the position taken by Inkeles and Levinson (1954) and Kaplan (1954, 1957, and Kaplan, Rickers–Ovsiankina, and Joseph 1956) who, genuinely disturbed by the stereotypy and lack of sophistication of the unimodal viewpoint, argue that cultural groups are characterized by a plurality of personality patterns. Kaplan's arguments are particularly compelling in that he bolsters them with empirical cross-cultural evidence, although he himself admits (1954) that his results may be a consequence of his particular sorting and categorizing techniques. He concludes his comparative study of Navaho and Zuni TAT's with the statement that (1957): "The influence of culture on personality does not appear to create a common personality configuration in its members, but instead tends to foster a variety of personality tendencies in small groups or clusters of individuals while leaving many aspects of personality free to vary without respect to group membership."

My position, in comparison, is that the cases for complete unimodality and complete multimodality are both overstated. What both viewpoints seem to overlook is the likelihood of there being *specific areas* of psychocultural functioning in which a high degree of homogeneity exists and *other specific areas* in which a high degree of heterogeneity comes into play. This more flexible formulation not only provides a more realistic picture of modal personality than can be had from ascriptions of wholesale uniformity and diversity but directs our attention to identifying the areas of differential frequencies and attempting to account for them. For example, I suspect that those areas characterized by a high degree of homogeneity are ones likely to be surrounded by strong cultural sanctions, or are areas of psychological "focus" (psychological parallels to Herskovits' "cultural focus," [10] as it were) or, perhaps, are areas of greatest cultural conditioning; conversely, I would think that areas of high heterogeneity most likely do

[10] Although Herskovits seems to have changed his definition of "cultural focus" over time (1945 and 1948), his first definition is most relevant to our present meaning: "that area of activity or belief where the greatest awareness of form exists, the most discussion of values is heard, the widest difference in structure is to be discerned." However, unlike his formulation, which in practice assumes only one focus in one culture, our use of the term presupposes that a culture can have a number of psychological foci.

not involve important social stakes (although they may involve very important personal ones, their highly charged personal nature perhaps being the very source of the heterogeneity). In these terms, I would expect Bang Chan SCT responses to be highly unimodal in the realm of authority—an area of sharp psychological focus—but relatively multimodal in the area of friendship. In any case, it would seem to me that whatever the ultimate reasons for an area being unimodal or multimodal, the identification of these areas is in itself an important task.

In the light of these remarks, I have tried to avoid establishing rigid rules about the number of major themes which may emerge from the responses to the various SCT items. The discussion which follows, and the SCT material itself, is organized in terms of specific areas of psychological functioning, and a table accompanies each SCT item. The tables are organized thematically and are designed to exemplify characteristic responses for each theme discussed in the test, although some of the minor themes and sub-themes are excluded for the sake of simplicity. The number of responses given under each thematic heading reflects the *approximate* percentage of all responses which are included in that theme. A theme is defined as an underlying, generalized psychological orientation encompassing the raw responses of two or more informants—the supposition being that it takes at least two to make a theme shared or "cultural." [11] The determination of a theme is explicitly weighted in the unimodal direction but is constrained by the nature of the responses themselves. No explicit criteria have been established for deciding the number of themes which may emerge before declaring an item, and the area it represents, either unimodal or multimodal. In fact, in terms of our empirical operations, these terms are viewed simply as ideal types. Also, it should be remembered that some of our responses are multidimensional in nature; that is, like much communication they simultaneously reveal several meanings and are interpretable from several perspectives. In this case, each perspective can conceivably yield a different number of themes. The number of simultaneous themes that occur are determined solely by the patterning of the responses themselves. Given these considerations, the statements that are made about the unimodal or multimodal nature of an area are phrased simply in terms of general comparisons as we move from one area to another. Since we are not using any fine statistical methods, this procedure is clearly the most efficient to follow.

---

[11] It is recognized, of course, that it is possible for responses to be shared by two or more informants solely on the bases of fortuitous factors or on the basis of the principle of limited possibilities. All human behavior, cultural or otherwise, is ultimately limited by such simple statistical considerations.

V

Analysis: The SCT's Exploration
of Thai Personality[1]

Attitudes Toward Authority

The first area to be dealt with is in a sense the easiest. Thai attitudes toward authority represent what is perhaps the most explicitly expressed and highly ramified area of their social psychological life. The notion of authority—a sense of superordination and subordination—is an intrinsic part of their linguistic structure, it being impossible to address or refer to a person without indicating his social status relative to the self; two-week-old infants are taught to *waj,* or offer the gesture of obeisance to superiors; during elections, villagers say that they are going to vote for the prime minister because "he is our Master. He has been very good and kind to us. He is like our father, and we are like his children"; the entire structure of the family is predicated on a system of superordination and subordination, even to the extent of considering a twin born a few minutes ahead of his sibling the latter's social superior. Examples expressive of this emphasis in the workaday life of the villagers could be cited endlessly.

What is impressive in the data to follow is not only the near unanimity of villagers in responding positively to what are essentially neutral authority situations, but the tendency on the part of a large number to respond positively to the authority situation even when the authority figure is avowedly wrong. Many of their responses also make quite explicit the underlying ethical justifications for the authority system.

The first item, *"When the phuujiŋjaj told him to do it, he . . . ,"* is a

---

[1] Words and phrases appearing in parentheses in the responses on the following pages are for purposes of clarification. The few Thai words appearing in the responses are either "complex concepts" or "difficult to translate" terms, and have been retained mainly for those readers familiar with Thai. At the top of the table, the English language item that was originally prepared for the villagers appears first; it is followed by the best English translation of the actual Thai item given to informants, including the Thai pronouns that were used. Intra-sample differences (age, sex, religion, economic position), where important, are indicated in the text, not the tables.

simple statement of a common experience. A *phuujiŋjaj* generally means a "big person" or "big man," although in many contexts it has the same connotations as the American slang term, "big shot." (Occasionally when I used the term with Bangkokians I was laughingly told that it was not a "nice" word; however, Bang Chaners used it and responded to it in an entirely matter-of-fact way.) As it appeared in the SCT interviews, the item was clearly an abstract phrasing of a generic kind of authority situation, and could have referred to any individual the informant deemed to be a *phuujiŋjaj*.

TABLE 1

When the phuujiŋjaj *told him to do it, he* . . .
When the phuujiŋjaj *tells* raw *to work,* raw . . .

DIRECT, POSITIVE RESPONSE:	86%	had to do it.
		had to do it well, to be worthy of the *phuujiŋjaj*'s trust.
		had to hurry and do it.
		ought to do it *riab-rɔɔj* (in the neatest way).
		did as he was ordered.
		did it in accordance with the *phuujiŋjaj*'s wishes.
		did what he had been told to do.
		had to do it, so he would get credit (praise and goodness for doing it).
CONDITIONAL (PROPRIETY):	7%	ought to do only work which is proper work. If the work were not proper, he would avoid doing it.
CONDITIONAL (ABILITY):	5%	if we cannot do it, tell him we cannot. If we can do it, do it.
"RECONCILIATION":	—	if he knew the order was right, he was glad to carry it out; if it was a wrong order, according to the regulations, but if it was necessary, he had to carry it out. And when he had an opportunity, he would point out what was wrong with the order.

Examination of the responses indicates a single, overwhelming disposition on the part of villagers to accept and act upon the superior's authority. Four informants condition their response on the necessity, propriety, or reasonableness of the superior's order, but even in these cases the initial tendency is to respond positively; three others condition their response on their own capacity to fulfill the authority's expectations; and one villager does not reply. But all others, 86 percent, respond directly and positively to the authority demands made upon them.

The vast majority of these simply do, or feel they have to do, what the *phuujiŋjaj* tells them. Some of the sub-types of this major response, however, are interesting in their own right. Three individuals hurry to do what they are told, while two others, all young females, are concerned with being appealing and conscientious in their conformity. Three Bang Chaners are interested mainly in gaining the superior's praise, trust, or approval. On the other hand, two others view the situation largely in terms of naked power, e.g. ". . . did it; otherwise the *phuujiŋjaj* might beat her." Perhaps the most interesting response in the group (the last in table 1) is that of the informant who reacts positively but conditionally at first; then realizes the danger of setting up any condition, and volunteers to fulfill even improper orders (although not without providing justifications); and then realizing what he has done to himself, attempts to smooth over everything later. The afterthought of "reconciliation"—the *attempt* to smooth over and resolve conflicts, often in logically disarming, but psychologically satisfying, ways —is quite characteristic of village thought and shows up sharply in later items. In this particular instance, of course, the informant's resolution makes considerable sense.

From the point of view of the selectivity of the responses, what is perhaps most impressive here is the unanimous acceptance by the villagers of the prerogatives of the authority figure. Although a few informants condition their response on the propriety or appropriateness of his order, not one challenges his right to issue it or uses his authority as a counterpoint to one's own needs. No one tells the *phuujiŋjaj* to "jump in the lake" (or its Thai equivalent), to "mind his own business," or even has the boldness to ask him, "why?" There is no hint of defiance or of any need to undermine the premises of the authority situation.

The next item, *"When he is in the presence of a phuujiŋjaj, he feels . . . ,"* is even more neutral and behaviorally less demanding than the above. The informant does not have to do anything. Although the item produces three closely related themes, not a single informant expresses any negative feelings toward the superior (envy, jealousy). Interestingly, there is no sense of identification with the superior either, that is, ". . . he feels he might want to be a *phuujiŋjaj* himself"; ". . . he feels that he must work hard or obtain the merit to become like him." Informants that might be considered to approach this position, as in the first two responses, are more concerned with basking in the power of the authority than they are with being like him.

The major theme to emerge from the item is the sense of esteem— respect, pleasure, honor, admiration, and gratitude—that informants feel toward the superior. More than 64 percent of the responses are of this general type. Three of these persons (see the second and third examples)

TABLE 2

When he is in the presence of a phuujiŋjaj, *he feels* . . .
When raw *am* (*are*) *in the presence of a* phuujiŋjaj, raw *feel*(*s*) . . .

ESTEEM:	64%	pleased to see the face of a man who has *bun-waasanaa* (good fortune as the result of merit from previous lives). it is good. He will get some knowledge from him. The *phuujiŋjaj* is more intelligent (knowledgeable) than we are. glad that the *phuujiŋjaj* comes to visit her, comes to look after her. respect (for the *phuujiŋjaj*). respects and salutes him. honored, proud, and happy. respect and veneration for the *phuujiŋjaj*.
DISCOMFORT:	25%	that the man is big, but she is not afraid. uncomfortable. He would not be in *phuujiŋjaj*'s presence if it were not necessary. scared of him. He is afraid that the *phuujiŋjaj* might blame him and scold him. anxiously frightened (*kreeŋklua*) because he (the *phuujiŋjaj*) is more fortunate (*mii bunwaasanaa*: has more merit and good fortune from previous lives) than *raw*.
PASSIVITY:	8%	*chəəj-chəəj*; she is not afraid.
"BLESSING":	—	loves and *waj*'s (salutes) the *phuujiŋjaj*.

are especially interesting in that they make relatively explicit the basis of their pleasure: they assume that the superior is helping them or giving them something, as a *phuujiŋjaj* might be expected to do.

The second theme, covering 25 percent of the responses, represents the obverse of the above: a sense of diffidence and self-abnegation that ranges from awe through discomfort to fear of dealing with the superior. From an interpretive point of view, the major analytic difference between this theme and the one above is of course, the object of attention. In this situation the informant cannot forget about himself and intensifies his own sense of subordination. However, with the single exception of the informant who wishes that he were not in the situation, there is no indication that such feelings, or the situation that causes them, are unacceptable to the self. The informants' readiness to articulate them, in fact, implies precisely the opposite. What might be suggested here is that although the internalization of the Thai authority system might not be as painless as overt behavior typically leads one to believe, villagers obviously tolerate such "pain" with little difficulty.

The third theme encompasses the responses of four villagers who by being *chəəj-chəəj* either avoid declaring their feelings toward the superior or shift their attention from their feelings to behaving in a properly passive manner while dealing with the superior. This latter interpretation is based upon a Thai reading of the meaning of a *chəəj-chəəj* response in an authority situaticn. To be stoically passive, to speak only when spoken to, is not only proper but psychologically prudent. Thus, these individuals manage to meet the requirements of the authority situation without really committing themselves.

TABLE 3

When his superior gave him an order which he knew was wrong, he . . .
When a superior gives raw an order that raw know(s) is wrong, raw . . .

DO NOT FULFILL (53%)		
UNELABORATED:	37%	did not do it.
		would not do it.
		did not do it, if it was wrong.
TROUBLED:	16%	was afraid and did not like to do it.
		was uncomfortable in her heart; she did not do it.
DO FULFILL (36%)		
UNELABORATED:	22%	had to do it.
		had to do it. For *raw* to go against him can't be done.
JUSTIFIED:	14%	had to do it, because he had higher status than *raw*. He might very well *daa* (denounce, scold) *raw*, if *raw* didn't do it.
		sometimes had to do it, because he wanted money from the superior.
MISCELLANEOUS:	10%	had to consider the kind of person who gave the order. If the man was an ordinary man, he would not do it. If it was necessary, he would do it.
		ought to show that he would do it, but he ought to find a way, gently, to contradict the order without letting his superior know that he did so.

There is one additional theme cutting across all three of the above that merits mention. This is the attention that is given to social forms; that is, although the item explicitly asks for the *feelings* of the informant, a large number from all three categories, 20 percent of the sample manage to work into their response their need to *waj*, bless, or otherwise fulfill their ritualistic obligations to the superior. For some of the informants described in the first theme, the form is equivalent to the feeling.

The next item represents what might be considered a test case of the above. "*When his superior gave him an order which he knew was wrong, he . . ."* describes what is essentially a conflict between the authority system and another principle external to the system which has its own powerful validity.

Examination of the responses indicates that although 53 percent of the informants do not fulfill the wrong order, as many as 36 percent do. (There are crucial qualifications involved here: more than one-third of those who do not fulfill the order are distressed about it, and approximately one-third of those who do are not without their resistances.) The remaining responses are distributed among individuals who simply cannot act; whose decision is dependent on how high in rank the superior is; or who, like the last informant in the table, manage both to fulfill the order and evade it. However, what is most striking about the villagers' cognitive structuring of the item is the complete lack of negative reference to the authority. Three informants protest the order, one "by giving reasons," another *in order to* avoid being personally harmed, for example, ". . . had to argue. Why should he do it? In all probability, he might be easily damaged if he followed such an order." However, these are not reflections on the competence or privileges of the superior. In fact, two other villagers either cannot quite understand the premise of a superior issuing an incorrect order or are certain that he will correct it (". . . would not like to do it. Because why didn't he give a correct order?"). There are no completions here which read: ". . . he knew that the superior was not clever"; ". . . he told the superior's superior about the wrong order"; ". . . he did it knowing that it would harm the superior." The entire emphasis is on meeting or not meeting the order itself.

Of the villagers who do not fulfill the wrong order, the majority, 37 percent of the sample, present what are essentially flat, unelaborated expressions of unwillingness. However, another 16 percent are troubled by their refusal, and feel compelled to report their hesitation, their fear, and their perplexity over why the order was not correct. Two of these do take it upon themselves to ask the superior for a new order, but do it ever so gently: ". . . told him that such an order was perhaps wrong. *Raw* need not tell him point-blank. Maybe then he might change his order." Similarly, even though 22 percent simply agree to follow the superior's order, another 14 percent try to mitigate or justify their conformity by pleading that they would correct the error later, that they would not take the responsibility for the error, that the superior would denounce them for not conforming, or that they followed his order mainly because they wanted something from him.

The above results, of course, raise a fundamental question about the nature of Thai attitudes toward authority. That is, accepting the premise that none of the responses reflect directly on the competence or prerogatives of the superior, does the fact that as many as 53 percent of the villagers decline to carry out an incorrect order of his tell us anything about the *efficacy* of his authority or of the motivational import of the attitudes previously expressed? More broadly, is the villagers' respect, admiration, and diffidence toward the authority figure a psychologically interesting but functionally meaningless pose? The answer to this question must for the most part be negative. The most important consideration operating here is the premise that the superior's order is wrong. That as many as 36 percent should agree to follow such an order and another 16 percent feel squeamish because they do not is considerable testimony to the efficacy of his influence. This is further underscored by the fact that so few informants, only three, take issue with his order, *i.e.,* they are more concerned with not doing wrong than they are with disobeying him. At the same time, the results from this item clearly indicate that deference to authority is not *the* dominant motivation of the villagers. It might well be one of the most easily recognized and clearly expressed, but this should not be confused with its psychic priority.[2]

The discussion till now has focused on villagers' attitudes toward external authorities. We now shift attention to how they themselves respond to acting as authority figures and to how they perceive the role of the authority figure. The item, *"When he was placed in a position of power, he . . . ,"* gives the informant considerable latitude to describe how he would behave or feel in the situation, to muse over the personal meaning and significance of the position, to wonder why he obtained it, or to express satisfaction over the fact that he did.

Examination of the responses indicates that the overwhelming tendency of the villagers is to structure the item in terms of how they would perform under the circumstances. No informant ". . . wondered why" he was given the position, or ". . . felt that he had been given his due," or ". . . realized that he finally achieved what he always wanted." With the exception of *one* informant who was simply "pleased," no villager perceives the experience in terms of its *personal* rewards. It is as if they had just happened on the experience and would attempt to acquit themselves well. Considering that most of them are peasants who, outside the family, have never actually experienced the role of being a superior, this is perhaps not surprising. Perhaps even more important is the fact that good fortune, which being in a power position implies, is so unpredictable in their minds: they have little reason to feel personal reward when they are never sure when and if the power position may be attained, nor are clear about their own role in achieving it. It might be noted that those villagers whose

---

[2] Neither do I mean to suggest that the desire to avoid doing wrong has psychic priority in the minds of the villagers. Unfortunately, I do not know how they might resolve the following hypothetical item: *"When he was doing something which he knew was wrong, but which he really wanted to do, he. . . ."*

TABLE 4

When he was placed in a position of power he . . .
When placed in a position of power, raw . . .

ACQUITTING WELL:	67%	ought to be sympathetic toward his neighbors. Should not bully (molest) them so that they suffer and become poor. had to maintain his dignity. must be just; must not be biased; must reprimand those who do wrong and praise those who do good. gave her money to the poor. had to behave well and tell his subordinates to behave well too. had to try to train his subordinates to know how to do the work.
NO COMMITMENT:	8%	had to assume the position.
MINIMAL PERFORMANCE:	4%	would use that power as little as possible.
REJECTION OF POSSIBILITY:	14%	wouldn't accept (that position). didn't want power at all. did not know what to do; she just kept growing rice.

responses most closely approximate a sense of convincing psychological investment in the position are two young women, who are disturbed and depressed about it, *e.g.*, ". . . was depressed, if the work was beyond her capacity and she was not familiar with the work." However, even here it is clear that they are most distressed about their capacity to fulfill the social and technical demands of the position.

Despite their lack of explicit personal investment or identification with the power role, the majority of informants are concerned with acquitting themselves well. Sixty-seven percent of the sample respond to the item along these lines. Of these, approximately 60 percent are relatively explicit in how they perceive themselves performing the role, and specify such traits as being sympathetic and non-bullying, not negligent, dignified, just, concerned with the poor, and attentive to the needs of their subordinates. The emphasis is on being a benevolent, just, but no-nonsense superior. The remaining individuals in this category are similar to the informant who says simply and abstractly that he "must behave himself well; be honest to others."

Excluding the "no answer" and idiosyncratic responses, the remaining members of the sample offer completions which fall along a three-category continuum emphasizing degrees of non-involvement in the power position: "non-committed performance of the job," "minimal performance," and "rejection of the position and what it entails." It is probably not insignificant that all eight individuals in this last category, 14 percent of the sample, are females who are least likely to find themselves in formal power positions.

These results suggest, of course, that although the majority of villagers have a relatively clear notion of how they would behave in an authority position (their ideas emerge with considerably greater clarity in the items below), they hold no strong conviction about the desirability of assuming such a role themselves, at least outside of those normal authority roles that they hold by virtue of their position in the family, their age, and the like. Their responses imply, more on the basis of what they fail to say than what they do say, a basic acceptance of their present positions in the authority hierarchy.

This implication becomes quite explicit in their responses to the item, *"When he was asked if he wanted to become boss, he. . . ."* This item was originally developed to tap reactions to responsibility in the general area of "Achievement-Failure." However, because it is so appropriate to the present discussion it will be reviewed here. Sixty-nine percent of the villagers say that they do not want to become boss and an additional 9 percent say that they would become boss only if they were really wanted, or if they were sure that it was a job that they were capable of doing. The majority of informants who reject the authority position do so flatly. However, 30 percent of this group justify their rejection on the basis of their assumed lack of knowledge or ability; their fear (because of the responsibility); because they do not have sufficient status (presumably a prerequisite for the position); or because they are just villagers. One informant's justification is perhaps the most absolute: she would not become boss because she does not have sufficient good fortune from previous existences (*waasanaa*) to permit her to fulfill the role adequately. This response and two "lack of status" responses (see the third response in the table) are expressions of the "after-the-fact" type of thinking that animates many village explanations, and which is rooted partially in the villagers' translation of Buddhist doctrine. That is, they assume that status and "boss-hood" are reciprocals of one another: only one who already has sufficient status or *waasanaa* could possibly be a boss, and one who is not already a boss lacks the status or good fortune to become one. In essence, the role of "boss" is self-fulfilling.

The twelve villagers (21 percent) who would like to become bosses for the most part do not attempt to justify themselves. The few who desire the role simply mention the honor, respect, and money that they perceive as going along with it. However, the response of one villager in this category is worth noting. This informant enjoys being a boss because "she would not have to be under anyone's control." Although a deviant response in terms of the distribution on this item, I have often heard villagers express this sentiment as one of the major reasons why they do not want to work for

TABLE 5

When he was asked if he wanted to become boss, he . . .
When asked if raw wanted to become boss, raw . . .

REJECT OFFER:	69%	she did not want to.
		would say she did not want to be boss.
		would not take the position, because his status was insufficient.
		did not want to become boss, because he is a villager.
		did not want to.
UNSURE:	9%	if he could, he would like to become one. But there are some jobs he cannot do; then he would not become boss.
ACCEPT OFFER:	21%	wanted to.
		wanted to become boss if he could, because a boss is more honored and respected, and gets more money.

anyone else, and also as one of the major reasons why they do not want to leave the land for a position in Bangkok.

The final two items in this section focus on the villagers' definitions of the proper ways to treat social subordinates. Since the items *"The best way to treat a subordinate is . . ."* and *"The worst way to treat a subordinate is . . ."* are simply obverse expressions of one another, they will be handled together. Note, however, that the informants on the two items are different: the first was a Form A item, the second a Form B item. The striking similarity in the content and style of the responses is partial testimony to the "reliability" of the two forms.

Whether in responding to these cues the villagers saw themselves mainly as the source or recipient of the treatment is unknown. However, the relative specificity of their completions suggests a richness of identification with these items greater than that obtained with some of the other SCT materials.

With the exception of one informant, whose deviancy suggests personal difficulty in this area,[3] the universal response of the villagers to the "best way to treat a subordinate" is to be benevolent, kind, attentive, and to satisfy his bodily and psychological needs. The *method* of expressing kindness and benevolence and the *specifications* of his bodily and psychological needs are perhaps what are most interesting here. Thirty-five percent of the informants specifically mention the desirability of using nice-sounding, pleasing, and agreeable words with the person of lower status. In

---

[3] This unique villager said *"The best way to treat a subordinate is . . . to scold him; to keep him at home and not let him go out."* In Thai terms, this Dickensian type of reaction is possible, rather than funny.

TABLE 6

The best way to treat a subordinate is . . .
The best way to treat a person of lower status or rank is (namely) . . .

"AGREEABLE WORDS"	35%	we have to speak to him nicely. Agreeable words alone can make people like us.
		to talk nicely to him; he will then have the heart (the desire) to work.
		to speak to him in a nice-sounding way. If anything happens, then it should be dealt with by compromise. And we should please (humor, pamper) him somewhat.
		to show a good heart and a good mood when giving orders. Speaking nicely will make for good service. If you speak badly, he will not work.
		to talk to him nicely. Everybody likes a person whose words are agreeable to the ear.
FEED WELL:	19%	to feed him the same food that you eat; to talk to him nicely.
		to give him food; not to work him too hard.
		to look after him, giving him food. If he did not have enough to eat, he would speak badly of you.
NOT OVERWORK:	15%	not to give him too much work to do and allow him time to rest.
		by letting him work and letting him rest; not to work him so that he has no time to rest.

fact, the responses of two villagers (see the first response in table 6) make "agreeable words" the *sine qua non* of social appreciation. The same pattern is repeated on the "worst way to treat a subordinate" item, although the frequency of references to using bad, rude, insulting words is lower, only 18 percent of the sample. However, if one adds the "to scold" and "to damn" references to the "bad language" references, the total amounts to 35 percent, precisely the same as the above. This emphasis on pleasant and agreeable words—on the style of language, rather than specifically on its content—reveals an extreme sensitivity to the social psychological, rather than to the functional, nature of the hierarchical relationship. There is an implicit recognition here both of the necessity to motivate the subordinate to participate in the relationship and of his freedom to disengage himself from it. His performance in the role is not assumed. Rather, he must be induced by "sweet talk" and an agreeable "front" (cf. Goffman 1959) to respond to his superior. There are no completions here which emphasize the satisfactions that the subordinate might derive from the job he has to do (*"The best way to treat a subordinate is . . .* to ask him for his best

TABLE 7

The worst way to treat a subordinate is . . .
The worst way to treat a person in your service (someone whom you are using to do something for you) is (namely) . . .

"BAD LANGUAGE":	35%	to scold him every day. Scold him when he does anything. Never praise him when he does well. There are some people who act just like this.
		to scold and damn him in anger. Not to see his goodness.
		to reprove him and hurt his feelings.
		to use insulting language.
		to curse at him.
UNDERFEED:	13%	to give him bad food and bad clothes.
		to be grudging about food. To let the subordinate go hungry. To want only to get the job done. Like having a water buffalo and working it without giving it food. It will soon die.
OVERWORK:	20%	to have him work without any rest. To use him like cattle or a buffalo.
		by putting him to work without giving him time to stop and rest; by sticking to the rules too closely.

work"), although two informants on the "worst way to treat" item suggest this as a counter-balance to scolding him or to not looking after his physical well-being (see the first completion in table 7). Neither are there many responses that focus on the structural attributes of the relationship, that is, that the subordinate should be treated with "dignity," "respect," or "in a manner appropriate to his status." On the contrary, the completions are highly personalized and are addressed directly to the psychobiological needs of the subordinate.

The attention that is given to the physical well-being of the subordinate is apparent on both items. Two considerations are primary: that the subordinate be fed well (19 percent on one item; 13 percent on the other); and that he be permitted to rest, sleep, or not be worked too hard (15 percent on one item; 2 percent on the other item). The concern with having sufficient relaxation is highly congruent with a more generalized "low pressure" orientation of the villagers. Although this desire usually remains unarticulated, it tends to arise in contexts such as this where demands might be made upon the staying power and social responsiveness of the individual. The villagers' wish for relaxation is probably not so much a plea for relief from fatigue as it is an expression of wanting to be free from constant attentiveness to the superior's needs and desires.

The concern with being well fed, or interest in food in general, is one of the great preoccupations of the villagers. It appears in several items—particularly those aimed at discovering the villagers' ambitions and their notions of the most important things in life—although not always with sufficiently high frequency to be considered a "dominant" response. (In the statistical sense, it is not a "dominant" response here either.) The ethnographic reports on Bang Chan (Sharp et al., 1953, Janlekha 1955, L. M. Hanks 1959b and 1959c, Jane R. Hanks 1961) have all made reference to the recurrent expression of this concern. The concern of the villagers seems especially pronounced to an outside observer not only because of its ubiquity but because in terms of the availability of food, no Bang Chaner —no matter how great his poverty—need starve. From an objective and comparative point of view, the vast majority of the villagers are very well fed indeed. The question that then arises is, why do they feel such anxiety about food? What symbolic function might their preoccupation serve?

Although this food fixation, like many symbolic acts, probably has several functions, its purpose here appears to be quite simple: it represents the munificence, security, and benevolence of the authority figure. Since the food-giving process is the prototype of all nurturance, it seems reasonable that individuals seeking a definition of the authority situation should look for evidence of the authority's nurturing and benevolent qualities in the food-giving act. The authority who feeds his subordinate well loves him.

Having analyzed the above SCT materials, what might we say with reasonable certainty concerning Bang Chan villagers' predispositions to authority? The data clearly confirm the generally recognized willingness of villagers to respond positively and undefiantly to authority figures. Their response is accompanied by feelings of esteem, admiration, and often diffidence toward the authority figure. However, their behavioral and emotional responses toward the authority are not absolute: when the authority is wrong they are most likely to ignore him. They do this, however, without in any way challenging the prerogatives of his authority or pointing to his error. Their structuring of the situation indicates that they are more interested in avoiding the error, and the blame that might be associated with it, than in taking issue with him. At the same time, a large minority are willing to implement the error in order to conform to his authority demands.

Perhaps the most important finding of our review is that although most villagers know how to acquit themselves well in the authority role, they would not like to become authority figures themselves. They have no strong emotional orientation toward the role, and, on practical grounds, feel that they do not have sufficient ability, knowledge, and status to fulfill it adequately. The latter is related in part, in their own minds, to some of their fundamental notions of causation.

In addition, they have very clear and explicit ideas of the way the authority figure should behave toward the subordinate. His proper role is that of a benevolent, nurturing individual who attends to the elemental psychobiological needs of the subordinate in order to maintain the latter's service and loyalty.

Finally, the most substantial contribution of the data is the extraordinary homogeneity that they reveal in the villagers' attitudes toward the authority system. Excepting the *"When his superior gave him an order which he knew was wrong, he . . ."* item, this homogeneity is apparent even at the most manifest levels of analysis. At the somewhat more abstract levels, it increases considerably. "Attitudes Toward Authority" clearly represents one of the more "unimodal" areas of Thai psychological life.

Predispositions to "Dependency"

Most of the items appearing in this category were originally developed in terms of Occidental, and particularly American, assumptions concerning the nature of dependency. However, after a preliminary examination of the data, it became clear that the items were not tapping dependency needs so much as they were getting at the nature of reciprocal relationships in Bang Chan. It is for this reason that the above title appears in quotes.

Whether the unilateral type of dependency that we are familiar with in the West—based on the *assumption* that one can depend on another with no expectation that such dependency be returned, and the *assumption* that to the person being depended on dependency is its own reward—could ever be applied to the villagers of Bang Chan is doubtful. It is clear that although some villagers are aware of such alternatives, most do not utilize them as part of their normal cognitive and emotional assumptions when dealing with other people. Rather, they seem to assume that all human contact is fundamentally bilateral in nature—a "contract" between independent souls—and that dependency is simply a special case of this. In the same way, it is uncertain whether villagers of Bang Chan could come to share Western assumptions about the negative sides of dependency: that people need each other so much as a source of emotional satisfaction and self-esteem that rejection by others is to be felt as painful or is taken as a sign of the diminution of one's own worth. Rather, they seem to assume that the primary reference of rejection is the party who rejected them or is some objective condition which makes the rejection appropriate. When the rejection is not appropriate (e.g., *"When he found out that his best friend spoke against him, he . . ."*) they are unable to see this as any reflection upon themselves, but rather assign blame to the other party. In all cases, the vast majority accept and are willing to maintain the breakdown in the social relationship that the rejection creates. One gains the distinct impression that to the emotionally self-concerned and self-sufficient villager (for whatever reasons he became self-concerned and self-sufficient) it is generally not worth the trouble to reaffirm the relationship.

None of the above should be taken to mean that the villagers do not *behave* in a dependent manner. Nothing could be further from the truth. The entire authority system is based upon the individual's willingness to consider himself a dependent subordinate to somebody else. But this dependency is phrased in terms of the reciprocal relationship existing between the subordinate and his superior. He remains dependent only as long as the superior satisfies his individual needs. From a social psychological point of view, his superior is actually just as "dependent" upon him.

The villagers' distinctive phrasing of their "dependency" needs is perhaps revealed most clearly in their structuring of the items, *"When he thinks of his mother, he thinks of . . ."* and *"When he thinks of his father, he thinks of. . . ."* These stimuli are related to dependency in the simplest possible way: they ask the informant to organize his thoughts and perceptions about those individuals who have been his greatest sources of dependency. Perhaps the most striking attribute of the responses is that, with the exception of two informants on the "mother" item, every villager explicitly thinks of his parents in terms of himself rather than in terms of what the parents are in their own right. There are simply no completions here on the order of "how wise she was," "how strong he was," "what a wonderful person he was," and the like. It is as if disinterested appreciation were simply not one of the villagers' cognitive and emotional premises.

TABLE 8

When he thinks of his mother, he thinks of . . .
When raw think of mother, raw think of . . .

SELF-BENEFIT:	46%	her love and her kindness and her protection. the good deeds she has done for him; her taking care of him since he was a little boy. her bringing him food and water ever since he was a child. her bringing him up.
OBLIGATION:	43%	making merit for her, as she died a long time ago. her well-being; he is concerned about it. her goodness. He had fed from her breast; it was her blood that fed him. He must not forget her kindness (her *bunkhun*). her kindness (*bunkhun*) to him. He must obey his mother.

TABLE 9

When he thinks of his father, he thinks of . . .
When thinking of father, raw think of . . .

SELF-BENEFIT:	36%	the protection which his father offered to him.
		the good deeds his father has done for him; his father has taken care of him since he was a little boy.
		the time when he looked after him, taking care of him in sickness. If he had no father, he might not be alive.
OBLIGATION:	50%	he prays for him on Friday.
		his goodness in bringing us up from childhood. It is essential that children repay their father's goodness when he is old and can no longer work.
		if father is alive, he should go visit him and bring food. If father is dead, he should make merit for him.
		his kindness (*bunkhun*) done for her.
		his kindness to him (*bunkhun*). He obeys his father and repays the debt of kindness.

In thinking about their parents in terms of themselves, the informants give their responses in two closely related forms. They think of those characteristics of the parents that directly benefited them: their goodness and kindness to the informant; that they carried the informant in their womb or brought him into the world; that they reared the informant, took care of him when he was ill, or gave him money. Forty-six percent of the sample respond in this manner on the "mother" item and 36 percent on the "father" item. Some of their responses suggest that they were deeply touched by their recollections: one informant remembered her father "bringing her up, since the time her feet were as small as shells," and another thinks of the time her mother "brought me sweets and comforted me when I was frightened." The numerous references to food, as expressions of benevolent concern, should not be overlooked.

The other major form of the villagers' responses, and the one that bears out our earlier point, is the deep feeling of obligation that individuals feel toward their parents. In several instances, the obligation is simply assumed, and the informant gives a completion which describes the nature of his obligatory act: making merit for the parent, giving alms or blankets to monks, caring for the parent when he gets old. In most instances, however, informants indicate that they are obliged to their parents because of the kind and good things their parents have done for them. In a few cases, it is a moral imperative: "it is essential that the children repay their father's goodness when he is old and can no longer work"; "if you are a male, you must get ordained to redeem the sins of the parents. Just like sending them money." Many of the responses included in this category do not refer explicitly to the reciprocity of the child, but are phrased in terms of the *bunkhuns* that the parent has done for the child. Because the term *bunkhun* assumes reciprocity as part of its root meaning—good deeds which are reciprocated—references to the *bunkhuns* of the parents are included here. All told, 43 percent of the sample fall into this obligation category on the "mother" item and 50 percent on the "father" item.

The entire discussion above leads to the proposition that if the premise of reciprocity did not play such a major role in the villagers' assumptive world, there would be a few more informants who would be willing to perceive their parents as living an existence independent of themselves, and fewer informants so concerned with repaying their parents for fulfilling what is, after all, the parents' primary psychosocial role. Such a concern is likely to arise only when there is an underlying awareness that the parents have an option of fulfilling or not fulfilling their role, and that this has been impressed on the individual so dependent upon their choice.

The next item, in its manifest purpose and in its diversity of response, is less emotionally loaded than the above. In fact, perhaps the major function of the item, *"A real close friend is one who . . ."* (and its companion piece, *"The thing I want most in my closest friend is . . . ,"* which is so similar in response it will not be presented), is to indicate that there are no widely shared notions of a "real close friend" in Bang Chan. Whether this suggests that the figure of the "close friend" is unimportant to the villagers is uncertain. However, the diversity of the villagers' responses permits us to say relatively little about the typicality of the socially equal, yet dependent, figure in the village.[4]

Examination of the responses indicates that they fall into six different categories. Listed in the order of their frequency, "a real close friend is one who" has such qualities as faithfulness, loyalty, the willingness to die for his friend, and keeps his word (27 percent). Almost as many people (24 percent) agree that he is an individual who helps you, especially if you are poor or are in need of reminders to behave in a moral way. One informant in this category voices a definition of a "close friend" that I have heard on several occasions when villagers were discussing their relationships with kinsmen or neighbors: ". . . one who helps you when you are in trouble and goes away when you are happy." A third group (18 percent) perceives

---

[4] An earlier point by Hanks and Phillips (1961: 642) might not be insignificant in this regard. We noted that it "is difficult for an equal to give anything of value to an equal or to command his 'respect.' Indeed, he stands as a potential competitor for favors."

TABLE 10

A real close friend is one who . . .
A real close friend is (namely) one who . . .

IS LOYAL	27%	is such that we love each other truly and would die for each other.
		is dependable, stays with you in suffering and in happiness, gives you useful advice about things, and loves you as you love him.
		is loyal.
IS HELPFUL:	24%	tells beneficial, helpful things to us.
		always helps *raw*.
		has sympathy; helps his friend when he is in trouble.
DOES NOT HARM SPEAKER:	18%	does not slander or blame *raw*.
		does not accuse *raw* falsely.
IS LIKE SPEAKER:	15%	loves me as I love him, has same thoughts, and speaks the same things.
LOVES SPEAKER:	10%	loves us very much.
		loves us, may risk his life for us, shares his food with us, does not take advantage of us, and tells his secrets to us.

a close friend as an individual who, from a positive point of view, does not slander, blame, quarrel with you, or accuse you falsely. This attention to the lack of negative qualities—as if negative qualities were people's given attributes—is repeated below in several items. A fourth group (15 percent) defines the close friend as an individual who is essentially the same as oneself, who enjoys doing the same things as oneself, or who enjoys sharing things with oneself. A fifth group (10 percent) considers the close friend to be simply a person who loves you, and a sixth group (only 2 percent) identifies the close friend as a member of his own family. Two of the idiosyncratic responses are interesting in their own right: one villager says, "I have never had any one like that at all. I have only ordinary friends"; and another says that only a person who is innocuous enough to "not bother anybody" could be considered a real close friend.

Despite their lack of consensus about the nature of a close friend, Bang Chaners do tend to agree about how they would respond *"when they found out that their best friend had spoken against them."* This item asks the villagers to state how they would behave in a situation that has *direct* relevance to them, in contrast to the above, which aims mainly at a definition of another party, albeit a party who would be expected to have some relevance to the self. However, the difference in the tone of response to the two items is striking. Here 66 percent of the sample responds with immediate anger, declares that he will have nothing to do with the friend, or accepts the premise of the item as *prima facie* evidence of the friend's undesirability.

Only one of all the informants raises the possibility of there being some validity to the friend's remarks, and thus indicates some concern with the friend's *evaluation* of himself, as if his friend's opinion mattered to him. He says that he ". . . tried to find out whether there was any truth in what he said. If it was my fault, I would try to make it better and look for ways to come to an understanding." Four other villagers will go so far as to talk the matter over with the friend, but their phrasing indicates that they are concerned with finding out whether the friend did indeed say what he was reputed to say, rather than discussing the value of his remarks. Five other

TABLE 11

When he found out that his best friend spoke against him, he . . .
When finding out that raw *best friend speaks against* raw, raw *. . .*

ANGER:	66%	had to tell him off. A friend ought not to do **that**. felt angry with his friend and disliked him. was angry that his friend was a bad, bad person. was very angry and stopped going with him immediately. was angry.
TALK IT OVER:	10%	talked it over with him; talked about why he spoke against him. had to find out why his friend slandered him; if he was not a good man, he would stop being friends with him.
COUNSEL HIM:	13%	ought to advise him not to do it again. had to tell the friend to act correctly.
DISTRESS:	10%	felt *siacaj* (sorry, unhappy).

villagers also indicate a willingness to discuss the matter with the friend, but only to counsel him in the error of his ways: they are doing him the favor. It is probably not coincidental that four of these five counseling individuals are village monks. This is one of the few SCT items to which Buddhist monks, as a group, tend to give responses that are distinctively different from other informants. Finally, four villagers say that they are unhappy or distressed about the situation. A check of the translation of their responses indicates that although the reason for their distress is not absolutely certain, it can from the Thai point of view mean only that they are either unhappy about being slandered, or, like the preceding inform-ants, unhappy *for* the friend; but it does not mean that they are unhappy about having lost a friend, or about the fact that it was a "friend" who had such an opinion. In this latter respect, their meaning would be similar to the response of one informant who said that he "felt very angry because it is quite common for others to slander him, but it is very low thing for friends to slander." In both cases, the premise of being spoken against is accepted and is given priority over the strength of the friendly relationship.

In fact, perhaps the most impressive thing about this entire distribution is the overwhelming acceptance of the premise and a concomitant indifference to the source of information or the nature of the evidence, whether it be against the friend or themselves. Only six villagers suggest that they are thinking along these lines, and only one addresses herself explicitly to the reliability of her informants, when she says that she ". . . paid no attention to what they said about her best friend (or what they said her best friend said)." It is as if hearing such things about friends, or discovering such things being said by friends, were indeed, as I originally suggested to the villagers, one of those "things that happen every day in life; just plain, ordinary things."

In any event, no villager except one ever entertains the possibility of there being any value in what the friend said. Any merit in the comment or any positive motive that the friend, in his role of friend, might have had, is assumed by the villagers to be inconsequential to the act performed. The fact of his being a "best friend" does not give him any special prerogatives. In fact, the villagers give such little attention to the fact of friendship in this situation that the experience emerges largely as one of insult, rather than rejection.

The next two items differ from the preceding one in that the stakes in

TABLE 12

When he saw that they did not like him, he . . .
When seeing (realizing) that other khon do not like raw, raw . . .

WITHDRAWAL OR INDIFFERENCE:	60%	did not see them again.
		Oh! I don't feel anything. I never worry.
		did not go to have trouble with them.
		did not go to them; did not keep company with them.
		let them do as they pleased. He lived his own life. Who would say anything against him?
SELF-IMPROVEMENT:	15%	had to behave better.
		would try to improve himself, so that they would like him.
DISPLEASURE:	8%	was displeased, and did not like them either.
REGRET:	8%	felt sorry.

TABLE 13

When he saw that others avoided him, he . . .
When seeing that other khon do not want to stick around raw, raw . . .

WITHDRAWAL OR IN-DIFFERENCE:	53%	she would not hang around with them either. did not care; she would live to an old age and see how they liked it. would avoid them. did not bother with them and did not make friends with them again. he did not feel anything.
ACCEPTANCE:	24%	probably was not generous with them, so they avoided him. they probably felt that she wasn't good enough, so they avoided her.
UNHAPPINESS:	6%	felt unhappy and sorry and thought they hated him.
SELF-EXAMINATION:	3%	ought to examine himself and find out the reason.
DISPLEASURE:	3%	felt displeased. But she was *chɔɔj-chɔɔj;* she did not go hurt them (beat them up).

being rejected are clearly not as high. In the items, *"When he saw they did not like him, he . . ."* and *"When he saw that others avoided him, he . . ."* there are no friends involved and the reasons for rejection are unstated. The informant thus has greater freedom to respond. Nevertheless, the responses here are very similar in their over-all effect. While the angry reactions have all but disappeared, they have been replaced by a general indifference to the experience of rejection. Thus, although informants here are not as emotionally expressive as they were on the earlier item, they are just as willing to accept the breakdown in the social relationship that the item implies. In only one of the 111 responses is there any thought of mending the interpersonal rupture, and even this is conditioned by the necessity of the rejector being a kinsman or someone the informant likes, that is, "if it is a member of his family, he will ask him the reason. If it is an outsider, he does not care. If he does not like him, he will have nothing to do with him. He lives in his own house, works in his own field, and makes his own living."

Examination of the responses on the *"When he saw that they did not like him, he . . ."* item indicates that 60 percent of the sample responds either by saying that they will not have anything to do with the people who do not like them or that they do not care, and 53 percent responds similarly on the *"When he saw that others avoided him, he . . ."* item. What is most impressive about these highest frequency responses is the simple matter-of-factness with which they are articulated. The villagers' rejection of, or indifference to, the rejector lacks almost all sense of spleen or hurt. Many of them describe the experience as a simple transaction: *"When he saw that others avoided him, he* . . . also avoids them. If they are good to me, I shall be good to them. If the others are not good to me, I therefore avoid them"; ". . . did not want to stay around them. He would be good to those who were good to him. If they were not good to him, he would not be good to them"; ". . . did not want to associate with them, because one cannot force oneself." The basic rationality underlying the indifference of some of them is also striking: ". . . he feels *chɔɔj-chɔɔj* (cool, indifferent, self-possessed); does not feel glad or sad because he depends on himself, not on other people"; *"When he saw that they did not like him, he* . . . was not surprised; he was not sorry, because he did not have to ask anyone any favor"; ". . . let them feel and say whatever they like. He did not bother with them. We people have many minds, different hearts. Whatever they say, we can't be sure whether it is true or not."

Following the above dominant response, the distribution on the two items diverge a bit. A noteworthy minority, 24 percent, offer a series of responses on the "saw others avoided him" item that are not found on the other item. These responses describe a complete acceptance of the avoidance situation. That is, informants simply present reasons to explain or justify why others avoided them, for example, ". . . probably was not generous with them, so they avoided him"; ". . . felt that they might have been offended by something that he had done." (Note that the pronoun in the item is *"raw,"* the editorial "I," not "he.") This kind of response, where informants not only accept the experience of rejection but volunteer their own negative qualities as the objective reason for it, suggests of course an ultimate faith in themselves vis-à-vis their relations with other people. Other minority responses on the two items are as follows: on the "avoid him" item, 6 percent are unhappy, 3 percent examine themselves for the reasons for the avoidance, and 3 percent are displeased; on the "do not like" item, 15 percent want to improve themselves (although despite this Dale Carnegie approach, one villager in this category says: "Actually, it is difficult to please other people"); 8 percent are displeased with the situation; 8 percent are sorry others do not like them; and 3 percent cannot quite understand why they are disliked by others.

In summary of this section on predispositions to "dependency," the following points might be made. The data here tend to support earlier remarks on the importance of reciprocal relationships in Bang Chan. As a cognitive principle, the notion of reciprocity even extends to the rejection situation where many villagers say, "If people do not want to associate with me, I will not associate with them." (The percentage that say just this averages out to 40 percent.) There are no widely shared notions about the nature of a "close friend," an individual who, although a social equal, might be expected to be a source of dependence. When the quality of the friend's fellowship is challenged or placed in serious doubt, the majority of informants accept this as a reasonable possibility and exhibit little effort to reintegrate the social rupture that is thus created. In situations where the reasons for, and parties of, rejection are unknown, villagers respond with genuine self-confidence and equanimity. Excepting the "conception of friendship" item, predispositions in this area tend toward "unimodality," although not to the degree that we encountered in the area of authority.

Orienting Toward Others

The materials to be covered in this section aim mainly at the villagers' perceptions of the way human relations should be conducted and their notions of desirable and undesirable human qualities. To a certain extent, my purpose is to check how typical and representative many of the statements on interpersonal contact are that were made earlier in the text. However, two important points about the nature of this "check" are in order. First, it must be remembered that we are dealing here with the villagers' perceptions of desirable human qualities, not those that an outside observer identifies. Inevitably, there are certain areas that an outsider may consider primary, but which the villagers may simply take for granted, or vice versa. The complete absence of references to the desirability of *sanug* or being an "amusing talker" in the responses below is a case in point. Villagers, of course, are aware of the desirability of *sanug* and probably could not get along well without it. But the capacity to be "sanug-ful" is, in their environment, such a familiar and undistinguished human attribute that to them it does not merit being singled out for special regard. As a "check," therefore, these data serve mainly to identify any inconsistencies that may appear between our own perceptions and those of the villagers, rather than to provide full confirmation of the earlier observations. Likewise, it is possible that this material may reveal concerns not previously noted. Second, it should be clear that when there is confirmation, it will obviously be expressed in the villagers' idiom, not our own. Few informants below explicitly say that what they most like about others is their cordiality and affability. However, several (irrespective of sex) do say that they like the fact that others "talk sweetly," "are not coarse," or have "a soft and gentle way." This is their way of communicating the desirability of being polite and nonimposing toward others. Similarly, their indication that *"In their relations with people, the thing they are most careful of is . . .* talking to them correctly and properly"; ". . . manners and etiquette"; or

". . . to talk only about good things" is their own way of phrasing the significance of social cosmetics in their psychological life.

The first item to be examined, *"The thing I like most about him is . . ."* simply asks villagers to present their assessment of desirable human qualities. Although the variability on this item is considerable, encompassing at least eight qualitatively different categories [5] (more than any item heretofore encountered), one mode of response has obvious prominence. Not unexpectedly, this is the category that describes someone else's most favorable quality as doing favors for the informant, helping the informant, liking him, or loving him. The qualities are seen in terms of their direct relevance and utility to the self. Although this may be a reflection of the value that is placed upon "generosity" in Bang Chan, it is clearly also a reflection of the villagers' self-concern (or, perhaps more fundamentally, emotional honesty). Thirty-five percent of the sample responds in this manner, and another 8 percent, although not concerned principally with the self, build some self-reference into their reply, for example, ". . . he is not haughty; whenever he meets me, he greets me." The great variation in the tone of responses within this category, however, merits mention. One informant admits that he most likes the other person because of the gifts he receives from him; another says he enjoys the respect the other gives him; and still another (a monk) merges the teachings and language of Buddhism with his own self-interests: *"The thing I like most about him is . . .* that he relieves my suffering, he nurtures my happiness, and advises and teaches me in the good and likable way." (Although this response might seem paradoxical to Western sensibilities, it makes complete sense from a Thai point of view. As a monk, one of the major functions of this person is to present himself to others as a means by which they can do good: they can relieve his suffering, nurture his happiness, and the like. That other people do indeed take advantage of the opportunity he provides them indicates how desirable they are.)

The second major form of the villagers' responses, representing 15 percent of the sample, is the "nice talk" or "sweet speech" category mentioned above. Very similar to it in intent, but lacking the explicit reference to speech, are a set of responses held by 9 percent of the sample, which

---

[5] Many informants also cite not one, but several, desirable qualities. My practice here, as in all cases of plural entries, is to give each citation a percentage of credit: a half, a third, etc. This is not done, however, if the secondary citations are simply amplifications of the first, non-categorizable after-thoughts, non-categorizable in themselves, or are phrased as subordinate rather than equivalent considerations. No reliability check of this "coding" has been conducted, mainly because few reliability checkers know Thai culture well enough to assign the correct cultural meanings to the responses. (See my comments in the preceding chapter on the dangers of assigning American meanings to Thai responses without using native meanings as intervening correctives. The *bunkhun* responses presented earlier are an excellent illustration of the kinds of dangers involved.)

TABLE 14

The thing I like most about him is . . .
The thing which causes raw *to like him is* (*namely*) . . .

SELF-REFERRING (43%)		
PRINCIPALLY:	35%	that he is good to me.
		that he does good. He is our benefactor. He helps us in our work.
SECONDARILY:	8%	that he has a good heart; he loves me.
POLITENESS (24%)		
SWEET SPEECH:	15%	that he talks sweetly; he has gentle manners.
		that he speaks well.
OTHERS:	9%	that he has a soft and gentle way.
NO BAD QUALITIES (18%)		
NOT HAUGHTY:	9%	that she has a good character. She does not look down upon *raw*.
ALL OTHERS:	9%	that she speaks well and never encroaches on me.
OTHERS (15%)		
GOOD LOOKS:		that he is handsome.
DILIGENCE:		that he is good; he works well, so I like him; we do not like wayward people.
ABSTRACT QUALITIES:		his good character and inborn temperament.
STRAIGHTFORWARDNESS:		that he speaks to me directly.

describe lack of haughtiness or sense of social superiority as likable qualities. Although small in numbers, it is surprising that any informants in a community as socially homogeneous as Bang Chan would think of these as traits to be evaluated. These responses become even more apparent, although still clearly in a minority, in the next item, which focuses on "dislikable" qualities. It might well be that they reflect the sense of social class and intra-village status differences, and an accompanying status anxiety, that have been observed to be emerging in Bang Chan. (See Sharp *et al.* 1953.) It might also be noted that positive personal characteristics are again being phrased in negative terms, as the absence of undesirable characteristics. Eighteen percent of all the responses here are of this type. The four remaining categories, in no case encompassing the responses of more than three villagers, emphasize the handsomeness of the other person; that he works hard or diligently (to a certain extent, an emphasis on achievement); that he has some abstract qualities which, by definition, are desirable, and thus not further analyzable (that the person is good, has a good heart, or fine character); and that he speaks directly or truthfully.

This last may be a reflection of the dissatisfaction a few villagers may feel over the continuous emphasis given to sweet and appealing words.

The next item, *"The thing they most dislike about him is . . . ,"* is in its stimulus value essentially the obverse of the above. Thus, the negative counterparts of some of the characteristics noted above also appear here: 4 percent of the sample dislikes the lack of orderliness and a pleasing disposition in others; 13 percent dislikes haughtiness, conceit, or arrogance; and one villager dislikes a person who "does not know what work is." However, the dominant definitions of undesirable characteristics are not simply negative phrasings of the desirable. Although two villagers do dislike

TABLE 15

The thing they most dislike about him is . . .
The thing that makes khon *not like him is (namely) . . .*

TROUBLING OTHERS (64%)		
HURTFUL SPEECH:	30%	that he does not speak well and lies.
		her lies. No one likes those whose words cannot be trusted.
		that she damns others. Some people gossip about others.
ANNOYING OTHERS:	24%	that she is a troublemaker and does not speak nicely.
		that she likes to look for trouble.
THIEVERY:	10%	that he is a person who likes to steal.
BAD QUALITIES (17%)		
HAUGHTINESS:	13%	that he is conceited and lofty.
OTHERS:	4%	his bad manners; he is not *riabrɔɔj* (he lacks neatness, good order, finesse, etc.); his coarse way of speaking.

people who are ungrateful for the help they have received or who do not help others, most accept these sins of omission as realistic possibilities. (Although *bunkhuns* assume reciprocation, one always has the option of terminating the relationship.) Rather, most villagers perceive undesirable qualities in terms of the trouble that individuals actively cause others.

This trouble takes at least three forms. The first, representing the responses of 30 percent of the sample, is the deceptive or otherwise painful use of language: lying, gossiping, using rude and insulting forms to deal with others. This last, of course, means the expression of aggression: indifference to the feelings and dignity of other people. Lying and gossiping, however, reflect the sensitivity that some villagers have about the untrustworthiness of others: that beneath the gloss of smiles and amicable face-to-face contacts, people often do hurt one another. This suggests, of course, some of the ambivalence that villagers feel about "nice words" and "sweet speech." The second major response, representing 24 percent of the sample, is more generic in nature: it encompasses the trait of inciting other people to have arguments; the capacity to annoy people, in a manner akin to what is connoted by the American slang term, "to bug" a person; and the capacity actually to threaten others. The emphasis here is on intruding on the peace, stability, and self-concerns of other people. The last response, representing 10 percent of the sample, is interesting because of its rather non-psychological, highly practical, nature: people are disliked because they steal. Theft is something that one *hears* about in Bang Chan very frequently, but actual cases are almost never encountered. What its symbolic significance may be is unknown, unless it is simply a more concrete expression of the concern about the untrustworthiness of others.

The most striking characteristic of the above responses is that despite their diversity they almost all emphasize qualities that are directly interpersonal, rather than intrapersonal, in nature. There are no responses here which say that the most dislikable thing about a person is "his stupidity"; "his weakness"; "his incompetence." It is only when unattractiveness takes on a manifestly social dimension, when a person's activities can actually harm others, that most villagers become exercised. Otherwise, Bang Chaners seem to assume (and it is the assumption that is important) that a person can be any way he wants. To a large extent, this same assumption was implicit in the villagers' structuring of the previous item on "likable" qualities, and may help to explain why they often define positive qualities as the absence of negative ones. In that item, if a person could not be of direct help to the self or love the self (the major response), villagers desired that he deal with others in a "soft spoken" and gentle way (the second most frequent response) or at least lack offensive qualities (the third most frequent response). They seem to assume that it is better not to have a relationship at all than to have one that admits unpleasantness. Or, phrased in another way, they seem to assume that if a relationship is even to occur, it must be useful, pleasant, or harmless. What the person is otherwise like, outside of the relationship, is irrelevant to one's assessment of him.

This attention to the manifest nature of social relationships and to the necessity of keeping the relationships smooth and uncomplicated is revealed most sharply in the next two items, "*People who never show their feelings are . . .*" and "*It is sometimes good to hide your true feelings about a person because. . . .*" The latter item is clearly biased in the direction of sanctioning the social pose, and is valuable mainly for the kinds of justifications it reveals. The former item, however, has no evaluative connotations and permits villagers to respond in any direction. Examination of the responses indicates overwhelming agreement on the part of villagers about the desirability of hiding one's feelings. Eighty percent of the sample responds approvingly; 12 percent responds disapprovingly (three quarters of whom are disturbed by the deceptiveness involved); and 6 percent responds in a non-committed way. One of the non-committed is almost literary as he describes a person who never shows his feelings as "a man who is like a sword in a scabbard." (His non-committment derives from the protective, as contrasted to the obviously aggressive, symbolism of the sword.)

In the majority group, more than half the informants describe people who hide their feelings as "good," "persons who do not want to cause trouble," "just men," and perhaps most cogently from a Thai point of view, "persons who realize that hiding one's feelings is a virtue that helps men to live together happily." Three of the majority informants, however, are

TABLE 16

People who never show their feelings are . . .
Khon who never show their feelings are . . .

APPROVAL:	80%	good people, because others do not know their feelings. thoughtful people. real men, serious men, men who do things seriously. careful people who do not want to cause trouble. people who do not want to be blamed. people who have very brave hearts.
DISAPPROVAL:	12%	bad people, because their mouths are one thing but their hearts are another.
NON-COMMITTAL:	6%	both good people and bad people.

more defensive in their justifications: they say that people who do not show their feelings do not want to be disliked or blamed by others. The balance of the majority (a dozen villagers) are the most expressive in their approval: they say that people who conceal their feelings are "patient," "brave," "pure," and "thoughtful." Their emphasis is on the highly desirable stoicism of such individuals.

Perhaps the most revealing aspect of the responses of the minority group who disapprove of the concealment of feelings is, again, the interpersonal point of departure that is used to evaluate the behavior. Such individuals are viewed mainly as deceptive, although one informant says they are cruel and another says that they are difficult to get along with. But nowhere is there any reference to the possibility of such concealment being undesirable because it makes psychic demands on the concealer or because it might be expressive of inadequacy on his part. There is no concern here over the possibility of these individuals being "fearful of others," "tight," or to use a readily available Thai term, *cuu cii* (compulsive, exacting). Why people do not show their feelings is their own business and their own problem (if not showing one's feelings could be thought of as a "problem"). As in the approving responses, the interpersonal effect of their behavior is what is most important.

The justifications with which villagers respond to the stimulus, *"It is sometimes good to hide your true feelings about a person because . . ."* are of three general, but closely related, types.

TABLE 17

It is sometimes good to hide your true feelings about a person be-cause . . .

Sometimes it is good to hide true feelings about another khon *be-cause . . .*

AVOIDS ANGER:	37%	people will not be able to say that *raw* is not a good person; it makes them not angry with *raw* or dislike *raw*. he will not hate you. he will not detest *raw* and will give *raw* help. they will not hate *raw* in return.
AVOIDS TROUBLE:	26%	it prevents people from quarreling. it preserves friendships; it prevents quarrels and fights which break up friendships. there will be no trouble.
UNDERSCORING:	20%	it is not letting him see anything in our outward behavior. We don't let him see that we are angry and that we are controlling our feelings. you will not tell him what your true feelings are. it is bad if you do not hide your feelings.

The most frequent response, held by 37 percent of the villagers, is that by concealing their true feelings about another person that person will not dislike, hate, or be angry with them. Whether this response involves a projection (an unconscious attribution) onto others of their own aggressive feelings, which the concealment suggests to them they harbor, is uncertain. The response may simply reflect the omission of certain logical steps in the psychodynamic process, that is, "that if I did not conceal my feelings, and expressed what I felt, it could only lead to a series of events culminating in their hating me." It is interesting to note, however, that only one of all our informants makes the effort to point out that the point of the concealment may be to avoid hurting that other person ("it prevents the man from having bad feelings and you do not lose anything"). All the other informants who are concerned about the other person (several are not) either invert the item to protect themselves or speak in more general terms of the concealment's value in preventing quarrels, preserving friendships, and the like. This kind of response is the second major justification, representing the responses of 26 percent of the sample: individuals holding this position point out that by not expressing their feelings, quarrels are precluded, "the work will not be messed up," and "coöperation and understanding" can be maintained. The third major group of informants, 20 percent of the sample, accept the value of concealing one's feelings as self-evident, and use the item to underscore the point. One informant offers a highly articulate justification for her concealment which, in its stoical overtones, is suggestive of some of the tenets of Buddhism: "one should not show one's happiness, attachment, or sorrow to anyone." Basic to this person's response is the emphasis in Buddhist doctrine on the ultimate psychological isolation of every soul.

The final item in this section, *"In his relations with people, the thing he is most careful of is . . ."* asks villagers to specify their major form of interpersonal anxiety. The "anxiety" here is intentionally low-keyed. Villagers are asked what they are careful of, not what they are frightened of.

TABLE 18

In his relations with people, the thing he is most careful of is . . .
In relations with other khon, *the thing* raw *is most careful of is* (*namely*) . . .

OWN BEHAVIOR (55%)		
NATURE OF WORDS:	37%	words and promises.
		that he speaks well (politely, pleasantly).
		that her words might be insulting to them.
		his own words.
MANNERS:	6%	his manners, his etiquette.
GOOD SELECTION:	6%	to try to associate with good people only.
OWN "HEART":	6%	his own feelings (mood), for fear that they will be angry with him.
OTHERS' BEHAVIOR (37%)		
THEFT:	13%	she is afraid they will steal her things.
		he is afraid that they might be thieves.
TREACHERY:	7%	he is afraid that they will double-cross raw.
PHYSICAL HARM:	6%	she is afraid they will attack her.

Examination of the responses reveals two major reference points. Fifty-five percent of the sample responds in terms of what it is about their own behavior that makes them anxious; 37 percent respond in terms of what they are anxious about in the behavior of others toward them. Of those responses in the first category, the majority (in fact equal in number to all the responses in the second category) refer once more to the nature of their words. One informant sums up almost everything we have been saying about the villagers' concern with social cosmetics. He says that "*in his relations with people, the thing he is most careful of is . . .* not to talk about important matters." Other villagers point to words as the *sine qua non* of obtaining social admiration: one informant says that he is most careful of "talking. It is most important. If you talk well, people love you. If you talk badly people hate you"; another says, "his words; if a person does not speak well, he can't get anything from anybody; nobody loves him." Other informants anxious about their own behavior in this situation divide their responses equally (6 percent each) among three sub-categories: they say that they are most careful about having good manners; about being sure that they select only good, non-troublemaking individuals with whom to deal (involving an assumption that they do indeed have considerable control over the situations into which they place themselves); and a third group says that they are most careful about their own feelings and their own "hearts," indicating the concern they feel over controlling their own impulses in order to deal with others in a comfortable and amicable way.

Among the villagers who respond in terms of anxiety about what other people will do to them, the majority, 20 percent of the total sample, says that they are careful about other people stealing from them (13 percent) or being treacherous and cunning toward them (7 percent). Another 6 percent are careful lest others attack them and do them physical harm. The extremity of the replies of this sizable minority (26 percent) is perhaps what is most interesting, and somewhat surprising. The balance of responses in this category are mainly expressions of a diffuse wariness about the intentions of others ("he must keep watching and listening"; "that she must know whether they are good persons or not"), although two informants specify that they must be careful about the words, promises, or criticisms of others.

The foregoing discussion of the villagers' modes of "orienting toward others" may be summed up in the following manner. Despite the obvious tendency toward "multimodality," or high variability of response, on all items excepting the "*People who never show their feelings are . . .*" item, the villagers' reactions to the above stimuli go far in supporting our earlier remarks on the nature of social contact in Bang Chan. Villagers evaluate other people mainly in terms of how well they treat the self or how well they manage not to harm the self. The interpersonal relationship is the major component of their evaluation in the sense that they are either indifferent to, or highly tolerant of, character traits of other people that exist outside the purview of their contact with them. In effect, villagers seem to assume that a person can be anything he wants to be, so long as his behavior is not detrimental to others. Villagers respond in a highly favorable manner to persons who conceal their feelings, and explain their approval by saying that such behavior helps minimize social conflict, particularly conflict of which they may be the object. Their commendation of people who control their feelings is extreme, taking the form of calling them "just," "good," "brave," "pure," and "thoughtful." In their interpersonal contacts, villagers say they are most careful about the effect of their words on others, and one informant presents what is perhaps the perfect summation of the role of politeness in their lives when he says that, in his relations with people, he is most careful "not to talk about important matters." For a sizable minority of villagers, the data also indicate a sense of untrustworthiness about the motives of others. The major forms of this lack of trust are that others will steal from or physically harm them, be treacherous, slander, or gossip about them. Our observational materials suggest that although their anxiety may have realistic foundation with regard to others gossiping about them, and perhaps slandering them, this would not be true in the case of others stealing or doing them physical harm. These fears are probably symbolic expressions of a more diffuse anxiety about harm to the self through the medium of interpersonal relationships. Whether anxiety about interpersonal relationships is indeed the major form of anxiety in Bang Chan will be investigated in the next section.

Anxiety and Reactions to Crises

In this section we are dealing with materials that present the most ticklish analytic problems we will encounter. We know from American culture that persons identify as sources of anxiety issues which are genuine existential problems (illness; payment of bills; how to deal with an arbitrary boss); issues which by most culturally "reasonable" standards should not be sources of anxiety, but which are nevertheless felt that way (how to obtain a beautiful or handsome figure with the least amount of effort); and issues which by both cultural and personal standards of "reasonableness" are not considered valid sources of anxiety, but which are nevertheless "understood" and tolerated (fear of thunder, wild animals, flying insects). In the last two cases, we know that the expressed anxiety usually symbolizes some other threat, which is considerably more crucial but unknown. And in the last instance, we know that the fanciful fear often serves the vital function of binding what might otherwise be extremely painful free-floating anxiety.[6] We also know from American culture that there are many objective sources of threat existing in the environment which are rarely identified as objects of anxiety, unless directly or imminently encountered, e.g., being struck by an automobile. Finally, we know that there are objects or sources of anxiety that may be denied as such because of the cultural values associated with being fearful or brave: it is possible for a teen-ager to admit anxiety over an examination or an important "date," but usually not when he is asked to perform a daring deed by a group of his peers.

The point of these remarks is that despite our familiarity with the various forms and functions of anxiety, we are still hard put in most instances to identify the precise psychodynamic role of an anxiety response when it is expressed by individuals in our own culture. The problem is compounded immeasurably when we attempt to do this with members of another culture. It is for this reason that the responses below will be accepted as those things which actually frighten or worry the villagers of Bang Chan, and will not be examined for any intrapsychic functions that they may serve. The few interpretive excursions of this type that we took earlier in the text (e.g., the villagers' concern about a superior feeding them well) were sanctioned principally by the context in which the responses were made. Here, informants are asked to indicate their anxieties under a completely unspecified set of conditions.

Actually, most of the responses given below are, in terms of the villagers' culturally constituted reality, of a highly reasonable nature, suggesting that informants are reacting in terms of their genuine existential concerns. Being bitten by a cobra is a dangerous (although not a likely) possibility, and although a few villagers may hesitate on direct questioning to declare their belief in malevolent spirits (translated below as "ghosts"), all know about such spirits and at one time or another have performed acts to propitiate them, indicating considerable psychic investment in their reality. Although in some cases one might wonder about the motivations behind them, the responses make complete sense.

The responses to the first item, "He was most afraid of . . ." fall into three major categories. The vast majority of villagers (61 percent) are frightened by experiences, actually possibilities (and again, in their unpredictable world, the possible is psychologically critical) which threaten

---

[6] The major analytic difference between anxiety and fear is, in fact, that the latter is "bound" anxiety, i.e., the anxiety has assumed a concrete, objective representation which the individual at least can deal with: by avoidance, doing battle with it, laughing over it, and the like.

their physical well-being.[7] They specify such threats as poverty (15 informants), not having enough to eat (11), illness (4), flood and fire (3), death (3), and being bitten by poisonous snakes (2). There is no significant difference in the economic statuses of individuals who mention either poverty or famine as their greatest fear. While there are six references to these fears on the part of "poor" villagers, there are sixteen references on the part of "average" villagers and four references on the part of "rich" villagers, all accurate reflections of their representation in the sample. The second major category of responses, held by 20 percent of the informants, describe the actions of people as the source of greatest fear. In all cases, these refer to actions of people other than the self, and the reference in more than half the responses is specifically to thieves. In a few cases, younger informants speak of their parents scolding them or beating them. As suggested earlier, no villager recognizes any personal inadequacies as sources of fear, although the idiosyncratic *karma* (or *kam*) response, mentioned below, suggests this in a superficial way. In this regard, it might be noted that three informants assert that they are afraid of nothing. The third category, encompassing the responses of 10 percent of the villagers, mentions malevolent spirits as the sources of greatest fear. Interestingly, one of these informants tries to pooh-pooh her fear by noting that if there were no way to escape the spirit she could manage.

From the point of view of one of the major concerns of this book, the most significant finding of the above data, replicated in part and in an even more apposite way in the next item, is that only a minority of villagers admit to any fear, symbolic or otherwise, of the actions of other persons, and none indicate any anxiety over their own actions toward others. The relevance of this finding is, of course, that it places our earlier remarks in the "Orienting Toward Others" section in proper perspective. In that section, where we were concerned explicitly with interpersonal relationships, it was perhaps inevitable that the interpersonal mode of anxiety would loom large. Here, however, villagers are permitted to express any kind of anxiety—physical, interpersonal, intrapersonal, fanciful, magical—and only a minority do indeed give their anxiety an interpersonal form. In this connection, a remark made much earlier in the text might be recalled. In discussing the uneasiness that villagers frequently betray in their interpersonal contacts (nervous laughter and concern with inconsequential

---

[7] By way of general intellectual interest, it might be noted that this finding, as well as the one emerging from our next item, offers strong support to some "admittedly impressionistic and unverified" observations of Skinner (1957: 309–310) who, in discussing the major concerns of the lower class Thai members of Bangkok society, who are mainly transplanted peasants, singles out as primary their concern with "basic well-being, *i.e.*, the health and safety of the organism."

TABLE 19

He was most afraid of . . .
The thing raw *is most afraid of is (namely) . . .*

THREATS TO PHYSI-CAL WELL-BEING:	61%	poverty. If he had enough, he would not be afraid. having nothing to eat. I mean when there is a flood, and all the paddy is lost, and we will starve because there is no rice to eat. not having enough to eat. having fever; getting sick and having no money. fire, because when a house catches fire it is a great loss. death. snakes. He is not afraid of ghosts. He can walk in the dark. But snakes are dangerous. He does not like to go anywhere after dark.
ACTIONS OF OTHERS:	20%	people. When she had money, she was afraid she would be robbed. When she did not have any, she was in difficulty. her father beating her.
MALEVOLENT SPIRITS:	10%	ghosts; but if there were no choice (no place to go, no way to get out of the situation), then she could manage. death; of ghosts haunting him. If the ghosts don't haunt him, he is not afraid.

topics) it was noted that, "uneasiness, when it occurs, is accepted as a social psychological fact of life; it is not felt as a threat to the integrity of the personality." The data here would tend to reinforce that conclusion. At the same time, however, it must be remembered that 20 percent of the informants do give what is at least symbolic expression to their fear of others, and it would, therefore, be most inappropriate to go to the other extreme and assert that villagers have no anxiety about interpersonal relationships. I also noted in the earlier discussion that "the nervousness that is betrayed indicates some of the internal strain that villagers undergo in having to maintain a constant front of politeness." This appears to be a case of their simply accepting—without worry, shame, or any other secondary anxiety—their own shortcomings. The anxiety that is experienced is just not *felt* as a psychological burden.

One of the responses above, although idiosyncratic, merits attention. This is the response of the villager, age 52, who says that she is frightened by her *karma:* "it depends on *raw's* mind [or heart]. Some people are afraid of ghosts. They see things and they believe that they see ghosts. That is not right. They see falling leaves and they think that is a ghost. There is nothing when they approach. The most frightening thing is bad *karma.* It follows you. If you kill a living thing in this life, a living thing will kill you in the next life." What is surprising is that there are not more responses of this type, especially from older villagers. The psychological significance of this kind of response is of course most difficult to assess. Although on the surface it is an expression of personal inadequacy—an expression that the informant has not done as well for herself as she could have—its essentially timeless and unpredictable quality (one never knows when the product of bad *kam* will issue) almost takes it out of the sphere of direct emotional import. It is in fact an inordinately intellectualized response, probably just as expressive of the informant's sense of psychological security as it is expressive of her anxiety. Although bad *kam* is an omnipresent and unavoidable anxiety, the fact that one can make merit to reduce such *kam* and the possibility that one might in fact have less bad *kam* than one's anxiety would lead one to believe (one never knows) is a source of considerable psychological comfort.

The next item, *"His greatest problem was . . ."* is somewhat more cerebral and reflective than the preceding one. Villagers are asked to indicate not what frightens them, but what worries and generally concerns them. Thus, although their responses are in many ways similar to those given on the previous item, they are also considerably less extreme. All reference to malevolent spirits, for example, is missing here. Again, the majority of villagers (57 percent) describe as their greatest problem their well-being and survival. Their responses, however, lack the sense of trepidation that colored their earlier replies. Here, twelve villagers phrase their replies in terms of worrying about obtaining money, being rich, having money to spend, and the like, rather than in the more plaintive terms of being anxious about poverty, a response given by only one villager. Thirteen informants also say that they are worried about "making a living" or their "work," responses that are more ambiguous than the above in that it is difficult to determine whether villagers are worried about having sufficient income from the work or are disturbed by difficulties involved in the work itself (how their rice crop is coming along). Nine informants say that they are worried about starving, not having enough to eat; one is worried about illness; one about floods; and none about death or poisonous snakes. The reappearance of the food response should not of course be overlooked.

The second major category, encompassing the responses of 24 percent of the sample, relates to worrying about other people. However, almost half these responses (11 percent of the total) are protective and succoring responses, where ego is concerned with preventing harm to his family. The other 13 percent describe ego's concern about getting along with other people. Two of these responses refer explicitly to the informant's worry over the words he chooses in relating to others or that he speak sensibly.

TABLE 20

His greatest problem was . . .
Raw greatest problem is (namely) . . .

SURVIVAL:	57%	how to have money to spend and not starve.
		earning his living, day after day, and finding money to spend.
		her occupation; which career was good for her, and also continuing to do it.
		making his living in the future.
		rice and fish: food. If one does not have enough to eat, life is difficult.
		having money and food to eat.
WORRY OVER OTHERS (24%)		
"PROTECTIVE":	11%	the happiness of *raw* family.
		the complicated events in the nation that brought trouble to his family.
"GETTING ALONG WITH":	13%	relations with people. ("Going to visit people and have them visit us.")
		if it concerns the affairs of other people's hearts, we cannot solve it.
HAPPINESS:	8%	how to be rich. When one has money, one has happiness.

Interestingly, these two completions reflect ego's concern about his own capacity for dealing with others, not about how others might affect him. Also, in contrast to the preceding item, few of the responses in this category seem symbolic of any interpersonal anxiety that the villagers might feel. Here when a villager says, *"His greatest problem was . . .* his relations with people," or *". . .* when she got married, she was afraid of trouble," the villager is pointing directly at the cause of his anxiety.[8] In the second response, incidentally, the cause of worry may not be relationships with other people so much as it is the burdens which such relationships create: having to be responsible for and responsive to others; having to make oneself get along with them; and in this case, with the informant a young female, perhaps the burden of having children and the loss of personal freedom that this inevitably involves.

The fact that so few (but nevertheless some) villagers structure this item in terms of interpersonal problems is, of course, congruent with the

---

[8] On the other hand, some of the responses describing anxiety over lack of food and rice might be expressive of an anxiety over loss of self-esteem, *i.e.*, individuals who have no food are incompetent and must depend on others. Three informants (two of "average" economic status and one "poor") actually make this point explicit: ". . . what to do to have something to eat and not starve. Starvation, in addition to being uncomfortable, makes one feel ashamed in front of one's neighbors."

findings of the previous item, as is the fact that the majority structure it in terms of survival issues. The relative differences between the two items in the percentage of individuals holding these views (20 percent vs. 13 percent regarding interpersonal anxieties; 61 percent vs. 57 percent regarding survival anxieties) are obviously not significant.

The remaining responses on this item resist easy categorization. Eight percent of the villagers speak in general terms about their greatest problem being their desire for happiness, a response whose major significance is probably the fact that it is given by such a small number of persons. This is not to suggest that the majority of villagers are either happy or unhappy; it is simply to indicate that few have the need to articulate a general sense of unhappiness. (Indeed, from a few of the items in the "Dominant Drives and Wishes" section, it is clear that a sizable minority of villagers feel that given the possibilities of this world, they are in fact quite content. See particularly the item, *"He wishes he were. . . ."*) A few villagers here, both young males, also speak about the uncertainty of their futures as sources of worry. One villager says that her greatest problem is that she wants too much, suggesting a desire on her part for greater self-control.

The remaining items in this section are of a different order from the above. They ask villagers to describe how they would react to frightening or worrisome situations. The items are, *"If one is frightened, the best thing to do is . . ."* and *"When something worried him, he usually. . . ."* One of the more interesting attributes of the responses to both items is the sense of familiarity with these situations that they reveal. The responses are pointed, emotionally loaded (although not excessively so), and unembarrassed, suggesting again the villagers' tolerance of their own existential limitations. Their emotional tone also suggests that my assistant was originally correct when he said that it was "easy" for villagers to express their feelings of fear. In both cases, the responses tend to follow a bi-modal distribution, although the two modes are clearly related to each other psychologically.

To *"If one is frightened, the best thing to do is . . ."* 40 percent of the informants respond by saying that they would keep cool, calm, and *chəəj*. However, what is intriguing is that this is all that they would do. Their aim is to get their emotions back under control, their personal stability being paramount to any other consideration, such as discovering what caused the fright, how they might deal with the cause, or fighting that cause. The other major response, held by 31 percent of the villagers, is to express dependency. However, what is most important here is that this is a metaphorical dependency, involving seeking help from the Lord Buddha or from Allah (for Moslems) or from one's "soul-stuff," rather than from other human beings. In fact, the absence of any reference to other human beings, especially parents, is striking.

Of the seventeen persons who ask for supernatural help, seven, all women, explicitly say that they would call their *khwaan* (or "soul-stuff") back. Since this is a distinctively Thai concept, it merits a few words of explanation. Thai ontology holds that every individual is inhabited by a *khwaan*, who during childhood (when the individual is unstable and immature) or during a crisis can escape the body through an invisible hole in the head. One of the major functions of the top-knot worn by half the children of Bang Chan is to cover the invisible hole so that the *khwaan*

TABLE 21

If one is frightened, the best thing to do is . . .
If raw is frightened, the best thing raw ought to do is (namely) . . .

EQUANIMITY:	40%	to keep his heart calm.
		to pull yourself together (to try to compose yourself). Sometimes, just run away.
		to control oneself.
		to control your emotions until they are better.
		to stay *chəəj-chəəj*.
DEPENDENCY:	31%	to exclaim, "Lord help me!"
		to call one's soul-stuff back; call upon God, Allah.
		to think of Lord Buddha, his teaching, and his priests.
		to sometimes exclaim, *"phra chuaj"* ("Lord Buddha, or Buddhism, or monks—help me.")
FLIGHT:	8%	to avoid the situation; to run away.

cannot escape; also most life-cycle ceremonies have a special ritual devoted to "calling the *khwaan*," who although obviously not absent from the individual at the time, is called to reaffirm the necessity of his being in his place when the individual needs him most. At the same time, the formal ritual of "calling the *khwaan*" memorializes the fact that the *khwaan* is in his proper place, thus indicating that the individual in whom he resides has had the internal stability to reach the point in life that he has in fact reached. The "calling of the *khwaan*" is usually, although not always, performed by women, which might explain why all the villagers who give this response are female. The *khwaan* has four crucial attributes: (1) although he is of the self, he does have an independent existence of his own; (2) he is that part of the self that gives the self stability, and from an analytic point of view, is really an objectification of human stability; (3) he is recognized to be capricious; and (4) his departure from the body is both cause and effect of the loss of one's wits, steadiness, and equilibrium. If the *khwaan* stays away too long, the individual may become deranged and may die.

In these terms, the seven individuals who say that when they are frightened they would call back their "soul-stuff" seem to be expressing two related needs: a recognition of their ultimate dependence on supernatural forces and, very much like the majority group of informants, a preoccupation with psychological stability. There is in fact implicit to these responses almost an assumption that one of the marks of an adult, civilized "human being" (in its basic ontological sense) is the achievement of stability, orderliness, and stoicism in a universe—both inner and outer—that at any time may regress to a more primitive, chaotic state. The great attention that villagers give to being *riab-rɔɔj* (neat, clean, well-organized in appearance, demeanor, and speech); the fact that they often distinguish between adults and children in terms of the disorganization and randomness of the latter's behavior; the very fact that an individual's *khwaan* is most wayward during childhood; the high value that is placed upon being *chəəj* and the negative value that is placed on having a "hot heart" (*caj rɔɔn*) are all expressive of this assumption.

There are a few other categories of response to the above item that should be mentioned, although none is held by more than 8 percent of the sample. Four villagers say that the best thing to do when frightened is to run away; three villagers assert that they are never frightened; three do say that they would investigate the cause of the fright, indicating that this response is not completely lacking in Bang Chan; two say that they would comfort themselves; two are simply afraid; and two more have no idea of what to do under the circumstances.

To the item, *"When something worried him, he usually . . ."* 45 percent of the sample responds by saying that they would feel anxious, uneasy, uncomfortable, or unhappy. In essence, they seek no solution to their hypothetical problem, but simply accept the state of anxiety that has been created. For a few of them, the anxiety is extreme: they say they "could not eat, could not sleep, could not work," a response that I have heard several times in Bang Chan from villagers who were actually worrying through a problem. The other major response, held by 40 percent of the sample, is to perseverate over the problem: to keep thinking about it, to think about it constantly, or, as one villager expresses it, *"When something worried him, he usually . . . thought about it. Sometimes he dreamt of it too."*

The major theme of both the above responses is, of course, that although villagers handle their worries in an emotionally meaningful way,

TABLE 22

When something worried him, he usually . . .
When something worries raw, raw, usually . . .

DISCOMFORT:	45%	felt rather uneasy about it.
		was worried, anxious and uncomfortable.
		suffered and felt down in the dumps.
		was anxious; wanted to know what would come next.
PERSEVERATION:	40%	paid attention to it; continually thought of it.
		thought of it and worried about it all the time.
		could not go anywhere until she solved the problem first.
		kept thinking about it; couldn't do other things easily because he couldn't help thinking about it.
SOLUTION:	6%	had to go and find the truth (find out whether the thing that was worrying him was true or not).
NO WORRIES:	6%	he has never been worried, so he does not know.

they never really resolve them or even hold out the hope of resolving them. They simply accept worry as an inherent, enervating, but tolerable part of their experience.

The minority responses here are not wholly insignificant: 6 percent of the informants do describe a happy solution of their problem in that they "find a way out," or "try to settle it first before going somewhere else"; 6 percent claim that they never worry; and a few say that although they worry, they try not to show it.

This section on "anxiety" may be summarized in the following way. In answer to a question posed at the end of the last section, the data indicate that anxiety about interpersonal relationships is not the major anxiety of the villagers. Rather, the responses of the majority of the informants focus on matters relating to survival and the physical and material well-being of the individual. However, a noteworthy minority, averaging 16 percent of the sample, do reveal symbolic or direct anxiety about their interpersonal relationships, suggesting that beneath the affable or *chɔɔj* exteriors of at least a few villagers there is some distress about the social psychological pressures placed upon them. On the other hand, when we consider that for most human beings the most important fact about the environment is the presence in that environment of other human beings and the pressures that they inevitably place upon the individual, it is impressive that a larger number of villagers do not phrase their anxieties in interpersonal terms. The only possible explanation for this is that most Bang Chaners feel a

fundamental security about their own *psychological* worth. This is undoubtedly abetted by the fact that the modes of social interaction in Bang
Chan do not demand too much from the individual, as well as the fact that
the individual, with his profound sense of free choice, often ignores or
isolates himself from the impingements of others. (That a stance of psychic
isolation is not necessarily maladaptive will be discussed in the final chapter.) When asked how they would react to frightening or worrisome
situations, most villagers respond in terms of maintaining their inner
psychic stability and in terms of accepting and tolerating these familiar
psychic pressures. Their responses are non-constructive, but are highly
congruent with their passive and secure orientations to the world. Their
responses to "anxiety" tend toward psychological "unimodality" at an interpretive level, although in the last two cases the descriptive similarity of the
responses first suggest a bi-modal distribution.

Aggression: Causes and Reactions

Analyzing "aggression" in Bang Chan is very much like analyzing "sex" in
contemporary American culture. The category represents at one and the
same time one of the most obvious and one of the most convoluted areas of
the villagers' psychological lives.

The most obvious fact about aggression in Bang Chan is that villagers
cannot tolerate its spontaneous, direct expression in face-to-face relationships. This is demonstrated not only by the general absence of overt
aggression in such relationships but by the elaborate array of devices that
villagers use to control its expression: giggling when making or receiving an
untoward request, using a go-between to soften the demand of an interpersonal lien, leaving the field at the slightest hint of provocation (whether
the provocation is intended or not), as well as the more general use of
flattery, comedy, and self-effacement (*kreeŋcaj*). The repeated use of these
devices as well as the villagers' evaluations of "people who never show their
feelings" (see tables 16 and 17) reveal their sensitivity to aggression as a
latent, but intrinsic, attribute of most social encounters. In fact, their
evaluations of people who inhibit their feelings—or their *assumptions* about
the inherently hostile nature of such feelings—suggest that their recognition of the potentiality of aggression (whether in themselves or others) is
quite conscious.

The net result of these orientations is to give face-to-face contacts an
aura of surface pleasantness, but at the same time a high degree of brittle-
ness. Over and over again, villagers indicate that they prefer not to have
any relationship at all than to have one that is even tinged with hostility.

Thus, in explaining why he loves one of his closest friends, a villager says:

> We love each other because we never contradict each other or disagree. That is why we love each other. If we disagreed, there would be no love. [Investigator: "It is normal sometimes even for close friends to disagree. About what kind of things do you and your close friend disagree?"] We never disagree. Only people who are drunkards and take opium disagree. That is why our friendship has lasted so long. [Investigator: "What would happen if you disagreed?"] We would not love each other, and maybe he would take revenge on me.

In another place, this same informant says of his relationship with his wife: "My wife and I never quarrel. If we quarreled, we would have to separate. There would be nothing to divide—except the children." As indicated earlier, many villagers, fearing the volatility of a quarrel, actually do separate, often even before the dispute gets going. Similarly, individuals, particularly if they are in subordinate positions, hesitate even to approach others lest they stimulate, let alone elicit, anger. Villagers will hesitate to approach others even if they are not the object, but simply a possible catalyst, of another's potential aggression: witness the cases of the land sale deal and the broken noria cited earlier. Note that in these cases it is not manifest aggression but merely the anticipation of it that inhibits villagers from initiating or maintaining interpersonal involvements.

Although villagers decline to express or to be exposed to direct aggression, they do have several indirect, if somewhat more complicated, ways of venting these feelings. Of these, the simplest is to gossip nastily *about* people. The frequency of this characteristic peasant activity is considerable in the village: in fact, an uncharitable observer might, on the basis of Bang Chan, just as readily entitle a book about Thailand *Land of Gossip* as *Land of Smiles*. However, the very frequency of gossip seems to mitigate its intensity or effect. Villagers are so accustomed to it that it is almost a *way* of talking, a style of speech. And as is the case with much village speech, villagers listen to, but do not necessarily believe, the nasty things one person might say about another. Also, excepting those cases where a person's complaints are either realistic or justifiable, people are just as likely to listen to an individual's gossip for what it says about him as for what it says about the person whom he is criticizing. None of this is to suggest that the person gossiping does not attain release, or that the person about whom he is gossiping, *if* he found out, would not be hurt or peeved. Rather, it is the situation in which the hostility is expressed that mitigates its effect.

Less frequent and more painful than the above are the formal, almost ritualized, ways of expressing hostility. What is significant about these particular procedures is that their very formalism serves to keep the aggression controlled and within bounds. Thus, everybody knows precisely how to behave when a buffalo disappears in the middle of the night and an intermediary arrives the next day to arrange the price for its return. Similarly, the aggressor, his victim, and everyone else present knows what is meant when someone calls a dog by the name of a person who is within hearing range and claims it was simply a slip of the tongue. The victim might respond by stealing his antagonist's boat and returning it a few weeks later, after his adversary has suffered sufficient anxiety. Note that in all these cases a face-to-face confrontation is either avoided or concealed.

Related to the above is the use of magical aggression. Textor (1960) points out that magical aggression—from one *person* to another *person*—is on the wane in Bang Chan. Also, it is clear from his exhaustive inventory of the magical practices in the village that interpersonal aggression has a very minor part in what is otherwise an extremely elaborate belief and ritual system: there are no more than three or four supernatural "objects," out of more than one hundred and seventy, that even suggest witchcraft, and although these objects are considered highly potent, they are rarely used. Even in the most extreme case—a young man using the oil from the chin of a corpse to induce hysteria in a maiden who has rebuffed his advances [9]—the victim is held partially responsible for having succumbed to the magic, a consideration that diminishes the "magical" implications of the ritual.[10]

Finally, a word should be said about the most convoluted way of expressing aggression. This is suicide, a procedure which, obviously, is applicable to only a small number of people. Nevertheless, during the relatively brief period that I was in the field, three Bang Chaners (out of a population of 1,771) attempted to do away with themselves by hanging. They always selected a conspicuous place (a tree on the Minburi highway or over the main canal) and were always unsuccessful. The aggression here is convoluted not only because it is turned inward, but also because it is

---

[9] This blending of sex and aggression does not have the same meaning in Bang Chan as it has in the West. Although the young man is concerned with punishing the girl for not responding to him, he is more concerned with breaking down her defenses and equilibrium, the very factors which denied him access. In English terminology, he wants to "unhinge" her, with all the duality that such symbolism might imply.

[10] While magical aggression between people is relatively minor, magical means of averting aggression by non-human forces is not. In fact, the largest number of magical practices in Bang Chan relate to protecting the health and welfare of the organism from malevolent spirits, accidents, and dangerous animals. These data, of course, are quite consistent with the SCT data on "anxiety," presented in the preceding section.

intended to hurt others. The explicit justification in all three suicide attempts was to make a spouse feel "sorry and unhappy."

What is perhaps most intriguing about all these naturalistic ways of expressing aggression (even the last, which, despite its drama, is attempted, not actual, suicide) is that in their formalism and indirection they are actually quite flaccid. An obvious question, therefore, is whether the villagers' aggressive tendencies are, at bottom, quite weak, or whether they are simply bottled up, never to emerge in any but controlled and disguised ways. The answer to this question seems to be "both," depending upon one's analytic perspective. On the one hand, the villagers are so attentive in their relationships to shutting off aggression before it gets up a head of steam, that these relationships provide little basis—in an objective, realistic sense—for the development of aggressive feelings. When a potentially hostile act does not even take place, there is simply no reason to feel angry, other than perhaps to be angered because one's anticipations have been frustrated. However, the likelihood that overt hostility will be suppressed is itself so expectable that such secondary anger, if present, is minimal. Further, the villagers' self-concern is so great that they simply do not have that much to gain, psycho-dynamically, from being intensely angry at others. An act of interpersonal aggression assumes emotional investment in others (or obversely, that others provide the self with major emotional satisfaction). If such investment is hesitant, guarded, or otherwise weakened—as almost all of our materials have indicated—the aggression that normally accompanies that investment, or is allowed by it, will also be weakened. Simply stated: it is difficult for a person to be angry at people with whom he does not have much of an emotional relationship.

On the other hand, the great attention that villagers give to the control of aggression indicates that they are by no means at peace with these feelings. In fact, what is most impressive about aggression in Bang Chan is not its absence, but the amount and kinds of control that are exercised over it. This very process of control probably intensifies whatever "realistically derived" aggressive feelings they already harbor. Thus, although their overt social behavior does not provide a basis for the development of aggressive feelings, their covert behavior—vis-à-vis themselves—certainly does.

The fundamental issue, of course, is why villagers should be so concerned with controlling their aggressions in the first instance. This is not an easy question to answer. However, there are at least three considerations which, if taken together, might account for it. First, much of their aggression control might derive from the more generalized fear of losing equilibrium—of "falling apart" or becoming psychically disassembled; of losing their *khwaan,* as it were—if they release their anger. This is the fear of "letting go" and of regressing to a primitive psychological state. Every impulse of an adult villager is to fight this tendency. Second, by controlling their aggressions, they are not imposing their own problems on others and are maintaining the attitudes of "respect" and tolerance—as well as emotional indifference—that are otherwise so important to them. This consideration obviously does not account for the absence of aggression; it simply points up the fact that the aggression that does exist is dealt with internally, rather than socially. Finally, their aggression control seems to be based upon fear of reprisal. Although in a few instances this may be a realistic fear, it is principally a straightforward projection: they know only too well how painful the reprisals would be of people who hold the feelings of hostility that they themselves hold. This consideration is not inconsistent with my earlier remarks on the difficulty villagers have in investing hostility in others. Rather, it follows directly: the villagers' difficulty is not based upon lack of hostility, but upon the lack of social relationships which are sufficiently meaningful to merit that hostility. Rather than work out their aggressions behaviorally—in and with other human beings—they work them out in the isolation of their own inner psychodynamics.

I have gone into considerable detail here because "aggression" is the one area of the villagers' lives where the meaning of behavior is not at all apparent from its manifestations. Without such background material, the following SCT results would probably also have little significance.

The first item, *"He most often gets angry when . . . ,"* reveals some of those patterns with unexpected clarity. Ostensibly, the item asks informants simply to identify the various sources of aggression. However, the term for "angry" (*krood*) in this sentence explicitly means "angry toward other people." [11] Thus, one would expect villagers to focus on the activities or characteristics of others—or, at minimum, on some dimension of a social relationship—which elicits their ire. However, their most frequent response is to ignore the semantic pressure to refer to others and to dwell on characteristics within themselves that cause their anger. Thirty percent of

---

[11] The importance of this point becomes apparent when *krood* is contrasted with some of the other "angrys" in the Thai lexicon: *moohoo,* angry at the situation in which one is entangled rather than toward another person; *chun,* angry at the action of another person, but not the person himself, with a suggestion of helplessness (the blast of a radio as one is falling asleep); *chiw,* to *feel* angry at another person, but to conceal its expression; *moohoochunchiaw,* angry all the time, at anything, because one has a character trait to be angry; *khunkhɛɛn,* revengeful. That the villagers should have such a rich set of lexical contrasts in this area—and I have excluded terms which are simply variations on the intensity of "angry" ("irritated" vs. "enraged") —is not without significance. "Anger" obviously is an emotion to which villagers attend.

the sample responds in this manner. Thus, they say that they are hostile toward other people when they themselves are "in a bad mood and tired," "are rattled," "have done wrong," or "are old. When one gets old, one's tongue becomes sharp and one gets angry easily." The emphasis on the loss of control or psychic equilibrium can be noted here, as well as the fact that although these disequilibrium forces are in themselves not very extreme, they are presented as ample justification for anger. Even when villagers do mention others, it is not in reference to others' actions so much as it is in reference to the emotions that those actions elicit, that is, *"He most often gets angry at other people when . . .* he is cross, such as, when other people are infuriating or annoying."

TABLE 23

He most often gets angry when . . .
Khon most often get angry at other people when . . .

SELF-REFERENCE:	30%	when *raw* make an error in the work. I, too, get angry.
		she has done something wrong.
		he is in a temper.
		he is drinking, drunk. If he is not drunk he does not become angry easily.
OTHERS DO NOT SATISFY SELF:	19%	they disobey him.
		they are not good to her.
GOSSIP:	23%	people say bad things about him.
		other people accuse him about something that has no truth.
QUARRELING:	23%	they quarrel.
		he has no happiness; when other people molest him often.

Related to the above are the responses given by 19 percent of the sample which, although referring to others, focus not on any objective negative quality or action of others (as in the two categories to follow) but on the simple fact that others do not satisfy the wishes and demands of the self. Again, the self—its needs, value, and significance—is primary. Villagers falling in this category say that they are most often angry at others when "people do not do what *raw* have told them to do," "they are not good to her," "people do not do things according to my wish." Informants giving these responses fall in all age and socioeconomic categories, suggesting that they are not necessarily the attitudes of social superordinates, which an older age or "wealthy" economic position might otherwise imply.

The final two categories, each representing 23 percent of the sample, describe as the causes of anger the direct actions of others. In one case, others deride and gossip about the self: "people speak of him in an envious way"; "they blame her according to what is not true." In the other case, people quarrel, scold, and otherwise aggress overtly toward one another: "people come to look for trouble and damn him"; "people pick a quarrel with her." It might be added that excepting two villagers, none of the overt hostility specified by the villagers is even suggestive of physical aggression. More important, there are no completions at all which are suggestive of Bang Chaners being angry because they have been taken advantage of or because their competence has been challenged or threatened. There are no thoughts on the order of: "when they have pulled a fast one on him"; "when he has been tricked"; "when he has been cheated." The point is important because being tricked, cheated, or otherwise "one-upped" are events which some Western observers (leMay 1930, Textor 1959) have seen as occurring with considerable frequency in Thailand. The point has been implied in a few places in this book as well. These data would suggest that although such events occur, in a behavioral sense, they have little *motivational* significance to the villagers; that is, villagers seem to assume that an act of trickery or cheating is not necessarily prompted by the desire to hurt or to be hostile toward others. To them, the intrinsic attribute of trickery or cheating is self-advancement, not aggression or a sense of evil. These latter elements are by-products, and they are not so much by-products of the cheater's motivations as they are of the situation into which the cheated party was foolish enough to place himself. *If* the cheated party were to feel anger in such a situation it would be toward himself, not toward the individual who simply "took advantage of a good opportunity."

The next two items ask for the villagers' reactions to being annoyed and insulted by others. Since these two experiences are essentially intensity variations on the same theme, they will be dealt with together.

The overwhelming response of the villagers to both experiences is to avoid action and to respond internally with emotion and feeling. This is the response of 66 percent of the sample to *"When people annoy me, I . . ."* and 69 percent to *"When he insulted me, I. . . ."* (Note that in the original Thai the annoyance is explicitly interpersonal; the insult, although not explicitly interpersonal, assumes a human agent.) Even when villagers do act out their responses in behavior it is mainly to flee, avoid, or get away from the annoyance (20 percent) or to improve themselves *in order* not to merit the insult (14 percent). Thus, even in these variant cases, there is no contact between the annoyer or insulter and the self, and informants, although acting out their responses, do so in isolation. Only three villagers indicate any propensity to retaliate against others (and, by definition, deal with them directly and overtly: they scold their annoyers) while another three, in inimitable Thai fashion, hedge their retaliations with conditions, or phrase them as intentions ("I would scold them if I could"; "I would like to rail at them, but I am not sure I can.").

In the item, *"When people annoy me, I . . . ,"* 43 percent of the sample responds either by feeling angry or by indicating that they dislike being annoyed. The majority of these informants state their anger or dislike flatly, although a few justify it by adding that the anger or its external

TABLE 24

When people annoy me, I . . .
When someone annoys raw, raw *. . .*

EMOTION (66%)		
ANGER:	43%	am slightly angry.
		seethe inside.
		feel annoyed because I want to stay peaceful and cannot.
		dislike them.
		feel angry at them and I want them to go away quickly.
NO FEELINGS:	10%	well, well, I feel *chɔɔj-chɔɔj*. Nothing happens.
		have no feelings about being annoyed.
DEPRESSION:	13%	my heart and feelings are unhappy.
		am down in the dumps.
ACTION (30%)		
LEAVE THE FIELD:	20%	want to be far away. I don't want to be annoyed.
		want to get away from them.
		run away to find peace somewhere else.
ACTUAL RETALIATION:	5%	rail at them. Why should I spare them? They are not my parents.
INTENDED RETALIATION:	5%	scold them to stop annoying *raw*. If *raw* can find some way to make them stop annoying, *raw* will do it.

cause prevents them from "being at peace." Different from the above in content, but similar in its emphasis on inactivity, is the response of 10 percent of the villagers who say either that they have no feelings about being annoyed or simply feel *chɔɔj-chɔɔj*. In effect, these informants avoid or deny any reaction to the experience. Another 13 percent are also inactive, but instead of responding with stoicism or indifference, they perceive the annoyance as cause for feeling depressed and unhappy. Although not a complete withdrawal, as is the case in the category to follow, the response is another example of the villagers' emotional passivity in

TABLE 25

When he insulted me, I . . .
When there is an insult to raw, raw . . .

EMOTION (69%)		
ANGER:	40%	felt raŋkiad (disgusted or repelled by what the insulter did) and I did not want to speak with her either. A person who speaks too much, who is too sociable, is no good.
		felt a little angry, that was all. I did not feel much more than that.
		was annoyed. It was none of his business.
		felt displeased, as was natural, and I wondered why he insulted me.
NO FEELINGS:	16%	tried to control myself and not be perturbed. I tried not to let my base nature take control of me. Everyone suffers from contempt and backbiting: it is inevitable. If we remain undisturbed, they will stop of their own accord.
		was indifferent to him. I live my own life; I have my own work. I do not make my living by taking advantage of others or by cheating others. I do not steal from anybody in order to take care of my wife and children.
DEPRESSION:	13%	felt sorry. I live my own life; I do not trouble anyone; I earn my own living.
		felt unhappy and sorry. In the future I will try not to let him insult me again.
ACTION (28%)		
IMPROVE SELF:	14%	felt hurt and tried to improve myself.
		would behave better, so that they would stop insulting me.
"AVOID STIMULUS":	14%	it is not good to insult someone for no reason. There are a lot of people who like to insult others; they are men who like to gossip.
		no one ever insulted me, because I never said anything bad about anybody. Therefore, they never said anything bad about me.

psychologically stressful situations. Finally, 20 percent of the sample responds simply by leaving the field: they go away or run away from those who annoy them. Although an "active" response in the sense that energy is expended in overt behavior, the reaction is a patent evasion of the annoyance and its perpetrators.

The total of these various categories is 86 percent, indicating that the villagers' tendency to avoid dealing directly with people who annoy them is highly unimodal indeed.

The distribution of responses to *"When he insulted me, I . . ."* is strikingly similar to the above. Because it is a more extreme expression of hurt, some of the responses are a bit more dramatic; also, the internal frequencies of a few of the categories are a bit different. However, the overriding tendency is to deal with the insult by avoiding the insulter and simply feeling internally—angrily, "indifferently," or unhappily. Here, 40 percent of the sample responds with anger or dislike; 16 percent indicate that they have no feelings about the insult or are *chǝǝj-chǝǝj*; and 13 percent are depressed, sorry, or unhappy. Only a single individual, however, reacts by leaving the field.

There are two categories of response for which there are no equivalents on the earlier item. Fourteen percent of the informants indicate that the insult has provoked them into improving themselves or behaving better. However, they are explicit in indicating that this is principally a means of ridding themselves of their antagonists. Another 14 percent present what are essentially "avoidance of the stimulus" responses. They say that they have never been insulted or they discuss the immorality of insults. Not surprisingly, all but two of the Buddhist monks in the sample react in this manner.

In summary, the SCT data strongly confirm the villagers' behavioral tendencies to control, deny, and inhibit their aggressive impulses. The data indicate that they do not lack such impulses, but rather that they are unable to act them out in an overt, social manner. Instead, they respond internally and live with the hostility (in an angry, "indifferent," or unhappy fashion) or work it out in the privacy of their own minds. The data also indicate that this tendency is culturally unimodal.

Dominant Drives and Wishes

The materials covered in this section are to the author the most interesting of all the SCT data, not so much from the point of view of what they reveal about the villagers' psychic life as from that of providing answers to questions about an area that is virtually unknown. There are numerous things that the villagers do—make merit, grow rice, tell funny stories, treat others politely, and the like—which, on the basis of the time and effort given to them, an observer might point to as representing the villagers' major concerns. To a certain extent, I did this myself in the earlier, "naturalistic observation" chapter. However, there are no available data on what villagers *themselves* perceive as the most important things in life or what *they* identify as their hopes and aspirations. Although few of the responses below are in themselves startling, what is revealing is the relative weight given to the considerations that are mentioned.

It must be emphasized that the first two items here permit villagers to move in almost any direction and, if they wish, to indulge their fondest fancies. The fact that only a few take advantage of the latter is testament to the deeply ingrained sense of self-constraint and personal limitation ("I know my place: not too high and not too low") that they impose upon themselves.

To the item, *"He wishes he were . . ."* (in Thai, *"Raw wants to be . . ."*) all but five villagers respond in terms of what is essentially their public role or public image. Of the five who do not, two are individuals who do not want to suffer or do not want to have anything to worry about; one wishes he were intelligent and clever; and the other two phrase their wishes in such abstract terms ("a person who behaves well") that they simply resist further explication. In any event, these are the individuals whose responses most closely approximate what could be called "responses of psychic introspection," an area which villagers for the most part ignore.

The majority of the responses fall into three major categories. Forty percent of the villagers respond in terms of either specifying a particular status they might achieve ("an army officer"; "a big shot"; "a government official who is comfortable and has honor"; "the mother of a doctor, district officer, or governor"); saying that they would like to be rich; or simply by saying that they would like to be good and diligent workers "growing a lot of paddy" or "having good jobs." Within this majority category, nine individuals specify the first type of wish, the examples cited being the most self-indulgent replies; seven respond in terms of becoming wealthy; and six want to be competent workers. This last response is essentially a more optimistic or assertive phrasing of the one to follow—villagers want to be a better version of what they are already—and could just as readily be included there.

The second major response, held by 25 percent of the sample, is to be just what they are now. This is a description of their responses rather than a deduction from them. They explicitly say that they "do not want to change"; "my status compels me to be what I am"; "only want to be a rice farmer, to earn my living by raising rice, as I do now." Although a minority group, the fact that so many villagers should go so far as to deny the premise of the item in order to express their satisfaction over their present and traditional state is not without significance. It is important to note that were we to deduct the six "competent worker" responses from the previous category, this category would then represent the majority.

The third major response, given by 20 percent of the sample, describes being a "good," "respected," and "non-trouble-making" individual as the principal wish of the informant. A few of these villagers want to be "good

TABLE 26

He wishes he were . . .
Raw wants to be . . .

STATUS:	40%	a rich man. Then he could do anything he wanted.
		a teacher, in order to teach children so that they will have knowledge and be good children.
		an army officer.
		a person who has a lot of money and paddy fields, because I have many children. I have ten *raj* (four acres) of land now. What will the children do when they grow up? It worries me.
		a good worker, growing a lot of paddy.
STASIS:	25%	he does not want to be anything.
		he never wishes anything, because his status compels him to be what he is.
		he is quite content to remain a farmer.
GOOD PERSON:	20%	a man who behaves well and has goodness, virture, and honesty.
		a good person, not a *nagkleeng;* one who does not *thiawtree* (go out, enjoy oneself, leave the family).

citizens," a response which, although small in number, reflects the importance that villagers attach to being members of the nation-state. (Considering all the different things that they might wish to be, how many Americans would complete the item, *"He wishes he were . . ."* with the statement: ". . . a good American"?) More than half these informants, however, build an interpersonal dimension explicitly into their replies by saying that they either want to be persons who "do not lie or incite people, do not have trouble with others" or are persons "whom others trust and respect."

What is most revealing about the above responses are the unexpected omissions. There are no references at all to religious considerations, even on the part of older people.[12] Particularly obvious is the absence of any reference to accumulating Buddhist merit. Neither is there any reference to the pleasures derived from dealing happily or enjoyably with other people. The closest we get to this is with the responses of two informants who are concerned mainly with the welfare of their children, and who speak in terms of "inspiring respect" in their children or assuming the role of "doctor" who, either by his knowledge (in case the children are ill) or wealth, could take care of them. Given all the conceivable things that villagers might wish to be—fanciful, real, personal, social, of this world, and of any world—the dominant wish is to have status, wealth, and respectability within their prevailing peasant context.

The next item, *"Most of all he wants to . . ."* is essentially a confirmation of the above findings. However, perhaps because of the syntax of the Thai version of the item and the inclusion of the word, "most" (*"The thing which raw wants the most is (namely) . . ."*) the responses assume a considerably more extreme and "unimodal" form. The overwhelming majority of the informants, 77 percent, want only one thing: money. A few of them say that they want what are essentially cultural variations of money: property, rice fields, land, cattle, and jewelry. Several of them almost wax purple about the significance of money in their lives: *"The thing which raw wants the most is (namely)* . . . have money and gold, because money can help us all the time. Whatever one wishes to have, one can use money to buy it all. Even when one wants a wife, if one has a lot of money one can have anyone's daughter"; ". . . have money. Money is better than anything else. It is only the moon and stars that money cannot buy"; ". . . to have money. She wants money very much because when she lacks other things she can find something to take their place, but when she lacks money she is most unhappy"; ". . . have wealth because everything else comes after that." These responses, of course, explicate the major function of money. They indicate that money is not an end in itself, but a means by which to achieve some of the other life goals appearing here.

The minority responses to this item are in no case held by more than four individuals. Four villagers do give religious responses, saying that what they want most is to accumulate merit (one mentions both merit and money); three refer to maintaining the welfare of their families (one of them merging money and succorance by saying that he wants enough money to provide for his family); and four say that they want happiness (again, two of them linking money and happiness together).

---

[12] There is nothing in the grammatical-semantic structure of the Thai version of this item inhibiting a religiously oriented response. The Thai cognate for the verb "to be" here is *"pen,"* which could easily result in a response such as ". . . *pen khon thii mii bun,"* or ". . . a person who has merit." This would be the most obvious "religious" completion under the circumstances.

TABLE 27

Most of all, he wants to . . .
The thing which raw *wants the most is* (*namely*) *. . .*

MONEY:	77%	have wealth, because everything else comes after that. have money. have money. Only one thing. have money. have money, clothes, and ornaments. have money so that he can buy things. have money. get money.
MERIT:	8%	get some merit. *Raw* want only to make merit.
FAMILY:	6%	to have knowledge; have a happy and prosperous family.
HAPPINESS:	8%	have happiness of body and mind.

The next two items differ from the preceding primarily in being more realistic and constraining. The items, *"The most important thing in his life is . . ."* and *"His greatest ambition is . . ."* ask the villagers to specify their real life goals rather than to indulge themselves (if they wish) and express their dreams and fancies. This difference in stimulus value seems to have charged their responses with a greater sense of seriousness and personal involvement than was the case on the earlier items, although from a substantive point of view the differences are not very divergent. The concerns expressed are obviously cut from the same cloth.

TABLE 28

The most important thing in life is . . .
The most important thing in raw *life is* (*namely*) *. . .*

SUBSISTENCE AND WEALTH:	57%	earning a living is the most important thing. to earn a living. What he should do to get a good job. food. having enough money to spend. a good career; a lot of money.
RELIGION:	10%	that one must make merit, so that in the future and in his next life he will have something to depend on.
FAMILY: OTHERS (LESS THAN 10% EACH):	10%	her father and mother. his father and mother, who have done *raw* good. He must repay the *bunkhun* (good deeds which assume reciprocation). how to be happy. death. Death is final. Beyond death is nothing. things concerning the heart.

To the item, *"The most important thing in life is . . ."* 57 percent of the sample responds in terms of earning a living or food and money. Most of the "earning a living" responses are expressed quite flatly, but some of the food responses are presented almost with a note of urgency: ". . . rice. Very important. If there's no rice to eat, then life is very bad"; ". . . having or not having something to eat. If you have something to eat: good. If you have nothing: trouble. We people are born in order to find things to fill our mouths and stomachs. . . ." As noted earlier, the concern with elemental subsistence is primary here. The minority responses, although encompassing several categories, which thus reduces the representation in each one, are by no means insignificant. (Taken as a whole, they represent almost half the informants.) Five villagers here do stress the importance of

TABLE 29

His greatest ambition is . . .
Raw greatest ambition is (namely) . . .

SUBSISTENCE AND WEALTH:	44%	to be rich.
		to have a place to live and food to eat all the time, so that nobody will look down on him.
		to have money.
		in regard to his daily living. How can one count on stealing things?
MERIT:	12%	to have happiness in the present and in the future. Must try to build up goodness and to avoid different kinds of badness which will bring punishment in the next life.
HAPPINESS:	10%	to have happiness in life, because her own life has met mostly with failures.
STATUS:	10%	to have a better status than *raw* now have.

religion and making merit; and five others point to their parents or their families as the most important things in life, responses which are slightly suggestive of a concern with fulfilling interpersonal obligations or with succorance. Three others explicitly mention the fulfillment of interpersonal obligations as important. One of these individuals is concerned with others paying a debt of kindness to him; one with doing good things for others; and one makes the relationship perfectly reciprocal. Three villagers also speak of happiness as important; two, with perfect realism, mention death. Finally, two villagers mention the importance of human feelings; this is the only reference that is made to an inner psychological state in all the responses presented to the items in this section.

The responses to the item, *"His greatest ambition is . . ."* are very similar to the above. The "earning a living" reply is replaced in frequency by the more assertive desire to be wealthy, but the food reply is just as common. Together, they encompass the responses of 44 percent of the informants. A third type of reply comes into evidence here, and while it is substantively not at all different from the foregoing responses, it is stylistically interesting because it represents such an excellent summation of the ambitions of the villagers: ". . . to have a place to live and food to eat; to have clothes to wear to protect himself from the sun and the wind. That's enough." The minority responses to the item again encompass several categories: six villagers wish to make merit; five want happiness, five want higher status than they presently have; two want their families to be happy; three want to behave well; and two are simply concerned about their daily living. One of the latter raises the rhetorical question: "How can one count on stealing things?"

Analysis of the villagers' definitions of the most desirable things in life reveal an overriding concern with practical matters: money, earning a living, achieving status, and having sufficient food. Some, but relatively little, attention is given to religious concerns or to satisfactions of an interpersonal nature, including even family. Psychological satisfactions that are specified relate to abstract states of happiness or to satisfactions derived from knowing that one is "behaving well," although in both cases the number of villagers who actually point to such satisfactions is relatively low. Immanent to the responses of other villagers, but again, in relatively small number, are the satisfactions to be had from being a competent farmer who, through hard work, achieves a good harvest and "a place to live and food to eat; . . . clothes to wear to protect himself from the sun and the wind. That's enough." This careful and constrained conception of the good life extends even to situations where when given license to indulge their most extravagant desires, villagers will go no further than to admit that they might wish to be "a government official who is comfortable and has honor" or "the *mother* of a doctor, district officer, or governor." (Italics added.) Excepting this area of psychological license, the villagers descriptions of their dominant drives and wishes tend toward psychological unimodality, although the minority responses *in toto* are not at all insubstantial.

VI

Lessons from Thai Culture

The materials in this volume have been addressed to several issues: methodological, theoretical, and descriptive. My purpose in this final chapter is to reflect on some of these points and to examine them for their relevance to the main currents of contemporary social science research.

Turning first to the more obvious methodological issue, it is clear that of the two descriptive methods used in this study, the first, presented in the chapter on "naturalistic observation," while essentially anecdotal and less systematic than the Sentence Completion materials, was the more sensitive of the two approaches. The very fact that the discussion was not governed by a pre-planned methodological framework permitted pursuing certain issues that were central in the psychological life of the villagers, but which might not otherwise appear in a culture-personality study. On the other hand, it is also clear that the materials thus gathered have little *direct* utility for cross-cultural studies, other than to indicate that other field workers look for similar or contrasting psychological manifestations among the people with whom they are working.

The Sentence Completion materials, while descriptively less sensitive and graphic than the above, afford the great advantage of being directly translatable to any other culture, of providing a check on the typicality of the earlier conclusions, and of providing a description of the villagers' subjectively held behavioral dispositions.

While the materials were qualitatively different—one "natural," the other "instrumental"; one behavioral, the other verbal; one descriptive of action, the other descriptive of predispositions to action—they produced no striking empirical inconsistencies. Much of this may have been due to the fact that many of the SCT items focused on relatively specific interactional situations—those descriptive of face-to-face contacts—which tend to be highly patterned in Bang Chan, and into which "loosely structured" considerations rarely enter. Under these circumstances, any carefully applied method might be expected to obtain roughly equivalent data. On the other hand, the fact that much of what is analytically meaningful about Thai personality occurs before, after, or between face-to-face contacts suggests that an instrument such as the SCT should never be used by itself, or at least not without some reference to behavioral data. The SCT, or my particular version of it, could not readily get at the process of psychological commitment that plays such an important role in the lives of the villagers, and which underlies their "loosely structured social system." In fact, the handling of this process may well be one of the most interesting things about the villagers. In a somewhat oblique way, the SCT data implied the importance of this process: so many of the villagers' responses were phrased in terms of fulfilling social forms and rituals, that an analyst might question the degree of psychological commitment behind them. However, "psychological commitment"—the reliability, depth, and constancy of relationships; the degree of involvement necessary for insuring that an interactional event will even take place—cannot begin to be recognized as an analytic problem until one sees beyond the very social situations that presume it, and this can probably only be done by naturalistic observation and interpretation.

While the SCT and observational data did not contain any striking empirical inconsistencies, they did demonstrate the significance of an issue raised early in this study: the problem of whether the culturally interesting or distinctive is the same as the culturally frequent or modal. The analyses indicated that for the most part these two types of characterization were not incongruent. Thus, the extreme individualism and self-concern of the villagers emerged unmistakably from both sets of data. However, there were instances when the two kinds of characterization were not isomorphic, and resulted in conclusions quite different from those originally expected. Thus, on the basis of the observational materials, I fully anticipated that anxiety about interpersonal relationships would emerge in the SCT responses as the villagers' most frequent form of anxiety. The amount of gossip that occurs in the community, the references that one hears to slander, the touchiness that villagers exhibit in their actual relations with others, all pointed to this conclusion. These were the appraisals of an outside observer struck by the "different" and "unusual" facets of the culture he was studying. Yet the SCT data indicated beyond all doubt that interpersonal anxieties were not, from the villagers' point of view, their most typical form of anxiety. They were worried more about their stomachs than their hearts.[1] This conclusion, deduced from the villagers' own per-

---

[1] One might argue here from a psychoanalytic point of view that the stomach is simply a substitute for the heart. However, one might also argue from a psychoanalytic point of view that the heart is simply a substitute for the stomach. This Freudian principle of the substitutability of needs cannot by itself account for the *direction* of the substitution (unless one assumes a doctrinaire early Freudian or neo-Freudian position) nor can it prove the *existence* of the hypothetical substitution. These can be demonstrated only by detailed, empirical data on the traumata, repressions, fixations,

ceptions, took on additional significance when related to the sense of psychological worth and self-love that the people of Bang Chan *also* exhibit. Again, the essential issue here is not the presence or absence of anxiety about interpersonal relationships. There is little doubt that villagers do suffer such anxiety. Rather, the question is one of *relative* frequency, and, by implication, the *relative* importance of such suffering to the *total* need and deprivation system of the villagers. It is precisely with regard to this larger kind of question that an instrument such as the SCT can provide context and perspective.

Turning to the theoretical issues that have been raised or suggested by the data, perhaps the most important is the problem of "conformity" as it relates to the villagers' loosely structured social system. This problem is of course at the center of all social psychological research. It is concerned with how, why, and the extent to which individuals relate to their social environments. In fact, in a recent paper aimed at synthesizing the theoretical premises underlying most current culture personality research, Bert Kaplan (1961*b*) presents a cogently argued case for the necessity of anthropologists and psychologists to shift their attention from the study of why individuals behave in particular ways to the study of this more generalized disposition. He says (665–666):

> Up to now our emerging theory appears to suggest a jungle-like situation in which wholly free and autonomous individuals, in a relatively opportunistic way, make use of the available channels of social partici-

---

regressions, and other psychodynamic processes of informants. Even so, it is highly unlikely that the anxiety responses of adults are *simply* the result of a series of unconscious processes—substitutive, projective, or otherwise. It must be remembered that an anxiety response is just as often a function of the ego, oriented to and in the service of the organism's reality needs, as it is a function of unconscious needs derived from the difficulties of the developmental process. When we consider that the villagers live in one of the most unpredictable universes imaginable and that they are a people entering the throes of a revolution of rising expectations, it is not at all surprising that they should feel anxious about threats to their physical well-being, expressed as a fear of going hungry or being poor. In fact, I would suggest that at bottom these are expressions of an existential anxiety about the essential instability, uncertainty, and impermanence of all life (including their own), an anxiety which has its cognitive basis in the "Wheel of Law" and other Buddhist doctrine. It might be argued that since, objectively viewed, the villagers are well fed and enjoy one of the highest standards of living in Asia, such anxieties are without foundation. I would answer by saying that the villagers are not aware of the per capita income figures for Asia, and that "reality" for any people is how they subjectively perceive and define it, not what it objectively is. To say that there is no realistic basis for the villagers' anxiety about going hungry and being poor is like saying that there is no realistic basis for their belief in interminable existences or in the timeless continuity of the self. In both instances they believe these things to be the case, and ultimately that is what is important.

pation and the rewards that are attached to them. . . . However, there is much evidence that conformity is ordinarily a generalized and diffuse disposition, not something that occurs only when some desired reward is in sight. One might say that it is the basic way of life of all but a few persons in any society. The essential meaning of most social action is not that the actor wishes to do this or that act, but that he wishes to stand in a conformative relationship to the social demands that exist in the situation. In the great majority of social situations most of us are not concerned with the problem of what to do, but much more with the problem of finding out what it is that would be appropriate. When we know what this is, compliance follows almost automatically. The basic fact is that we are mostly good citizens, persons who want to do what is right, correct, decent, and fitting. The culture and personality issue that we have been working to define so far, is not why persons wish to do this or that act, but why they are good citizens. Or, in other terms, what is the motivational basis for the generalized disposition to conformity. . . .

. The approach outlined in this highly persuasive argument would clearly contribute to increased understanding of the functioning of social systems, particularly complex, smoothly operating ones. However, on the basis of our Thai materials, I wonder if it is not in fact based on the highly debatable assumptions that (a) all social systems function *equally* smoothly; (b) that all social systems are *equally* demanding in their functional requirements for people to conform; and (c) that persons in *different* societies are *equally* motivated, through socialization or otherwise, to conform. Kaplan in fact says: "One might say that it [conformity] is the basic way of life of all but a few persons in *any* society." (Italics added.) It seems to me that Thai culture provides a powerful argument for the capacity of a social system to function and of its members to have reasonably satisfying relationships with one another (they get done in a pleasant way the things that have to be done) while the standards for and dispositions to conformity are very low indeed. Again, it is perfectly true that Bang Chaners are highly motivated to conform, and even to over-conform, in face-to-face relationships. However, the most striking characteristic of these relationships is not the conformity exhibited in them. It is rather that there is never any assurance that the relationships will actually occur, or if they do occur, that the commitments undertaken in one face-to-face encounter will be carried over to the next. The conformity typically is immediate, short-lived, and uncertain. Bang Chaners may wish "to stand in a conformative relationship to the social demands that exist in the situation." But they first must make a judgment on whether or not to stand in that relationship, a decision that is very much based on their being "free and autonomous individuals, [who] in a relatively opportunistic way, make use of the available channels of social participation and the rewards that are attached to them. . . ."

Without claiming in any way to know the thinking that prompted Kaplan's provocative comments on the importance of the motivation of conformity in shaping action, I wonder if it is not based on the supposition that situations in all cultures are similar to those that we typically encounter in our own highly complex, functionally specific culture—a culture which, *if it is to operate in the highly complex and relatively efficient way we know it,* requires that individuals conform to the demands of their tasks. In other terms, to what extent is the argument for conformity based on the supposition that the majority of relationships in most societies are similar to those which obtain, for example, between workers on an assembly line or between a secretary and her employer, where, if conformity were not maintained most of the time, the consequences would be functionally disastrous, disastrous to the very *purpose* of the relationship? While I take issue here with Kaplan, there is one crucial aspect in which I am in complete agreement with what he seems to be aiming at. That is, if his argument is in fact based upon, and directed at understanding, a strictly American model, I can thoroughly understand the import of his question: "What is the motivational basis for the generalized disposition to conformity . . . [?]" After living in Thailand for several months and observing, and often identifying with, the ease with which individuals pursued their own purposes, oblivious to the requirements of conformity, I began to wonder not about the Thai capacity to maintain loosely structured relationships but about the considerably more mystifying American capacity to conform to the expectations of others. From a *psychological* point of view, the latter is by far the more difficult and demanding, requiring as it does inhibition of and control over one's own desires and a deeply developed predisposition to orient oneself to others. How this orientation is developed and sustained on such a pervasive scale as is found in American culture—particularly with regard to the rewards involved ("Are *instrumental* rewards such as money really sufficient to link person A to person B?")—is clearly, as Kaplan suggests by his posing of the issue, an analytic problem the motivational details of which we presently have only the dimmest understanding. To a certain extent this orientation is explicable in terms of the simple malleability of human beings; in terms of the consummatory rewards that instrumental satisfactions eventually lead to; or perhaps in terms of what Wallace (1957) calls, "cultural identification," or the love of one's culture patterns for their own sake (in this case, love of the modes of social interaction to be found in one's culture). This last would involve interactional patterns assuming a *motivational* "functional autonomy" (Allport 1937) of their own, that is, ego deriving an *intrinsic* satisfaction from fulfilling another's expectations. However, it is clear that the actual motivational process individuals go through in order to learn to be concerned with the expectations of others—and considering the pervasiveness of this concern, it must involve either intensive or sustained learning—has yet to be examined in a ramified way.[2]

To my knowledge, the only scholars to address themselves directly to the question of the motivations and rewards for conformity are Kaplan in an earlier paper (1957) and Parsons (1952, 1961, and Parsons et al. 1953). Kaplan argued that there are two motivational tendencies making for conformity: the desire to behave morally and the desire to please others. The former tendency is quite explicable in terms of the development and functioning of the super-ego (a universal human attribute), and by emphasizing this, particularly with his later use of the pointed phrase, "good citizen," Kaplan's contribution is considerable. However, the latter consideration begs the question of why individuals should be so motivated to please others, and raises the additional problem, as I have done here, of whether all people are equally motivated in such directions. Parsons' early discussions of conformity simply propound the "evaluative, cognitive, and cathectic" satisfactions that the fulfillment of prescribed patterns award to the individual. In his later, more carefully elaborated essay, he sees the roots of conformity in the inherent helplessness of the human infant. In what is essentially a masterful sociological translation of Freud, he argues that conformity develops into a "generalized goal" or "mode of organization of the ego" as the individual successively identifies with, cathects, and internalizes the attitudes of the powerful figures (his parents) who respond to his helplessness. In this sense, Parsons seems to be arguing that the individual's major initial reward for conformity is the maintenance of his own life. The individual's conformity is gradually generalized as he goes through successive developmental stages, reaching its crystallization—the "point of no return," as it were—in the painful options of the Oedipal

---

[2] The theories that have been most concerned with the nature of conformity and "self-other" orientations—role theory and "symbolic interactionist" theory—have for the most part viewed the *motivations* and *rewards* for conformity as self-evident. That is, the immense literature of these "schools" has tended to focus not on why individuals should wish to conform in the first place, but on the skills, consequences, and non-motivational processes of conformative behavior. Writers such as G. H. Mead (1934), Cameron and Magaret (1951), Sarbin (1954), Shibutani (1961), and Rose (1962) all recognize the necessity of individuals to be socialized into conformity, but they go no further than describing the manifest processes of socialization—"intentional instruction" and "incidental learning," "imitation" and "spontaneous play activities." Having once mentioned these processes, they simply go on to assume that the conformative motivation is thoroughly internalized and self-sustaining. The only exception I have found is Shibutani who addresses himself to the matter of reward in a single sentence (1961: 509): "For most children, the voluntary inhibition of impulses begins with attempts to please those whom they admire."

situation. It might be added that since the Oedipal situation is very much of a moral crisis, Parsons' arguments go far in supporting Kaplan's earlier contentions. Parsons, however, says little about the *different* ways in which parents respond to the child's helplessness and little about *variations* in the intensity and types of identifications, cathexes, and internalizations that the individual may implement—factors which would obviously lead to different kinds of conformative tendencies. Our earlier materials on Bang Chan socialization are particularly instructive on this point. In fact, if Parsons' formulation were linked to those data, it would go a long way to explain precisely why Bang Chaners have such a weakly developed sense of conformity. In the same way, the contrast helps to underscore the profound sense of interpersonal involvement, dependence, and concern inculcated in members of our own culture during the developmental process. To Parsons, the quintessence of these interpersonal investments is, of course, the Oedipal situation: the prototypic encounter with the power of external authority and all that such power implies for the individual's need to conform and to deny and control his own impulses. If this interpretation is correct, it would further suggest that the Oedipal situation must be based, *in the first instance,* on the developmental experience of close interpersonal involvement—an experience which, as our Thai data demonstrate, is subject to broad cross-cultural variation.

The problem of "conformity" raises an additional question, one that has been implicit to many of our earlier remarks, but which merits explicit consideration in these final pages. At several points in the text, it was suggested that the villagers, with their profound sense of self-concern and freedom of choice, often choose to ignore or to isolate themselves from the effects and influences of others. This kind of behavior is a major dimension of their loosely structured relationships; it appears as well in their handling of dependency, anxiety, and aggression. From a psychological point of view, the behavior can be interpreted in one of two ways. On the one hand, it can be interpreted to mean that the villagers have difficulty in relating themselves to others, and use isolation as a means of defense. Implicit here is the notion of emotional deprivation, for who but a deprived person should wish to withdraw from contact with others? On the other hand, the behavior can be read to mean that the villagers are emotionally tough, and simply do not need other people very much. Here isolation is seen as self-reliance and mature emotional security. Throughout this study, I have chosen to stress the latter interpretation.

This kind of interpretation is not an easy one to justify in contemporary Western social science. Implicit to almost all of our thinking is the Judaeo-Christian assumption (more recently codified by Durkheim and Freud) that the greatest psychological pleasures an individual experiences are

derived from his interpersonal contacts, commitments, and interdepend-
encies. In fact, I would suggest that perhaps the major reason that Freud
(although correct) placed so much emphasis on sex is because the sexual
experience is the most absolute expression of interdependency. My materials from this little community in Thailand, where psychological isolation is the norm and where this norm is so impressed upon the Western
observer, have stimulated me into wondering if perhaps our past assumption has represented only *half* the story. What we have failed to see (or if
we have seen, ignored) is that there is immense psychological satisfaction
to be gained through psychological isolation, or from experiences that
require or presuppose isolation. Such satisfactions are found in the pleasures of lonely creativity. (Has a committee, family, tribe, or neighborhood
ever written a symphony or a poem, or even a fable?) Additional examples
are sleep ("sweet sleep"); directing oneself toward the extremities of
human experience in matters of faith and religious belief (by definition, a
lonely, isolated experience); inducing mind-body alterations, as in halluci-
natory states. These are all pleasurable experiences that can be talked
about, but never shared. My point is of course that for historical and other
reasons we have come to assume that loneliness is maladaptive, something
which at best is to be avoided, at worst dreaded. And this is clearly not the
case: no more than is the experience of dealing with a spouse, a brother, a
child, a friend, or a teacher maladaptive.

What is perhaps most surprising is that the evidence for the need for
isolation and privacy has been so readily available, and yet until recently so
easily ignored. All of us who have observed children—in whom the elemental psychological needs of our species are most clearly and
unashamedly expressed—have been impressed by the child's need for contact, love, response, and stimulation. But equally apparent is the child's
need for privacy and lack of stimulation. Thus, we are just now beginning
to become aware that the child's use of his thumb (in Bang Chan, his
forefinger), his trips into quiet fantasy, his recurrent assertion, "Leave me
alone!" are not simply amusing infantile epiphenomena, nor even defenses
against an oppressive external world, but are expressions of a fundamental
human need to be with oneself.

The villagers of Bang Chan, of course, are not children. They are
people who for their own distinctive psychocultural reasons—their Buddhist ethos, their child-rearing practices, their loose and simple social
system—have heightened this essential human need to be left alone, and
express it in a mature, adult way. Unless one assumes that the only
universe is the social universe, theirs is not a case of emotional deprivation.
It is rather an honest and unabashed expression of another kind of psychological need, one which we in the Western world, for our own peculiar

psychocultural reasons, have chosen not to recognize.[3] They are "emotionally tough," as I described them earlier, to the extent that they squarely face such unavoidable facts of life as the presence in the world of other human beings who cannot be trusted; the absolute loneliness of birth, illness, and death in an endless cycle of existence; and the presence of inner feelings and impulses that can never be shared, and that are best "handled" by being stoical, *chɔɔj*, and even "sanug-ful."

In concluding, I wish to re-emphasize that this study does not purport to represent an exhaustive description of the personality characteristics of Bang Chan villagers. Most of the discussion is in fact given over to describing and analyzing dimensions of their interactions, refining and amplifying points in the previous literature that related to interaction, and working out the dynamics of social behavior and its meaning to the individual. However, there is little or no material here on the villagers' fantasy life, their unconscious mechanisms of defense, their cognitive processes, and other attributes of the total universe of events that comprise their psychological life. Even in the brief discussion above about their need for isolation, little is said about what they do when they are isolated. The major purpose has been to describe and interpret those characteristics that are revealed to an outside observer and, when possible, to dispel the penumbra that otherwise and, perhaps not unintentionally, obscures their psychic lives.

---

[3] This lack of recognition will probably not last long. The emerging concern in the Western intellectual community over the question of "personal identity"; the supposed search for "psychological freedom" expressed in the new interest in hallucinogens such as LSD and the faddish interest in the "incommunicable" elements of Zen Buddhism; the ferment created by the writings of Kierkegaard, Tillich, and Camus, all of whom emphasize the existential loneliness of man; and the emergence of Existential Psychoanalysis, will eventually work their way down into the thinking and the concrete research concerns of social scientists and into the popular mentality.

Bibliography

Allport, Gordon W.
  1937 *Personality: A Psychological Interpretation.* New York, Henry Holt
        & Company.
Andrews, James M.
  1935 *Siam: Second Rural Economic Survey, 1934–35.* Bangkok, Bangkok
        Times Press.
Barker, Roger G.
  1963 *The Stream of Behavior.* New York, Appleton-Century-Crofts.
Barker, Roger G., and Herbert F. Wright
  1951 *One Boy's Day: A Specimen Record of Behavior.* New York, Harper &
        Bros.
Bateson, Gregory
  1949 "Bali: The Value System of a Steady State," in *Social Structure:
        Studies Presented to A. R. Radcliffe-Brown,* Meyer Fortes, editor.
        London, Oxford University Press.
  1954 "A Theory of Play and Fantasy," *Psychiatric Research Reports,
        American Psychiatric Association,* 2:39–51.
Belo, Jane
  1935 "The Balinese Temper," *Character and Personality,* 4:120–146.
Benedict, Paul K.
  1943 "Studies in Thai Kinship Terminology," *Journal of the American
        Oriental Society,* 63:168–175.
Benedict, Ruth Fulton
  1928 "Psychological Types in the Cultures of the Southwest," *Proceedings,
        International Congress of Americanists,* 23:572–581.
  1934 *Patterns of Culture.* Boston, Houghton Mifflin Company.
  1946 *Thai Culture and Behavior: An Unpublished Wartime Study
        Dated September 1943.* New York, Institute for Intercultural
        Studies, Inc. Reprinted as Data Paper No. 4, Cornell University
        Southeast Asia Program, Ithaca, N. Y.
Benton, Arthur L., Charles D. Windler, and Elizabeth Erdice
  1957 *A Review of Sentence Completion Techniques.* Project NR 151–
        075, Office of Naval Research, Department of the Navy, Washing-
        ton, D. C., and Department of Psychology, State University of
        Iowa.
Blanchard, Wendell, and others
  1958 *Thailand: Its People, Its Society, Its Culture.* New Haven, Conn.,
        Human Relations Area Files, Inc.

Boesch, Ernest E.
 1956 *Research Plan: International Institute for Child Study*. College of Education, Prasarnmitr Road, Bangkok.
Boggs, Stephen T.
 1956 "An Interactional Study of Ojibwa Socialization," *American Sociological Review, 21*, 2:191–198.
Bohannan, Paul
 1959 "Anthropological Theories," (A Reply to Morgenbesser), *Science, 129*, 3345:292–294.
Brown, Roger
 1958 *Words and Things*. Glencoe, Ill., The Free Press.
Burwen, Leroy S., Donald T. Campbell, and Jerry Kidd
 1956 "The Use of a Sentence Completion Test in Measuring Attitudes Toward Superiors and Inferiors," *Journal of Applied Psychology*, 40:248–250.
Callois, Roger
 1958 *Man, Play, and Games*. Translated from the French by Meyer Barash, 1961. New York, The Free Press of Glencoe, Inc., A Division of the Crowell-Collier Publishing Company.
Cameron, Norman, and Ann Magaret
 1951 *Behavior Pathology*. Boston, Houghton Mifflin Company.
Credner, Wilhelm
 1935 *Siam, das Land der Tai*. Stuttgart, J. Engelhorns Nachf. in Stuttgart.
Davids, Anthony
 1955 "Comparison of Three Methods of Personality Assessment: Direct, Indirect, and Projective," *Journal of Personality*, 23:423–440.
deYoung, John E.
 1955 *Village Life in Modern Thailand*. Berkeley, University of California Press.
Dobby, E. H. G.
 1950 *Southeast Asia*. New York, John Wiley & Sons.
DuBois, Cora
 1944 *The People of Alor*. Minneapolis, University of Minnesota Press.
Dyk, Walter
 1938 *Son of Old Man Hat, a Navaho Autobiography Recorded by Walter Dyk*. New York, Harcourt Brace & Company.
Edmonson, Munro S.
 1957 "Kinship Terms and Kinship Concepts," *American Anthropologist*, 59:393–433.
Eggan, Dorothy
 1943 "The General Problem of Hopi Adjustment," *American Anthropologist*, 45:357–373.
Embree, John F.
 1950 "Thailand—A Loosely Structured Social System," *American Anthropologist*, 52:181–193.
Erikson, Erik H.
 1950 *Childhood and Society*. New York, W. W. Norton & Company.
 1954 "On the Sense of Inner Identity," in *Psychoanalytic Psychiatry and Psychology, Volume 1*, R. P. Knight and C. R. Freidman, editors. New York, International Universities Press.

1959 "Identity and the Life Cycle," *Psychological Issues,* Monograph 1, Volume 1, No. 1, New York, International Universities Press.

Farber, Maurice L.
1950 "The Problem of National Character: A Methodological Analysis," *Journal of Psychology,* 30:307–316.
1951 "English and Americans: A Study of National Characteristics," *Journal of Psychology,* 32:241–249.
1955 "The Study of National Character: 1955," *Journal of Social Issues,* 11, 2:52–56.

Flugel, J. C.
1954 "Humor and Laughter," in *Handbook of Social Psychology, Volume II,* Gardner Lindzey, editor. Cambridge, Mass., Addison-Wesley Publishing Company.

Foster, George M.
1960–1961 "Interpersonal Relations in Peasant Society," *Human Organization,* 19:174–184.
1961 "The Dyadic Contract: A Model for the Social Structure of a Mexican Peasant Village," *American Anthropologist,* 63:1173–1192.
1963 "The Dyadic Contract in Tzintzuntzan, II: Patron-Client Relationships," *American Anthropologist,* 65:1280–1294.

Fraser, Thomas M., Jr.
1960 *Rusembilan: A Malay Fishing Village in Southern Thailand.* Ithaca, N. Y., Cornell University Press.

Freud, Sigmund
1904 "Psychopathology of Everyday Life," in *The Basic Writings of Sigmund Freud.* New York, Random House, 1938. (Translated from *Zur Psychopathologie des Alltagslebens,* Vienna, 1904.)
1905 *Wit and Its Relation to the Unconscious.* New York, Moffat Yard, 1916 (A. A. Brill, translator). First published in German by Deuticke, Leipzig and Vienna, 1905.
1928 "Humor," *International Journal of Psychoanalysis,* 9:1–6.

Fried, Marc
1953 *Relationships Between Personality and Attitudes Among Soviet Displaced Persons: A Technical Memorandum on the Derivation of Personality Variables From a Sentence Completion Test.* Papers of the Harvard Russian Research Center, Cambridge, Mass.

Geertz, Clifford
1956 "Religious Belief and Economic Behavior in a Central Javanese Town: Some Preliminary Considerations," *Economic Development and Cultural Change, IV,* 2:134–158.

Gladwin, Thomas, and Seymour B. Sarason
1953 *Truk: Man in Paradise.* Viking Fund Publications in Anthropology, No. 20. New York, Wenner-Gren Foundation for Anthropological Research, Inc.

Goffman, Erving
1959 *The Presentation of Self in Everyday Life.* Garden City, N. Y., Doubleday Anchor Books.
1963 *Behavior in Public Places.* New York, The Free Press of Glencoe, Crowell-Collier Publishing Company.

Goldfrank, Esther
    1945 "Socialization, Personality, and the Structure of Pueblo Society
          (With Particular Reference to Hopi and Zuni)," *American Anthro-
          pologist*, 47:516–539.
Goldsen, Rose K., and Max Ralis
    1957 *Factors Related To Acceptance of Innovations in Bang Chan,
          Thailand*. Data Paper No. 25, Cornell University Southeast Asia
          Program, Ithaca, N. Y.
Goldstein, Kurt
    1948 *Language and Language Disturbances*. New York, Grune & Stratton.
Gorer, Geoffrey
    1948 *The American People*. New York, W. W. Norton Company.
Haas, Mary R.
    1951 "Interlingual Word Taboos," *American Anthropologist*, 53, 3:338–
          344.
    1957 "Thai Word Games," *American Journal of Folklore*, 70:173–175.
Hallowell, A. Irving
    1941 "The Social Function of Anxiety in a Primitive Society," *American
          Sociological Review*, 6:869–881.
    1945 "The Rorschach Technique in the Study of Personality and
          Culture," *American Anthropologist*, 47:195–210.
    1950 "Personality Structure and the Evolution of Man," *American Anthro-
          pologist*, 52:159–173.
    1953 "Culture, Personality, and Society," in *Anthropology Today*, A. L.
          Kroeber, editor. Chicago, University of Chicago Press.
    1955a *Culture and Experience*. Philadelphia, University of Pennsylvania
          Press.
    1955b "The Rorschach Test in Personality and Culture Studies," in
          *Developments in the Rorschach Technique, Volume II: Fields of
          Application*, Bruno Klopfer, editor. Yonkers-on-Hudson, World
          Book Company.
    1955c "Symposium on Projective Tests in Ethnography," *American
          Anthropologist*, 57, 2:245–270.
Hanfmann, Eugenia, and J. W. Getzels
    1953 "Studies of the Sentence Completion Test," *Journal of Projective
          Techniques*, 17:280–294.
Hanks, Jane Richardson
    1959 *Thai Character and Its Development*. Thailand Project, Cornell
          University Southeast Asia Program, Ithaca, N. Y. (Unpublished
          MS.)
    1961 "Reflections on the Ontology of Rice," in *Culture in History:
          Essays in Honor of Paul Radin*, Stanley Diamond, editor. New
          York, Columbia University Press.
Hanks, Lucien M., Jr.
    1959a *The Cosmic View of Bang Chan*. Thailand Project, Cornell
          University Southeast Asia Program, Ithaca, N. Y. (Unpublished
          MS.)
    1959b *Changes in Social Organization*. Thailand Project, Cornell University
          Southeast Asia Program, Ithaca, N. Y. (Unpublished MS.)

1959c *Changes in Family Life.* Thailand Project, Cornell University Southeast Asia Program, Ithaca, N. Y. (Unpublished MS.)

Hanks, Lucien M., Jr., and Jane Richardson Hanks
1955 "Diphtheria Immunization in a Thai Community," in *Health, Culture, and Community,* Benjamin D. Paul and Walter B. Miller, editors. New York, Russell Sage Foundation.
1961 "Thailand: Equality Between the Sexes," in *Women in the New Asia,* Barbara E. Ward, editor. Paris, UNESCO.

Hanks, Lucien M., Jr., and Herbert P. Phillips
1961 "A Young Thai From the Countryside: A Psychosocial Analysis," in *Studying Personality Cross-Culturally,* Bert Kaplan, editor. Evanston, Ill., Row, Peterson and Company.

Hart, C. W. M.
1954 "The Sons of Turimpi," *American Anthropologist,* 56:242–261.

Henry, Jules
1955 "Rejoinder in Symposium on Projective Tests in Ethnography," *American Anthropologist,* 57, 2:245–270.
1958 *Naturalistic Observation of Family Cultures.* Paper presented at the Annual Meeting of the American Anthropological Association, Washington, D. C.

Henry, Jules, and Melford E. Spiro
1953 "Psychological Techniques: Projective Tests in Field Work," in *Anthropology Today,* A. L. Kroeber, editor. Chicago, University of Chicago Press.

Henry, William E.
1947 "The Thematic Apperception Test in the Study of Culture-Personality Relations," *Genetic Psychology Monographs,* 35:3–135.

Herskovits, Melville J.
1945 "The Process of Culture Change," in *The Science of Man in the World Crisis,* Ralph Linton, editor. New York, Columbia University Press.
1948 *Man and His Works.* New York, Alfred A. Knopf, Inc.
1954 "Some Problems of Method in Ethnography," in *Method and Perspective in Anthropology,* Robert F. Spencer, editor. Minneapolis, University of Minnesota Press.

Hockett, Charles F.
1958 *A Course in Modern Linguistics.* New York, Macmillan Company.
1959 "Animal 'Languages' and Human Language," in *The Evolution of Man's Capacity for Culture,* J. N. Spuhler, editor. Detroit, Mich., Wayne State University Press.

Holmberg, Allan R.
1950 *Nomads of the Long Bow.* Smithsonian Institution, Institute of Social Anthropology Publication No. 10. Washington, U. S. Government Printing Office.

Holsopple, James Q., and Florence R. Miale
1954 *Sentence Completion: A Projective Method for the Study of Personality.* Springfield, Ill., Charles C Thomas, Inc.

Homans, George C.
1961 *Social Behavior: Its Elementary Forms.* New York, Harcourt, Brace & World, Inc.

Huizinga, Johan
   1938   *Homo Ludens: A Study of the Play Element in Culture.* Translated
          into English 1950. London, Routledge and Kegan Paul, Ltd. (First
          Beacon paperback edition published 1955, Boston, The Beacon
          Press.)
Ingram, James C.
   1955   *Economic Change in Thailand Since 1850.* Stanford, Calif.,
          Stanford University Press.
Inkeles, Alex
   1956   "Some Sociological Observations on Culture and Personality Studies,"
          in *Personality in Nature, Society, and Culture,* 2d edition, Clyde
          Kluckhohn, Henry A. Murray, and David M. Schneider, editors.
          New York, Alfred A. Knopf, Inc.
   1959   "Personality and Social Structure," in *Sociology Today,* Robert K.
          Merton, Leonard Broom, and Leonard S. Cottrell, Jr., editors.
          New York, Basic Books, Inc.
Inkeles, Alex, and Daniel J. Levinson
   1954   "National Character: The Study of Modal Personality and Socio-
          Cultural Systems," in *Handbook of Social Psychology, Volume II,*
          Gardner Lindzey, editor. Cambridge, Mass., Addison-Wesley Publish-
          ing Company.
Jakobson, Roman
   1957   "The Cardinal Dichotomy in Language," in *Language: An Enquiry
          into Its Meaning and Function,* Ruth Nanda Anshen, editor. New
          York, Harper & Bros.
   1959   "Boas' View of Grammatical Meaning," in *The Anthropology of
          Franz Boas,* Memoir No. 89 of the American Anthropological
          Association.
Janlekha, Kamol Odd
   1955   *A Study of the Economy of a Rice Growing Village in Central
          Thailand.* Doctoral dissertation, Ithaca, N. Y., Cornell University.
          (Also published by Division of Agricultural Economics, Office of the
          Under-Secretary of State, Ministry of Agriculture, Bangkok, n.d.)
Joseph, Alice, and Veronica F. Murray
   1951   *Chamorros and Carolinians of Saipan.* Cambridge, Mass., Harvard
          University Press.
Kaplan, Bert
   1954   *A Study of Rorschach Responses in Four Cultures.* Papers of the
          Peabody Museum of American Archaeology and Ethnology, Harvard
          University, Volume 42, No. 2.
   1957   "Personality and Social Structure," in *Review of Sociology, Analysis
          of a Decade,* J. B. Gittler, editor. New York, John Wiley & Sons,
          Inc.
   1961a "Personality Study and Culture," in *Studying Personality Cross-
          Culturally,* Bert Kaplan, editor. Evanston, Ill., Row, Peterson and
          Company.
   1961b "Editor's Epilogue: A Final Word," in *Studying Personality Cross-
          Culturally,* Bert Kaplan, editor. Evanston, Ill., Row, Peterson and
          Company.

Kaplan, Bert, Maria Rickers-Ovsiankina, and Alice Joseph
1956 "An Attempt to Sort Rorschach Records from Four Cultures," *Journal of Projective Techniques*, 20:172–180.

Kardiner, Abram
1939 *The Individual and His Society*. New York, Columbia University Press.
1945 *The Psychological Frontiers of Society*. New York, Columbia University Press.

Kaufman, Howard Keva
1955 *Bangkhuad: A Community Study in Thailand*. Unpublished doctoral dissertation, Bloomington, Indiana University.
1960 *Bangkhuad: A Community Study in Thailand*. Monograph No. 10 of the Association for Asian Studies. Locust Valley, N. Y., J. J. Augustin, Inc.

Keesing, Felix H.
1960 "Recreative Behavior and Culture Change," in *Selected Papers of the Fifth International Congress of Anthropological and Ethnological Sciences*, Anthony F. C. Wallace, editor. Philadelphia, University of Pennsylvania Press.

Kingshill, Konrad
1960 *Ku Daeng, The Red Tomb: A Village Study in Northern Thailand*. Bangkok, The Siam Society.

Kluckhohn, Clyde
1943a *Navaho Witchcraft*. Papers of the Peabody Museum of American Archaeology and Ethnology, Harvard University, Volume 22, No. 2.
1943b "Covert Culture and Administrative Problems," *American Anthropologist*, 45:213–227.
1944 "The Influence of Psychiatry on Anthropology in America During the Last 100 Years," in *One Hundred Years of American Psychiatry*, J. K. Hall, G. Zilboorg, and H. A. Bunker, editors. New York, Columbia University Press.
1945 "A Navaho Personal Document With A Brief Paretian Analysis," *Southwestern Journal of Anthropology*, 1:260–283.
1951 "Values and Value Orientations in the Theory of Action: An Exploration in Definition and Classification," in *Toward A General Theory of Action*, Talcott Parsons and Edward A. Shils, editors. Cambridge, Mass., Harvard University Press.
1953 "Universal Categories of Culture," in *Anthropology Today*, A. L. Kroeber, editor. Chicago, University of Chicago Press.
1954a "Culture and Behavior," in *Handbook of Social Psychology, Volume II*, Gardner Lindzey, editor. Cambridge, Mass., Addison-Wesley Publishing Company.
1954b "Southwestern Studies of Culture and Personality," *American Anthropologist*, 56, 4:685–697.
1959 "Common Humanity and Diverse Cultures," in *The Human Meaning of the Social Sciences*, Daniel Lerner, editor. New York, Meridian Books, Inc.

Kluckhohn, Florence Rockwood
1960 "A Method for Eliciting Value Orientation," *Anthropological Linguistics*, 2, 2:1–23.
Kroeber, Alfred L.
1908 *Ethnology of the Gros Ventre.* Anthropological Papers of the American Museum of Natural History, Volume 1, Part 4, pp. 196–222.
1909 "Classificatory Systems of Relationship," *Journal of the Royal Anthropological Institute,* 39:77–84.
1948 *Anthropology.* New York, Harcourt, Brace & Company.
1952 *The Nature of Culture.* Chicago, University of Chicago Press.
1955a "History of Anthropological Thought," in *Current Anthropology: A Supplement to Anthropology Today,* William L. Thomas, Jr., editor. Chicago, University of Chicago Press.
1955b "On Human Nature," *Southwestern Journal of Anthropology,* 11:195–204.
LaBarre, Weston
1945 "Some Observations of Character Structure in the Orient: The Japanese," *Psychiatry,* 8:319–342.
1958 "The Influence of Freud on Anthropology," *The American Imago,* 15, 3:275–328.
Langer, Susan
1942 *Philosophy in a New Key.* New York, Mentor Books of the New American Library.
Leichty, Mary, and A. I. Rabin
1961 *Family Attitudes and Self Concept in Vietnamese and American Children.* MS, Michigan State University Department of Psychology.
Leighton, Dorothea, and Clyde Kluckhohn
1947 *Children of the People.* Cambridge, Mass., Harvard University Press.
leMay, Reginald
1930 *Siamese Tales, Old and New.* London, Noel Douglas, Ltd.
Lessa, William A., and Marvin Spiegelman
1954 *Ulithian Personality As Seen Through Ethnological Materials and Thematic Test Analysis.* University of California Publications in Culture and Society, Volume 2. Berkeley.
Levinson, Daniel J.
1959 "Role, Personality, and Social Structure in the Organizational Setting," *Journal of Abnormal and Social Psychology,* 58, 2:170–180.
Levy, Sidney
1952 "Sentence Completion and Word Association Tests," in *Progress in Clinical Psychology, Volume 1, Section 1,* Daniel Brower and Lawrence E. Abt, editors. New York, Grune & Stratton.
Lewis, Oscar
1955 "Comparisons in Cultural Anthropology," in *Current Anthropology, A Supplement to Anthropology Today,* William L. Thomas, Jr., editor. Chicago, University of Chicago Press.

Lindesmith, A. R., and Anslem Strauss
  1950   "A Critique of Culture-Personality Writings," *American Sociological Review*, 15:587–600.
Lingat, R.
  1936   "La Responsabilité Collective Au Siam," *Revue Historique de Droit Français et Etranger, Sr. 4*, 15:523–539.
  1952   *Les Régimes Matrimoniaux Du Sud-Est De L'Asie: Essai de Droit Comparé Indochinois*, Ecole Française D'Extrême-Orient. Paris, E. De Boccard.
Linton, Ralph
  1945   *The Cultural Background of Personality*. New York, Appleton-Century-Crofts, Inc.
Lorge, Irving and Edward L. Thorndike
  1941   "The Value of the Responses in a Completion Test as Indications of Personal Traits," *The Journal of Applied Psychology*, 25, 2:191–199.
Malinowski, Bronislaw
  1923   "The Problem of Meaning in Primitive Languages," in *The Meaning of Meaning*, C. K. Ogden and I. A. Richards. New York, Harcourt, Brace & Company.
  1927   *Sex and Repression in Savage Society*. New York, Meridian Books.
  1936   "Preface," in Raymond Firth's *We, The Tikopia*. London, George Allen & Unwin, Ltd.
Mandelbaum, David G.
  1953   "On the Study of National Character," *American Anthropologist*, 55:174–187.
Maslow, Abraham H.
  1954   *Motivation and Personality*. New York, Harper & Bros.
Mauss, Marcel (Ian Cunnison, translator)
  1954   *The Gift: Forms and Functions of Exchange in Archaic Societies*. Glencoe, Ill., The Free Press.
Mead, George Herbert
  1934   *Mind, Self, and Society*. Chicago, University of Chicago Press.
Mead, Margaret
  1928   *Coming of Age in Samoa*. New York, William Morrow & Company. (Mentor Books).
  1935   *Sex and Temperament in Three Primitive Societies*. New York, William Morrow & Company.
  1951   "The Study of National Character," in *The Policy Sciences*, Daniel Lerner and Harold D. Lasswell, editors. Stanford, Calif., Stanford University Press.
  1953   "National Character," in *Anthropology Today*, A. L. Kroeber, editor. Chicago, University of Chicago Press.
  1955   "Effects of Anthropological Field Work Models on Interdisciplinary Communication in the Study of National Character," *Journal of Social Issues*, 11, 2:3–11.
  1958   "Cultural Determinants of Behavior," in *Behavior and Evolution*, Anne Roe and George Gaylord Simpson, editors. New Haven, Conn., Yale University Press.

Mensh, I., and Jules Henry
  1953 "Direct Observation and Psychological Tests in Anthropological Field Work," *American Anthropologist*, 55:461–480.
Ministry of Education of Thailand
  1959 *Sombad Khɔɔŋ Phuu Dii (Characteristics of a Good Person)*. In Thai. A Handbook for Teachers Instructing in Proper Behavior.
Moerman, Michael
  1962 "Interconnections Between Clerical and Lay Statuses In A Thai-Lue Village." Paper delivered at a conference on *Theravada Buddhism in Southeast Asia*, University of Chicago, June 1962.
Mosel, James N.
  1957 "Thai Administrative Behavior," in *Toward the Comparative Study of Public Administration*, William J. Siffen, editor. Bloomington, Indiana University, Department of Government.
  1961 *Trends and Structure in Contemporary Thai Poetry*. Data Paper No. 43. Cornell University Southeast Asia Program, Ithaca, N. Y.
Murdock, George Peter
  1940 "The Cross-Cultural Survey," *American Sociological Review*, 5:361–370.
  1949 *Social Structure*. New York, Macmillan Company.
  1954 "Sociology and Anthropology," in *For A Science of Social Man*, John Gillin, editor. New York, Macmillan Company.
Nadel, S. F.
  1955 "Symposium on Projective Tests in Ethnography," *American Anthropologst*, 57, 2:245–270.
  1957 *The Theory of Social Structure*. Glencoe, Ill., The Free Press.
National FAO Committee on Thailand
  1949 *Thailand and Her Agricultural Problems*. Bangkok, Thai Ministry of Agriculture.
Opler, Morris Edward
  1936 "An Interpretation of Ambivalence of Two American Indian Tribes," *Journal of Social Psychology*, 7:83–116.
  1937 "Apache Data Concerning the Relation of Kinship Terminology to Social Classification," *American Anthropologist*, 39:201–212.
  1938 "Further Comparative Anthropological Data Bearing on the Solution of a Psychological Problem," *Journal of Social Psychology*, 9:447–483.
  1948 "Some Recently Developed Concepts Relating to Culture," *Southwestern Journal of Anthropology*, 4:107–122.
  1955 "An Outline of Chiricahua Apache Social Organization," in *Social Anthropology of North American Tribes*, 2d edition, Fred Eggan, editor. Chicago, University of Chicago Press.
Parsons, Elsie Clews, editor
  1922 *American Indian Life*. New York, B. W. Huebsch.
Parsons, Talcott
  1952 "The Super Ego and the Theory of Social Systems," *Psychiatry*, 15, 1:15–25.
  1961 "Social Structure and the Development of Personality," in *Studying Personality Cross-Culturally*, Bert Kaplan, editor. Evanston, Ill., Row, Peterson and Company.

Parsons, Talcott, Robert Freed Bales, and collaborators
1953 *Family, Socialization, and Interaction Process.* Glencoe, Ill., The Free Press.

Payne, A. F.
1928 *Sentence Completions.* New York, New York Guidance Clinic.

Pendleton, Robert L.
1962 *Thailand, Aspects of Landscape and Life.* New York, Duell, Sloan and Pearce.

Phillips, Herbert P.
1958 "The Election Ritual in a Thai Village," *Journal of Social Issues,* *14,* 4:36–50.
1959 *Independence and Dependence in the Thai Peasant Personality.* Thailand Project, Cornell University Southeast Asia Program, Ithaca, N. Y. (Unpublished MS)
1959–1960 "Problems of Meaning and Translation in Field Work," *Human Organization, 18,* 4: 184–192. Originally prepared for *Human Organization Research,* Richard N. Adams and Jack J. Preiss, editors. Homewood, Ill., The Dorsey Press, Inc., 1960.
1960 Review of *A Simple One: The Story of a Siamese Girlhood,* by Prajuab Tirabutana, *American Anthropologist, 62,* 3:536–537.
1963 "Relationships Between Personality and Social Structure in a Siamese Peasant Community," *Human Organization, 22,* 2:105–108.

Piaget, Jean
1932 *The Language and Thought of the Child.* New York, Harcourt Brace & Company.

Piddington, Ralph
1957 *An Introduction to Social Anthropology, Volume II.* New York, Macmillan Company.

Pramoj, Khukrit M. R.
1952 *Panhaa Pracamwan (Problems of Everyday Life), Volume IV.* In Thai. Bangkok, Phim Thai Saphan Press.

Rabin, A. I.
1959 "Comparisons of American and Israeli Children by Means of a Sentence Completion Technique," *Journal of Social Psychology,* 59:3–12.

Radcliffe-Brown, A. R.
1952 "On Joking Relationships," in *Structure and Function in Primitive Society.* London, Cohen & West, Ltd.

Radin, Paul
1913 "Personal Reminiscences of a Winnebago Indian," *Journal of American Folklore,* 26:293–318.
1926 *Crashing Thunder: The Autobiography of an American Indian,* New York, D. Appleton & Company.

Rajadhon, Phya Anuman (or "Sathien Koset")
1957 *Prapheenii Kaw Khong Thai (Ancient Customs of Thailand).* In Thai. Bangkok, Phraeae Phidthajaa Company, 718 Wang Buu-ra-pham Street.

1954   *The Story of Thai Marriage Custom.* Thailand Culture Series, No. 13. Bangkok, National Culture Institute.

1958   *Five Papers on Thai Custom.* Data Paper No. 28, Cornell University Southeast Asia Program, Ithaca, N. Y.

Ratankorn, Prasop

1955   *Thesis on Statistical and Clinical Studies of Mental Illness in Thailand.* Unpublished doctoral dissertation. Philadelphia, University of Pennsylvania Medical School.

Redfield, Robert

1941   *The Folk Culture of Yucatan.* Chicago, University of Chicago Press.

1953   *The Primitive World and Its Transformations.* Ithaca, N. Y., Cornell University Press.

1956   *Peasant Society and Culture.* Chicago, University of Chicago Press.

Redfield, Robert, and Milton B. Singer

1954   "The Cultural Role of Cities," *Economic Development and Culture Change,* 3, 1:53–73.

Riesman, David

1950   *The Lonely Crowd.* New Haven, Conn., Yale University Press.

Riesman, David, and Warren Bloomberg, Jr.

1957   "Work and Leisure: Fusion or Polarity," in *Research in Industrial Human Relations,* Conrad M. Arensberg and others, editorial board. New York, Harper & Bros.

Roberts, John M.

1951   *Three Navaho Households: A Comparative Study in Small Group Culture.* Papers of the Peabody Museum of American Archaeology and Ethnology, Harvard University, Volume 40, No. 3.

Rohde, Amanda R.

1957   *The Sentence Completion Method: Its Diagnostic and Clinical Application.* New York, Ronald Press Company.

Rose, Arnold M.

1962   "A Systematic Summary of Symbolic Interaction Theory," in *Human Behavior and Social Process,* Arnold Rose, editor. Boston, Houghton Mifflin Company.

Roseborough, H. E., and H. P. Phillips

1953   *A Comparative Analysis of the Responses to a Sentence Completion Test of a Matched Sample of American and Former Russian Subjects.* Papers of the Harvard Russian Research Center, Cambridge, Mass.

Rotter, Julian B.

1951   "Word Association and Sentence Completion Methods," in *An Introduction to Projective Techniques,* Harold H. Anderson and Gladys L. Anderson, editors. New York, Prentice-Hall, Inc.

Roy, Donald F.

1959–1960   " 'Banana Time': Job Satisfaction and Informal Interaction," *Human Organization, 18,* 4:158–168.

Rychlak, Joseph F.

1955   *Personality Correlates of Social Adjustment of Japanese Students.* M.A. dissertation, The Ohio State University.

Rychlak, Joseph F., Paul H. Mussen, and John W. Bennett

1957   "An Example of the Use of the Incomplete Sentence Test in

Applied Anthropological Research," *Human Organization,* 16, 1:25–29.

Sacks, Joseph M., and Sidney Levy
1952 "The Sentence Completion Test," in *Projective Psychology: Clinical Approaches to the Total Personality,* Lawrence E. Abt and Leopold Bellak, editors. New York, Alfred A. Knopf, Inc.

Sapir, Edward
1924 "Culture, Genuine and Spurious," *American Journal of Sociology,* 29:401–429.
1927 "The Unconscious Patterning of Behavior in Society," in *The Unconscious: A Symposium,* E. S. Dummer, editor. New York, Alfred A. Knopf, Inc.

Sarbin, Theodore R.
1954 "Role Theory," in *Handbook of Social Psychology, Volume I,* Gardner Lindzey, editor. Cambridge, Mass., Addison-Wesley Publishing Company.

Schachtel, Anna Hartoch, Jules Henry, and Zunia Henry
1942 "Rorschach Analysis of Pilaga Indian Children," *American Journal of Orthopsychiatry,* 12:679–712.

Schaffner, Bertram
1948 *Fatherland: A Study of Authoritarianism in the German Family.* New York, Columbia University Press.

Sears, Robert R.
1961 "Transcultural Variables and Conceptual Equivalence," in *Studying Personality Cross-Culturally,* Bert Kaplan, editor. Evanston, Ill., Row, Peterson and Company.

Seidenfaden, Erik
1958 *The Thai Peoples, Book 1: The Origins and Habitats of the Thai Peoples With A Sketch of Their Material and Spiritual Culture.* Bangkok, The Siam Society.

Sharp, Lauriston
1957 *Thai (Siamese) Social Structure.* Paper read at the Ninth Pacific Science Congress, Section of Anthropology and Social Sciences, Bangkok.

Sharp, Lauriston, Hazel M. Hauck, Kamol Janlekha, and Robert B. Textor
1953 *Siamese Rice Village: A Preliminary Study of Bang Chan 1948–1949.* Bangkok, Cornell Research Center.

Sharp, Lauriston, Frank J. Moore, Walter F. Vella, and associates
1956 *Thailand.* Subcontractor's Monograph. New Haven, Conn., Human Relations Area Files, Inc.

Shibutani, Tamotsu
1961 *Society and Personality.* New York, Prentice-Hall, Inc.

Singer, Milton
1961 "A Survey of Culture and Personality Theory and Researches," in *Studying Personality Cross-Culturally,* Bert Kaplan, editor. Evanston, Ill., Row, Peterson and Company.

Sjoberg, Gideon
1960 *The Preindustrial City.* Glencoe, Ill., The Free Press.

Skinner, G. William
1957 *Chinese Society in Thailand: An Analytical History.* Ithaca, N. Y., Cornell University Press.

Spindler, George D.
  1955*a*   *Sociocultural and Psychological Processes in Menomini Accultura-tion.* University of California Publications in Culture and Society, Volume 5. Berkeley, University of California Press.
  1955*b*   "Symposium on Projective Tests in Ethnography," *American Anthropologist, 57, 2:245–270.*
  1963   "Editorial Preview to Selected Papers in Method and Technique: A Special Issue," *American Anthropologist, 65,* 5:1001–1002.
Spiro, Melford E.
  1952   "Ghosts, Ifaluk, and Teleological Functionalism," *American Anthropologist, 54:497–503.*
  1954   "Human Nature in Its Psychological Dimensions," *American Anthroplogist, 56:19–30.*
  1955   "Symposium on Projective Tests in Ethnography," *American Anthropologist, 57, 2:245–270.*
  1958   *Children of the Kibbutz.* Cambridge, Mass., Harvard University Press.
Suchman, Edward A.
  1955   *The Comparative Method in Social Research.* Cross-Cultural Methods Project, Cornell University, Ithaca, N. Y. (Unpublished MS)
Tendler, A. D.
  1930   "A Preliminary Report on a Test For Emotional Insight," *Journal of Applied Psychology, 14:123–136.*
Textor, Robert B.
  1959   *Shared Images of Thai Modal Personality Held by Peasants in a Central Plain Thai Community.* Thailand Project, Cornell University Southeast Asia Program, Ithaca, N. Y. (Unpublished MS)
  1960   *An Inventory of Non-Buddhist Supernatural Objects in a Central Thai Village.* Unpublished doctoral dissertation, Ithaca, N. Y., Cornell University.
  1962   "A Statistical Method for the Study of Shamanism," *Human Organization, 21,* 1:56–60.
Thompson, Laura
  1945   "Logico-Aesthetic Integration in Hopi Culture," *American Anthropologist, 47:540–553.*
Thurnwald, R.
  1940   "Review of *Sex and Temperament in Three Primitive Societies,*" *American Anthropologist, 38:663–667.*
Tirabutana, Prajuab
  1958   *A Simple One: The Story of a Siamese Girlhood.* Data Paper No. 30, Cornell University Southeast Asia Program, Ithaca, N. Y.
Titiev, Mischa
  1944   *Old Oraibi. A Study of the Hopi Indians of Third Mesa.* Papers of the Peabody Museum of American Archaeology and Ethnology, Harvard University, Volume 22, No. 1.
  1946   "Review of *The Hopi Way,*" *American Anthropologist, 48:430–432.*
Trites, David K.
  1956   "Evaluation of Assumptions Underlying the Interpretation of the SCT," *Journal of Consulting Psychology, 20:8.*

Vella, Walter
  1955   *The Impact of the West on Government in Thailand*. University of
          California Publications in Political Science, Volume 4, No. 3. Berke-
          ley, University of California Press.
Wallace, Anthony F. C.
  1952   *The Modal Personality Structure of the Tuscarora Indians*. Bureau of
          American Ethnology, Smithsonian Institute, Bulletin 150. Washing-
          ton, U. S. Government Printing Office.
  1957   "Mazeway Disintegration: The Individual's Perception of Socio-
          Cultural Disorganization," *Human Organization, 19*, 2:23–27.
  1961a "The Psychic Unity of Human Groups," in *Studying Personality
          Cross-Culturally*, Bert Kaplan, editor. Evanston, Ill., Row, Peterson
          and Company.
  1961b *Culture and Personality*. New York, Random House, Inc.
Wallace, Anthony F. C. and John Atkins
  1960   "The Meaning of Kinship Terms," *American Anthropologist, 62*:
          58–80.
Wheelis, Allen
  1958   *The Quest for Identity*. New York, W. W. Norton & Company.
White, Robert W.
  1948   *The Abnormal Personality*. New York, Ronald Press Company.
Whiting, John W. M.
  1954   "The Cross-Cultural Method," in *Handbook of Social Psychology,
          Volume I*, Gardner Lindzey, editor. Cambridge, Mass., Addison-
          Wesley Publishing Company.
  1961   "Socialization Process and Personality," in *Psychological Anthro-
          pology*, Francis L. K. Hsu, editor. Homewood, Ill., Dorsey Press, Inc.
Whiting, John W. M., and Irvin L. Child
  1953   *Child Training and Personality: A Cross-Cultural Study*. New
          Haven, Conn., Yale University Press.
Wilson, David A.
  1959a "Thailand and Marxism," in *Marxism in Southeast Asia*, Frank N.
          Trager, editor. Stanford, Calif., Stanford University Press.
  1959b *Politics in Thailand*. Unpublished doctoral dissertation, Ithaca,
          N. Y., Cornell University.
Wilson, David A., and Herbert P. Phillips
  1958   "Elections and Parties in Thailand," *Far Eastern Survey, 27*, 113–119.
Wood, W. A. R.
  1935   *Land of Smiles*. Bangkok, Krungdebarnagar Press.
Yerkes, Robert M.
  1943   *Chimpanzees: A Laboratory Colony*. New Haven, Conn., Yale Uni-
          versity Press.
Zimmer, Herbert
  1956   "Validity of Sentence Completion Tests and Human Figure Draw-
          ings," in *Progress in Clinical Psychology, Volume II*, Daniel Brower
          and Lawrence E. Abt, editors. New York, Grune & Stratton.
Zimmerman, Carle C.
  1931   *Siam: Rural Economic Survey, 1930–31*. Bangkok, Bangkok Times
          Press.

Index